# YOUNG STUDENTS
# Learning Library®

## VOLUME 7

Dentistry—
Elevators and Escalators

**NEWFIELD**
PUBLICATIONS
SHELTON, CONNECTICUT

# CREDITS

Page 772 NEI Reyolle Ltd; 773 Science Photo Library; 774 Bettmann Archive; 776 Bruce Coleman; 777 Hygena Polar White Kitchen from MFI furniture Centres (top right); The museum of Modern Art, New York. Gift of Herbert Bayer (middle); 778 Armando Curcio Editore; 779 ZEFA; 780 Bettmann Archive (bottom left); 781 Armando Curcio Editore (top right); Hodder & Stoughton (bottom left); 782 Armando Curcio Editore; 784 British Museum (middle); 789 Imitor; 792 ZEFA; 793 Mansell Collection; 797 Merke Sharp & Dohme (top left); Disney (middle right & bottom right); 800 View-Master Int. Group; 802 Armando Curcio Editor; 807 Michael Holford; 808 Smithsonian Institution photographic Services; 809 Armando Curcio Editore; 814 Armando Curcio Editore; 815 Armando Curcio Editore; 816 Armando Curcio Editore; 817 National Portrait Gallery; 820 Aquarius/Stuart Robinson (top); Los Angeles County Museum (bottom); 823 Armando Curcio Editore;

824 ZEFA; 826 Dave Collins; 827 ICI Pharmaceuticals; 828 Life File; 820 Brian Hawkes; 831 David Hosking; 832 Editorial Photocolor Archives (top left & right); 833 Armando Curcio Editore; 834 (Hulton Deutsch) Bettmann Archive (top left); Armando Curcio Editore (bottom left); National Gallery of Art, Washington (bottom right); 835 Staatliche Museum, Berlin; 836 Popperfoto; 839 National Air & Space Museum, Smithsonian Institution (top); Armando Curcio Editore (bottom); 842 NASA; 843 Geoscience; 848 Michael Chinnery; 857 British Library (top); I.L.N. (bottom); 858 ZEFA (bottom); 859 Florence Mallett; 863 ZEFA (top); Royal Library Windsor Castle (bottom); 864 Mansell Collection (middle); Camera Press (bottom left); 865 Permission of the Town of Bayeux; 868 Egyptian Museum; 871 Hulton Picture Company; 875 Photri; 887 ZEFA; 888 Science Museum; 894 Hutchison Library.

Young Students Learning Library and Newfield Publications are federally registered trademarks of Newfield Publications, Inc.

Copyright © 1994 by Newfield Publications, Inc.; 1974, 1972 by Funk & Wagnalls, Inc. & Newfield Publications, Inc.

Maps containing the appropriate Donnelley indication are copyright © 1994 by R.R. Donnelley and Sons Company. This product contains proprietary property of R.R. Donnelley & Sons Company.

Unauthorized use, including copying, of this product is expressly prohibited.

Printed in the U.S.A.

ISBN 0-8374-9814-7

# CONTENTS

▲ The mighty power of **ELECTRICITY** is shown by sparks produced in this **Van de Graaff generator.**

# DENTISTRY

Did you ever stop to think what a good friend your dentist is? A *dentist* is a doctor who takes care of your teeth and mouth. Your dentist tries to prevent tooth decay, or *cavities*. He or she shows you the best way to brush your teeth and use dental floss in order to prevent tooth decay. The dentist or an assistant, the *dental hygienist*, also cleans your teeth in a special way to remove any materials your toothbrush and dental floss cannot. A fluoride solution may be applied to your teeth to help prevent decay. If you do what the dentist tells you and eat nutritional foods, you will be doing all you can to grow up with healthy teeth. But, if you ignore what your dentist tells you or eat too many sweets, you will probably have painful toothaches or have to have the dentist repair many cavities.

When you visit the dentist, he or she uses sterilized tools to examine your mouth. The dentist inspects your teeth with a mirror and a needle-like instrument, looking for any changes in color or cracks in the teeth caused by decay or other problems. Any fillings you may have are checked. Sometimes the dentist takes X-ray pictures to find decay or problems that cannot be seen.

In earlier times, when a person had a bad toothache, the tooth was pulled. People with gum disease often lost many teeth. There was no way to take care of decayed teeth and diseased gums as dentists do today. Then early dentists learned that a tooth could sometimes be repaired instead of pulled. They first used wax and gums to fill cavities and, by the Middle Ages, began using gold and lead to fill them. Silver amalgam, porcelain, and other *synthetics* (man-made substances) are generally used today. Until the mid-1800s, a person learned dentistry by working for a dentist. The first dental school in the United States was established in Baltimore, Maryland, in 1841. Today most students who want to study dentistry attend college for four years before enrolling in a four-year dental program. These students take many of the same courses as medical students, learning about the body and various aspects of illness. They are taught how to prevent and treat *oral* (mouth) diseases. People who graduate from dental school must pass a state examination before they can set up a dental practice.

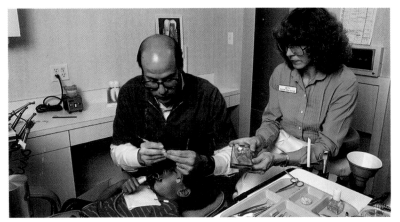

▼ Sometimes a visit to the dentist may mean that you need to have fillings. This dentist is filling the cavity in a child's tooth with a plastic material that is the same color as his tooth. The dentist is helped by his assistant.

Many dentists have helpers in their offices. Some are dental assistants, and some are dental hygienists. Each is educated to do special tasks to help the dentist with the patients.

Certain dentists specialize in various types of dentistry. Some take care of patients with diseases of the gums and the bones that support the teeth. This is known as *periodontics*. *Pedodontists* are dentists for children only. *Orthodontists* make sure that the teeth are correctly aligned and that they come together properly when the mouth is closed. The correct alignment of teeth is necessary to chew food properly and to prevent the teeth from being destroyed. Orthodontists make plaster impressions of the teeth and design corrective wire bands called "braces." These bands fit firmly on or around the teeth and are attached to specially designed wires that slowly move the teeth into the correct position. *Endodontists* specialize in root canals and implants.

> George Washington had several pairs of false teeth made for him. Historians have identified three pairs he once owned. The Smithsonian Institution has one pair on display.

Some dentists, called *prosthodontists*, make artificial teeth to replace teeth that must be pulled. Sometimes they make only a one-tooth bridge. *Partial dentures* replace several missing teeth. *Full dentures* contain all of the teeth belonging in one or both jaws. Other dentists, known as *oral surgeons*, correct deformities, injuries, and diseases of the mouth by operating. Oral surgeons also work with other dentists and physicians, for instance, in caring for persons injured in automobile accidents.

▶ ▶ ▶ ▶ **FIND OUT MORE** ◀ ◀ ◀ ◀
Teeth

▼ **Crowds gather outside the New York Stock Exchange on Wall Street in October 1929. When the stock market crashed suddenly, thousands of people who owned stocks and shares lost all their money. The "Crash" was the start of the Great Depression.**

## DEPRESSION

A low area of ground is called a "depression"; so is a low level of atmospheric pressure. Businesses depend on a certain level of demand for the goods and services they sell. If there is little or no demand, business suffers a depression.

To one family, a depression may mean buying no new clothes and eating low-cost meals. It may mean moving to a smaller house or apartment, and getting along without a car because a mother or father has lost a job.

To a country, a depression means a time when many stores and businesses close because people cannot

**The total earnings of everyone in the United States fell by half during the Great Depression. More than 85,000 businesses failed.**

afford to buy goods or use services. Large companies *down size* (become smaller) by laying off thousands of workers and cutting their production sharply.

The United States suffered serious depressions in the 1830s, the 1840s, the 1870s, and the 1890s. The most terrible depression of all began in 1929. This *Great Depression*, as it is called, paralyzed the country for 12 years and also affected many countries worldwide. Conditions in Germany were so bad that the Germans were prepared to listen to the Nazis. Adolf Hitler came to power and led them into World War II.

Not all economic slumps end in depressions. A less serious slowdown in business activity is called a *recession*. In the early 1990s, many countries, including the United States, felt the pressures of a world recession.

Economists think that many things can help cause a depression or recession. For example, if too many people save too much money, manufacturers have no customers for their products. Or if many manufacturers spend money for new machines and buildings at the same time, then a time follows when no one buys new machinery. Machine companies cannot find customers, so they lay off workers. Soon mining and transportation companies have fewer customers, so they lay off workers, too. Economists say that the way to avoid major depressions is to avoid major changes in the way a country spends its money.

▶ ▶ ▶ ▶ **FIND OUT MORE** ◀ ◀ ◀ ◀
American History; Economics; Hoover, Herbert; Roosevelt, Franklin

##  DESERT

A region so dry that most people, animals, and plants cannot live in it is called a *desert*. Many people think of deserts as being hot, burning areas covered with sand hills, called *dunes*. However, deserts can be found in cooler regions far away from the hot climate near the equator. Deserts may be covered with pebbles, large rocks, snow, or ice.

Low-latitude deserts (near the equator) and mid-latitude deserts (lying between 15 and 35 degrees in Northern and Southern Hemispheres) are alike in several ways. More moisture evaporates from the ground than enters it from rainfall. Infrequent rain usually pours down in great torrents. Because the hard, dry ground cannot absorb the rainwater

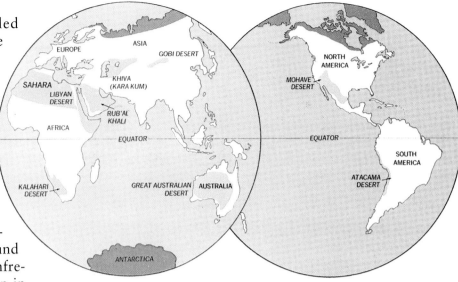

**DESERTS OF THE WORLD**

▦ HOT DESERT
▨ COLD DESERT

▲ **Before the invention of the car or airplane, travelers in Asia and the Middle East often had to cross vast areas of desert on camels. Special buildings, called *caravanserais*, provided food, water, and shelter.**

fast enough, flash floods often occur. Little soil exists because plant growth is needed for soil formation. Daytime temperatures may reach over 100°F (38°C). Nighttime temperatures may fall below the freezing point. The reason for the great variation in temperatures is that the ground is unable to hold the heat of the sun. Famous low-latitude deserts are the Sahara in northern Africa and the Arabian Desert in the Middle East. The

Mojave Desert and the Painted Desert lie in the western United States. The Atacama and much of the Patagonia region in South America, as well as the Gobi in central Asia, are other mid-latitude deserts.

Another kind of desert is found in northern Canada, northern Russia, Greenland, and Antarctica. These areas are ice-cap and tundra regions, or *cold deserts*. Cold deserts are dry because they have no water—it is all in the form of ice. Two million years ago, Canada and most of Europe were cold deserts. Very few plants and animals can survive in portions of these regions because of the cold, icy climate.

**QUIZ**

1. Are deserts always sandy?
2. What is the second-largest desert in the world?
3. Why is the Painted Desert called the Painted Desert?
4. Is an oasis different from a mirage?
5. What's inside a camel's hump?

*(Answers on page 896)*

| **FAMOUS DESERTS OF THE WORLD** | | | |
|---|---|---|---|
| **Desert** | **Location** | **Approximate Size** | |
| | | **(sq. miles)** | **(sq. km)** |
| Antarctica | South Pole | 5,500,000 | 14,245,000 |
| Sahara | North Africa | 3,500,000 | 9,065,000 |
| Great Australian | Australia | 420,000 | 1,087,800 |
| Libyan | Libya | 500,000 | 1,295,000 |
| Gobi | Mongolia | 300,000 | 777,000 |
| Rub'al Khali | Arabia | 250,000 | 647,500 |
| Kalahari | Southern Africa | 225,000 | 582,750 |
| Kara Kum | Turkmenistan | 110,000 | 284,900 |
| Atacama | Chile | 25,000 | 64,750 |
| Mojave (Mohave) | California, U.S. | 15,000 | 38,850 |

▲ Some desert oases are big enough to support large towns. Others are very small.

▼ Some of the many different plants and animals that can be found in the deserts of North America.

Certain plants are especially suited for desert living. Many hot and mid-latitude desert plants require very little moisture. Cacti, for example, store water in their thick stems. They do not have leaves that lose moisture. Some desert herbs and shrubs enter

▶ Not all deserts are hot. Antarctica is a vast expanse of pack ice covering 17 percent of the world's oceans.

a sleeplike state during the driest periods. They drop their leaves and wither up, but their roots stay alive. During wetter periods, these plants turn green again and bear flowers. Other kinds of plants have roots that go very deep underground to reach water. Certain mosses and lichens grow in parts of cold deserts during the short summer period.

Some animals are desert dwellers. Perhaps the camel is the most famous. It stores water in its stomach and can survive for a long period of time without drinking. The kangaroo rat does not drink water but

gets enough from the seeds it eats. Other animals that may live in deserts include foxes, hares, and gazelles, as well as certain insects, birds, and reptiles.

People may live in parts of hot deserts where there are oases (more than one oasis). There are no oases in cold deserts. An *oasis* is the area around a pool of surface water fed by an underground stream. People traveling through the desert stop at oases to replenish their water supplies. Farmers are sometimes able to grow a few crops around the larger oases.

▶ ▶ ▶ **FIND OUT MORE** ◀ ◀ ◀
Animal Distribution; Antarctica;
Cactus; Camel; Glacier; Gobi Desert;
Ice Age; Mirage; Mojave Desert;
Painted Desert; Sahara Desert

Elf owl

Pack rat

Bobcat

Saguaro cactus

Night-blooming cereus

Jumping cholla

Scorpion

Kangaroo rats

Barrel cactus

Jackrabbit

Rattlesnake

Collared lizard

Prickly pear

# DESIGN

*Design* is the arrangement of the different parts of something we can look at. Something looks pleasing when the parts fit together well. A cluster of buildings or the arrangement of furniture in a room is a design. The words and pictures in a book like this one, the clothes we wear, and other man-made objects are designed. People who create designs for man-made products are called *industrial designers*. Industrial designers must be able to create designs that are attractive and practical. Well-designed objects suit their purpose in addition to pleasing the eye. A telephone should fit nicely in the hand. A chair should be comfortable to sit in. Another type of designer is one who designs clothes. *Clothing designers* try to create new and beautiful fashions. They select fabrics, furs, leathers, and other materials that they use for dresses, suits, coats, shoes, underclothing, and even jewelry.

Some excellent designs are not man-made. Much can be learned from natural objects. If you cut an apple in half, you will see how beautifully it is "designed." You could make a collection of objects from nature, such as milkweed pods, leaves, seeds from different plants, pine cones, or flowers. All these objects differ in shape, color, and feel. Look at your collection through a magnifying glass. You will notice parts that you cannot usually see. Notice, also, how well the parts fit

together. Objects in nature not only look beautiful, but they also suit a particular purpose. The graceful shape of a bird is perfectly suited for flight. A gazelle is built for running, and a fish is shaped for swimming. Nature is constantly improving designs through evolution.

Variety is important in a design. The parts might be different in size, color, *tone* (dark and light), or *texture* (the feel or look of the surface). These differences will make the design more interesting. But the parts of a design must be carefully chosen

▲ **A beautiful example of a compact modern kitchen that is well designed and has all up-to-date conveniences.**

◀ **Marcel Breuer designed this chrome-plated steel tube chair in 1925. There are similar chairs made today. Design is concerned not only with making things look good, but also making them work well, too. This chair is both good-looking and comfortable.**

## LEARN BY DOING

You might make a *collage* using different materials. Collect scrap materials that have different textures. Some might be rough (sandpaper or burlap), others smooth (silk) or soft (feather, cotton). Arrange pieces of these materials into a design on a piece of cardboard. You can cut them into different shapes and sizes if you wish. Also try to find differences in color and tone. Arrange the materials until they look best to you. Glue them onto the cardboard with colorless liquid glue.

You could make another collage using clippings of pictures from old magazines. Cut out parts that look rough, smooth, or soft, and glue them onto another piece of cardboard.

► **The Pompidou Center in Paris has a very clever design. The inside of the building is supposed to have many uses, including being a museum and a library. The architects designed the building so that the elevators, stairs, lavatories, water pipes, heating, and electricity, would be on the outside of the building, leaving the inside with lots of open space.**

▲ **Hernando de Soto, Spanish explorer of the New World.**

▼ **Hernando de Soto's route. In his search for gold, de Soto explored much of Southeastern United States. He was the first European to reach and cross the Mississippi River.**

so that they look good when they are fitted together. A soaring skyscraper might be beautiful in itself. But if it is built in a street with tiny old houses, the design of the street will look strange. Everyone, though, has an idea of what a good design is. Each designer will arrange shapes and colors in a way that looks best to him or her.

▶▶▶▶ **FIND OUT MORE** ◀◀◀◀
Architecture; Commercial Art; Evolution; Graphic Arts; Interior Decorating; Painting

##  DE SOTO, HERNANDO (about 1500–1542)

Spain's desire for gold led Hernando de Soto to explore vast areas of southeastern North America. He sailed to the New World at age 19 and took part in the Spanish conquest of Central America.

De Soto joined Francisco Pizarro in 1532, in conquering the Inca tribe of Peru. His share of the Incas' gold made him a rich man. But he was still restless for more wealth. Rumors of a land of gold to the north persuaded him to explore Florida. With an army of about 600 men, de Soto landed near what is now Tampa Bay, Florida, in 1539.

De Soto's expedition marched north through the wilderness to the Carolinas, then southwest to what is now Alabama, where de Soto and many of his men were wounded in a battle with Native Americans.

Marching westward, he became the first European to reach and cross the Mississippi. He and his dwindling army explored the land as far west as Oklahoma. Three years passed without a trace of gold. Discouraged, de Soto turned back to the banks of the Mississippi, where he died of a fever. He was buried in the river.

▶▶▶▶ **FIND OUT MORE** ◀◀◀◀
Conquistador; Exploration; Pizarro, Francisco

## DETECTIVE

A detective is usually a special kind of police officer whose job is to *investigate* (ask questions about) crimes. He or she gathers *evidence* (or clues) that will lead to the arrest of a suspect. A police detective works for the township, city, county, or state police department.

Police detectives often have to work in dangerous surroundings and investigate dangerous individuals. They know that anything at the scene of a crime could be a clue—fingerprints, a strand of hair, a particle of clothing, the dirt on a person's shoes, or a tiny speck of blood. They work with *forensic scientists* in the police laboratory. A detective must search out people who can give information about a crime, and must be able to recognize any sign that would indicate a person is lying.

A *private investigator* is not a member of the police force. But former police detectives frequently become private detectives. They are often employed to trace missing persons, or are hired by hotels or stores to keep down theft.

▶▶▶▶ **FIND OUT MORE** ◀◀◀◀
Crime; Federal Bureau of Investigation; Fingerprint; Forensic Science; Police

## DETERGENTS

SEE SOAPS AND DETERGENTS

## DETROIT

With 1,027,974 people, Detroit is one of the ten largest cities in the United States. It is a major inland port, standing on the Detroit River, a busy waterway separating the United States from Canada in southeastern Michigan. Called "Motor City" or the "Automobile Capital of the World," Detroit is a great industrial center. Its large vehicle industry was founded in the early 1900s by men such as John and Horace Dodge, Henry Ford, and Ransom E. Olds. Besides vehicles, Detroit also makes many other things, including chemicals, machine tools, and medicines. Wayne State University and the University of Detroit are located here. The University of Michigan is at nearby Ann Arbor.

Detroit was founded in 1701, when Antoine de la Mothe Cadillac, leader of a group of French settlers, built a fort there. It was called "Fort Pont-chartrain du Détroit." But most people shortened this long name to Détroit, which means "on the strait." The fort was held by the British in 1760, but seized by American colonists in 1796. The modern city was built after 1805, when the original settlement was completely burned down. Detroit was captured by the British army during the War of 1812, but was retaken by U.S. forces under Commodore Oliver Perry and General William Henry Harrison.

The Detroit Museum of History has many items from the city's early days. The Henry Ford Museum at Dearborn has hundreds of antique vehicles. This museum is next door to Greenfield Village, where Henry Ford had more than 90 historical buildings restored. Detroit is also a sporting center. It contains the Joe Louis Arena for hockey and boxing, and the Pontiac Silverdome for basketball, baseball, and football.

### WHERE TO DISCOVER MORE

Wormser, Richard. *Pinkerton: America's First Private Eye.* New York: Walker & Co., 1990.

▼ **The skyscrapers of Detroit make an impressive sight set against the deep blue of the Detroit River.**

## DEWEY DECIMAL SYSTEM

SEE LIBRARY

## DIAGHILEV, SERGEI

SEE BALLET

▲ Of the two diamonds shown here, the one on the right is cut and polished. The other is still uncut.

Diamonds are made of very pure carbon that has been squeezed by enormous pressure deep underground. Scientists believe that diamonds are made at least 93 miles (150 km) underground. The diamonds have been slowly pushed up from these great depths.

▲ Bartholomeu Dias, Portuguese explorer. He discovered a sailing route around Africa.

## DIAMOND

Diamond is the hardest natural substance found on Earth. Jewelry often contains diamonds because the stones are so brilliant—especially when they are cut and polished to bring out their full beauty. When perfect, a diamond is clear, but it often contains *impurities* or flaws that color it. Diamonds that are too imperfect or too small to be used for jewelry are used in factories to cut and polish very hard metals and ceramics. These diamonds are called *industrial diamonds*. Some diamonds used in industry are made artificially from graphite, a form of carbon.

Diamonds were first discovered in India and Borneo. Large deposits were found near Bahia (Salvador), Brazil, about 1670. The greatest discovery of all was in Kimberley, South Africa, where "pipes" of blue earth containing many thousands of diamonds were found in 1870. This area is still the greatest diamond producer on Earth. The famous Jonker diamond comes from South Africa. Other famous diamonds are the Hope, Jubilee, Star of the South, Cullinan, and Koh-i-noor.

Diamonds are made of carbon. Coke is also made of carbon. But coke is black and softer than diamonds. The reason for the difference is that the carbon in diamonds is packed down much more tightly than it is in coke. Diamonds are formed below the Earth's crust at great pressure and heat. They are brought to the surface among other minerals in volcanic pipes.

▶ ▶ ▶ ▶ **FIND OUT MORE** ◀ ◀ ◀ ◀
Carbon; Gem; Mineral

## DIARY

Keeping a record of what happens each day can be interesting to do. People of all ages like to write down the things that they do. These records are called *diaries* or *journals*. Some children keep a diary of the things that happen to them or their families and friends. Others like to write about their own feelings and the way they think about certain problems and ideas.

When people keep diaries for several years, it is interesting to read them again and see how the people may have changed as they grew older. It is also fun for children to read diaries which were kept by their parents when they were young. Children learn how their parents spent their time and how they thought about things back then.

Some well-known people of history such as Samuel Pepys, Jonathan Swift, Queen Victoria, and Sir Walter Scott kept diaries. When we read these diaries today, we learn a lot about the writer and also about the way people lived when the writer was alive. *The Diary of a Young Girl* is a widely read book written by a 13-year-old girl named Anne Frank. Anne and her family lived in the Netherlands during World War II, and her diary tells about how they had to hide from the Nazis.

▶ ▶ ▶ ▶ **FIND OUT MORE** ◀ ◀ ◀ ◀
Biography

## DIAS, BARTHOLOMEU (about 1450–1500)

In the 15th century, spices and other Asian treasures were carried overland from India to the Mediterranean Sea, then by ship to Europe. The cities of Italy controlled the trade through the Mediterranean. The king of Portugal wanted to find a direct water route to India. He wanted

Portugal to have a share of the rich spice trade.

In 1487, the king commissioned Bartholomeu Dias (or Diaz) to look for a route around the southern end of Africa. Dias set sail with two ships. On New Year's Day in 1488, as he neared the Cape of Good Hope at the southern tip of Africa, a storm blew his ships far to the south. After 13 days, he was able to turn east, but found no land in that direction. He then sailed north and reached the east coast of Africa well past the Cape of Good Hope. He realized he had circled the tip of Africa. Dias wanted to sail to India, but his men made him return to Portugal.

In 1500, Dias was one of the captains in the Portuguese fleet that discovered what we now call Brazil. He went down with his ship when it sank in a storm.

▶▶▶▶ **FIND OUT MORE** ◀◀◀◀
Exploration; Da Gama, Vasco;
Henry the Navigator

▲ **Two characters from Dickens's,** *A Christmas Carol.* **Dickens's Bob Cratchit, watched by Scrooge, tries to keep warm.**

## DIATOM

SEE ALGAE; PLANKTON

## DICKENS, CHARLES (1812–1870)

Who can imagine Christmas without Charles Dickens's famous story "A Christmas Carol" being shown on television? In the days before television, some member of the family would often read this story aloud. It is the tale of the miser Ebenezer Scrooge, who is visited in a dream by the Ghosts of Christmas Past, Present, and Future. The ghosts persuade Scrooge to change his cruel ways. He becomes a good, kind person, to the joy of the little lame boy, Tiny Tim, whose words at the end of the story are: "God bless us, every one!"

Dickens was one of the most famous story-tellers of all time. He spent his childhood in Chatham and London, England. His family was very poor. Many of the most moving stories in his novels are drawn from his own experiences. He began his writing career as a newspaper reporter. His first novel, *Pickwick Papers* (1837), won him immediate popularity. *Oliver Twist* (1838), *Nicholas Nickleby* (1839), and *The Old Curiosity Shop* (1841) followed. Many of his novels were first published in monthly installments. Readers would wait in great excitement for the next part of the story.

His characters—with names such as the Artful Dodger, Uriah Heep, Mr. Micawber, and Jeremy Belcher—are often comic and always very realistic. Dickens described in vivid detail

▲ **Charles Dickens, the great British novelist of the 19th century, wrote books that told about the** *plight* **(conditions) of poor people.**

▲ **A scene from Charles Dickens's** *David Copperfield.* **Dickens drew from his own experiences to tell the story of David Copperfield's life.**

▲ Emily Dickinson, U.S. poet, who retreated from the world at age 26 and spent almost the rest of her life alone.

the cold, hunger, beatings, illness, cruel treatment, and other injustices and discomforts that poor people of his time suffered. His books created an interest in social reform.

Dickens married and had ten children. He enjoyed traveling and went to the United States twice. Part of his novel *Martin Chuzzlewit* (1843) takes place in the United States. Dickens was a friendly man who loved people, the theater, and writing to his friends. He is buried in Westminster Abbey in London. Some of his many other books are *David Copperfield* (1850), *A Tale of Two Cities* (1859), and *Great Expectations* (1861).

▶ ▶ ▶ ▶ **FIND OUT MORE** ◀ ◀ ◀ ◀
Literature; Novel

## DICKINSON, EMILY (1830–1886)

As a girl, Emily Dickinson was very lively, witty, and outgoing. She lived with her family in Amherst, Massachusetts. Her father was a lawyer and was elected to the U.S. Congress. Emily received a good education. When she was 26, she began to spend most of her time alone. She lived with her family but stayed in her room, coming out only once in awhile. She wore white all the time. She lived this way for the rest of her life. No one is sure why she retreated from the world. Some scholars think that she had fallen in love with a man who was already married.

Emily Dickinson wrote more than 1,700 poems in her solitude. She used scraps of paper and the backs of envelopes for writing. Only seven of her poems were published in her lifetime. Her family did not know about most of her poems until she died. They are short, beautiful poems about nature, love, and death. Today many people believe that this solitary New England woman is one of the greatest U.S. poets. Many books have been written about her.

▶ ▶ ▶ ▶ **FIND OUT MORE** ◀ ◀ ◀ ◀
Poetry

## DICTATOR

Sometimes a parent or a teacher will say that you must do a certain thing or else be punished. This is called *dictating*, or giving orders that must be obeyed.

A ruler of a country who behaves this way is called a *dictator*. Dictators have complete power over the people. They can make or unmake laws without consulting the people. They decide the policy of the government. They have the power to put to death or imprison anyone who disobeys or criticizes them.

A country may benefit from the strong control of a single ruler at times of war or national emergency. But a dictator must limit the peoples' freedom in order to retain complete power. Dictators were sometimes appointed in times of emergency in ancient Rome (Julius Caesar was one). But they were only allowed to stay in power for a limited time.

Dictators have ruled in several countries in recent times. Some came to power by gaining the support of a group, such as the army, and seizing control of a country by force. This is how Francisco Franco became dictator of Spain. But often dictators came to power legally and then took over complete control. Joseph Stalin of the

▼ **Dictator Adolf Hitler seized power in Germany when the country was suffering from economic hardship. He led the country into the terrible destruction of World War II.**

Soviet Union, Adolf Hitler of Germany, François Duvalier ("Papa Doc") of Haiti, and Juan Perón of Argentina all became dictators by these methods. Most of these dictators promised their people a better life. But then they repressed all individual freedom. Newspapers were shut down, and radio and television controlled by them. They used secret police to enforce their laws. Often, a revolution is needed to remove a dictator from office. But a revolution is almost impossible since the dictator controls the army and the police. However, in 1986, dictators Ferdinand Marcos of the Philippines, and Jean-Claude Duvalier ("Baby Doc") of Haiti were deposed, and in 1989, the dictator of Chile, General Pinochet, was removed from office when he was defeated in a presidential election.

▶ ▶ ▶ ▶ **FIND OUT MORE** ◀ ◀ ◀ ◀

Caesar, Julius; Franco, Francisco; Hitler, Adolf; Stalin, Joseph

## DICTIONARY

A *dictionary* is a book that tells us how to spell words, what the words mean, and how to pronounce them. Dictionaries are very useful reference books. They help students learn more about words and improve their writing skills.

A dictionary is arranged alphabetically. The most common type of dictionary is a collection of most of the words used in one language. It shows the usual pronunciation of the words, generally by using small symbols above or below the words. It gives the *definition* or meaning of the words and may include a sentence or phrase to show how the word is used. If a word has more than one definition, the separate definitions are listed.

A dictionary tells the part of speech, such as noun or adjective, of each word listed. This is usually shown by an abbreviation, as *n.* for noun or *adj.* for adjective.

Many different sizes and types of dictionaries are printed. The larger dictionaries tell the *etymology*, or origin and history, of words. Some words have come from other languages or have changed in spelling or meaning over the years. New words come into the language every day from science, technology, and many other sources. Dictionaries keep up-to-date with new words and also drop words if people stop using them.

A small dictionary, called a "glos-

> **ri·dent** (rīd′ənt), *adj.* laughing; smiling; cheerful. [< L *rīdent-* (s. of *rīdēns*, prp. of *rīdere*) = *rīd-* laugh + -*ent-* -ENT]
> **rid·er** (rī′dər), *n.* **1.** a person who rides a horse or other animal, a bicycle, or the like. **2.** that which rides. **3.** any object or device that straddles, is mounted upon, or is attached to something else. **4.** a rail or stake used to brace the corners in a snake fence. **5.** an additional clause attached to a legislative bill in passing it. **6.** an addition or amendment to a document. [ME, OE *ridere*] —**rid′er·less,** *adj.*
> **rid·er·ship** (rī′dər ship′), *n.* **1.** the people who ride a particular train, bus, subway, etc. **2.** the estimated number of such people.
> **ridge** (rij), *n., v.,* **ridged, ridg·ing.** —*n.* **1.** a long, narrow elevation of land; a chain of hills or mountains. **2.** the long and narrow upper edge, angle, or crest of something, as a hill, wave, vault, etc. **3.** the back of an animal. **4.** any raised, narrow strip, as on cloth. **5.** the horizontal line in which the tops of the rafters of a roof meet. **6.** (on a weather chart) a narrow, elongated area of high pressure. —*v.t.* **7.** to provide with or form into a ridge or ridges. **8.** to mark with or as with ridges. —*v.i.* **9.** to form ridges. [ME *rigge*, OE *hrycg* spine, crest, ridge; c. OIcel *hryggr*, D *rug*, G *Rücken*, L *crux*] —**ridge′like′,** *adj.*
> **ridge·ling** (rij′ling), *n. Vet. Med.* a colt with undescended testicles. Also, **ridg′ling.** Also called **ridg·el, ridg·il** (rij′əl). [? RIDGE + -LING², from the belief that the undescended organs were in the animal's back]
> **ridge·pole** (rij′pōl′), *n.* the horizontal timber or member at the top of a roof, to which the upper ends of the rafters are fastened. Also, **ridge′ pole′.** Also called **ridge·piece** (rij′pēs′), **ridge′ board′.** —**ridge′poled′,** *adj.*
> **Ridge·wood** (rij′woŏd′), *n.* a city in NE New Jersey. 27,547 (1970).
> **Ridg·way** (rij′wā), *n.* **Matthew (Bun·ker)** (buñg′kər), born 1895, U.S. general: chief of staff 1953–55.
> **ridg·y** (rij′ē), *adj.,* **ridg·i·er, ridg·i·est.** rising in a ridge or ridges.
> **rid·i·cule** (rid′ə kyōōl′), *n., v.,* **-culed, -cul·ing.** —*n.* **1.** speech or action intended to cause contemptuous laughter at a person or thing; derision. —*v.t.* **2.** to make fun of. [< L

sary," is sometimes included in a storybook or a nonfiction book. This is usually done if difficult words or words of another language have been used in the book.

Scholars in ancient Greece and Rome sometimes made lists of difficult or unusual words and gave their meanings. During the Middle Ages in Europe, most books were written in

▲ **An excerpt from a dictionary. Notice that some words have more than one meaning. The dictionary also gives** *synonyms* **for some words (abbreviation "syn"). A synonym is a word meaning the same, or almost the same, as another word.**

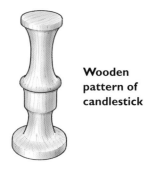

**Wooden pattern of candlestick**

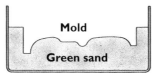

**Mold**

**Green sand**

**Metal box**

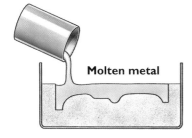

**Molten metal**

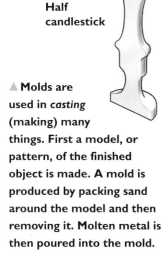

**Half candlestick**

▲ **Molds are used in** *casting* **(making) many things. First a model, or pattern, of the finished object is made. A mold is produced by packing sand around the model and then removing it. Molten metal is then poured into the mold.**

Latin. Students at this time used dictionaries that gave the Latin meanings of difficult Latin words. By the 1600s, people had begun to write books in their own languages. The earliest English dictionaries gave the definitions of only difficult English words. One of the first scholars to try to list most of the words in the English language was Samuel Johnson, in 1747–1755.

The first large U.S. dictionary was published by Noah Webster in 1828. It included the U.S. spelling and pronunciation of English words. It also included words of Native American origin, such as "wampum" and "tomahawk," which Americans were using. Webster's name is still used for a series of U.S. dictionaries put out by the Merriam-Webster company. The most complete U.S. dictionary is *Webster's International Dictionary*. Another one is the *Dictionary of Americanisms*, edited by Mitford M. Matthews.

Dictionaries that translate words of one language into another language are often used in schools, for example a "French-English dictionary." The *Oxford English Dictionary* is a very large and scholarly book that gives the complete etymology of each word. It has more than 400,000 entries. Dictionaries are also written for particular subjects, such as history, science, or music. The work of *updating* (adding and eliminating words) them goes on all the time.

▶ ▶ ▶ ▶ **FIND OUT MORE** ◀ ◀ ◀ ◀

Johnson, Samuel; Reference Book; Webster, Noah

## ☼ DIES AND MOLDS

Tom made delicious cookies called gingerbread men. He mixed the dough and spread it out on a board with a rolling pin. Then he took a little metal cutter made in the shape of a man and pressed it down on the dough. Each time he pressed it down, the figure of a gingerbread man was cut out of the dough, ready to be baked into a cookie.

The cookie cutter Tom used is one kind of *die*. A die is a metal pattern that stamps or cuts out something. Our coins are made by dies. Steel dies with coin designs in reverse are put

◀ **Even the earliest coins had designs stamped on them. A die, a metal block on which a pattern was cut, was used to press the design into the metal. This ancient Greek coin shows the head of Alexander the Great.**

into a coining press. These dies are patterns for the coins. One die is for the face of the coin, the other is for the back. The two dies come together under great pressure and strike a sheet of metal that is sandwiched between them. They press the metal into the shape of a coin.

Another kind of die is used to cut the threads on nuts and bolts. A block of metal with holes through it can also serve as a die. Strips of copper, aluminum, or another metal are forced into the holes on one side and come out the other side as wire of the same width as the holes. This process is called *extrusion*.

Another way to shape materials is to use a mold. A mold is simply a form that gives a desired shape to fluids or plastic materials that are poured or pressed into it. Perhaps you have used a mold in the kitchen to shape a gelatin dessert.

Molds are also used in *foundries*.

---

### LEARN BY DOING

Use a mold in your kitchen to turn a gelatin dessert into a special shape. Prepare the gelatin according to the package directions. Pour it into the mold. When the gelatin has cooled and set, place the bottom of the mold in a bowl of warm water for a few seconds. Turn the mold over onto a plate. Tap the mold and lift it off the gelatin.

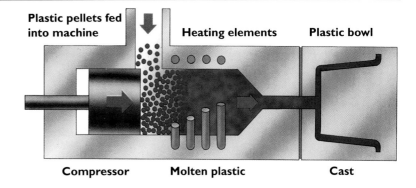

Plastic pellets fed into machine · Heating elements · Plastic bowl

Compressor · Molten plastic · Cast

Foundries are shops that make metal *castings*. For example, some workers in a foundry might want to make an iron wheel. First they make a model, or *pattern*. That is, they make a wheel out of wood in just the size and shape they want. They put this pattern wheel in an iron box full of wet sand and press it down. Next, they lift the wheel out of the sand. The shape of the wheel is left in the wet sand, the way you might make a footprint on the beach. The wet sand is the mold. The workers make two molds, one for each side of the wheel. After the sand hardens, they fasten the two molds together. The foundry workers pour molten iron into the space left by the pattern, then let it cool. When the iron hardens, they remove the sand, and there is an iron wheel which looks just like the pattern.

Other types of molds are used to make pottery, dishes, candles, and plastic goods.

▶ ▶ ▶ ▶ **FIND OUT MORE** ◀ ◀ ◀ ◀
Iron and Steel; Plastic

## ⚙ DIESEL ENGINE

A German engineer and inventor, Rudolf Diesel, built a new type of engine in the 1890s. His first version of the engine exploded and knocked him unconscious, but Diesel was not discouraged. He continued to work and completed his first working engine in 1897. It produced 25 horsepower (18,640 watts) with only one cylinder. During the following few years Diesel perfected his engine. Soon thousands of diesel engines were being made in many different sizes.

Modern diesel engines are used to power trucks, buses, construction equipment, locomotives, large ships, and some automobiles. These engines can be enormous, weighing as much as 2 million pounds

(907,000 kg) and delivering 25,000 horsepower (18,640 kW) or more— 200 times the power produced by most automobile engines.

The diesel engine works much like a gasoline engine, except it has no carburetor or spark plugs. Instead, the piston is used to squeeze the air into a very small volume. The air becomes very hot when tightly compressed. Fuel is simply sprayed into the cylinder, and the extremely hot air causes an explosion. The air must be tremendously compressed to become hot enough to ignite the fuel, so the cylinders of diesel engines must be very strong.

The diesel engine can use fuel more efficiently than the gasoline (*internal combustion*) engine, so a properly working diesel causes less air pollution than a gasoline engine. Diesel fuel oil is cheaper to produce than gasoline. Diesels are therefore

▲ Injection molding is often used to make objects out of plastic. Two halves of a mold are clamped together. Molten plastic is then forced into the mold. After the plastic cools and sets, the mold is split apart.

▼ How a diesel engine works. I. Air is drawn downward into the cylinder through a valve. 2. The air is put under pressure and becomes very hot. 3. Fuel is injected into the hot air and catches fire. This explosion forces the piston back and thus turns the wheel. 4. The piston pushes the exhaust gases out through another valve. Then the whole cycle begins again.

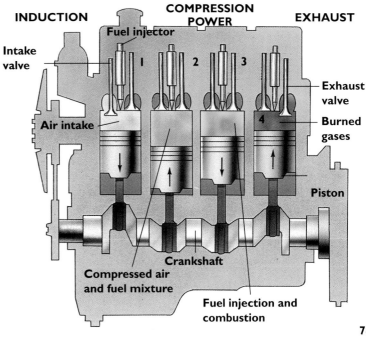

INDUCTION · COMPRESSION POWER · EXHAUST

Fuel injector
Intake valve
Air intake
Exhaust valve
Burned gases
Piston
Crankshaft
Compressed air and fuel mixture
Fuel injection and combustion

▶ Digestion starts in the mouth, where saliva mixes with food as it is chewed. Food travels down the esophagus to the stomach and is churned and partly digested. Most digestion occurs in the small intestine. Here the food is mixed with bile and digestive juices from the pancreas. Proteins and fats are broken down by enzymes and absorbed into the body. The rest passes to the large intestine and the water is taken back into the body. The waste goes to the rectum and is eliminated.

The crocodile's digestion juices contain so much hydrochloric acid that they have been known to dissolve large metal objects such as spearheads.

▼ All animals must digest the food they eat. Digestion involves breaking food into smaller and smaller pieces, until it consists of relatively small molecules. These pass through the gut lining into the body.

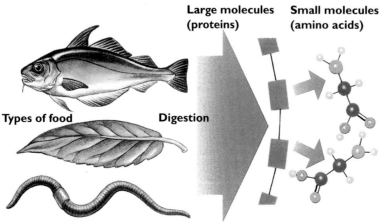

Types of food          Digestion

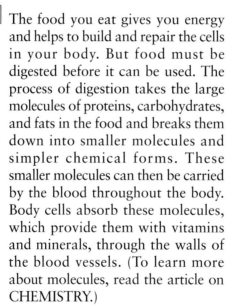

Large molecules (proteins)     Small molecules (amino acids)

more economical to use, although a diesel costs more to buy than a comparable gasoline engine.

Diesel engines are used to power electric generators in many ships and locomotives. The electricity is then used by the electric motors that actually turn the propellers or wheels. This is called the *diesel-electric system*.

▶▶▶▶ **FIND OUT MORE** ◀◀◀◀
Automobile; Engine; Petroleum

## DIET

SEE FOOD; NUTRITION

## DIGESTION

The food you eat gives you energy and helps to build and repair the cells in your body. But food must be digested before it can be used. The process of digestion takes the large molecules of proteins, carbohydrates, and fats in the food and breaks them down into smaller molecules and simpler chemical forms. These smaller molecules can then be carried by the blood throughout the body. Body cells absorb these molecules, which provide them with vitamins and minerals, through the walls of the blood vessels. (To learn more about molecules, read the article on CHEMISTRY.)

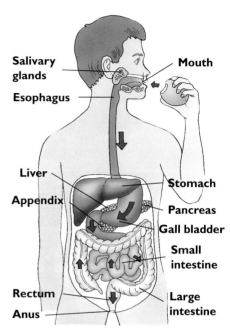

Salivary glands
Esophagus
Liver
Appendix
Rectum
Anus
Mouth
Stomach
Pancreas
Gall bladder
Small intestine
Large intestine

Digestion takes place in the *alimentary canal*, a long coiled tube extending from the mouth to the anus. The main parts of the tube are the mouth, esophagus, stomach, small intestine, and large intestine. The final part of the large intestine is called the rectum. Here undigested food is stored before being expelled from the body through the anus.

Food passing through the alimentary canal is moistened, ground up, churned, broken down by *acids* and *enzymes* (chemicals that make other chemicals change), temporarily stored, and finally, *absorbed* (passed through the walls of the intestine into the blood). The parts of food that cannot be digested or used are *eliminated* (thrown out) from the body via the anus.

### In the Mouth
Many organs, glands, and muscles work together to complete digestion. Digestion begins in the mouth. When you take a bite of bread, for example, *saliva* pours into your mouth from three pairs of glands located under your tongue, beneath your jaw, and in the sides of your mouth. In fact, just looking at, smelling, or imagining your favorite food can "make your mouth water," or produce saliva.

Saliva contains water and a sticky substance called *mucin*, which makes food soft and moist so that it can be swallowed. It also contains the enzyme *ptyalin*, which begins the digestion of starch (a carbohydrate). Ptyalin changes the starch in your bite of bread into a simpler chemical form—a sugar called *maltose*. Other enzymes will break down the maltose into simpler forms of sugar as the food moves through the alimentary canal.

Chewing plays an important part in digestion for many mammals. A cow, for example, chews its food, swallows it, then brings it back into its mouth and chews it again. You may have seen cows in a field chewing their "cuds" steadily even when they are not *cropping* (eating) grass. Some other animals, such as cats and dogs, do not chew, but bite or tear at their food. They then swallow it down in unchewed lumps.

Humans both tear and chew their food. You use your front teeth for biting or tearing and your flat-topped back teeth for chewing. The chewing helps break down solid food into small pieces. A lump of food is ready for swallowing when it is thoroughly coated with saliva. Then the tongue forces the food to the back of the mouth and down the throat. A flap called the *epiglottis* closes off the wind pipe so that no food can get caught there and cause choking or loss of breath. Muscles in the wall of the throat move the food into the next area, the *esophagus*. No digestion takes place in the esophagus. It is simply a tunnel that leads to the stomach. The wavelike movements or *peristalsis* of small muscles in the walls of the esophagus are so strong that your food would be forced into your stomach even if you were standing on your head while eating!

**The Stomach**

The *stomach* is a hollow, baglike organ. The lining of the stomach has glands that pour out *gastric juice*. This juice contains enzymes that continue the breaking down of food. Gastric juice also contains *hydrochloric acid*. It combines with protein in the food, making it easier for the enzyme *pepsin* to break down protein. Powerful muscles in the wall of the stomach churn the food so that it is well mixed with the gastric juice and forms a creamy liquid.

Food, depending on its nature, stays in the stomach for as long as one to four hours and sometimes even longer. Liquids pass through very quickly. When the stomach digests meat, it produces more gastric juice than it does in digesting potatoes or sugars. Fats, however, slow down the production of gastric

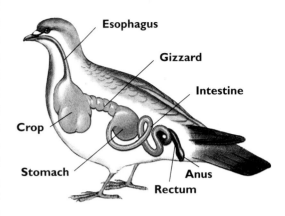

▲ The digestive system of a bird. It has a crop, a baglike organ, which expands and means that a bird can eat lots of food in a short time. The gizzard grinds up tough foods such as seeds.

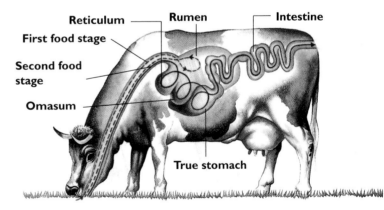

juice, so that a meal containing a large amount of fat stays longest in the stomach, and holds off hunger for longer periods, too.

Food is in a thick, liquid form by the time it is ready to leave the stomach. Small quantities at a time are moved from the stomach into the *small intestine*. The small intestine is the most important organ of the digestive system. Here the final steps are taken to prepare the food for absorption. More enzymes come into

▲ The digestive system of a cow. Its long intestine enables tough plant material to be broken down. A cow's stomach has four chambers. The first is called the rumen. The cow eats grass and swallows it whole into the rumen. After a while, the cow coughs up the grass and chews it in the mouth. This chewing the cud helps digestion.

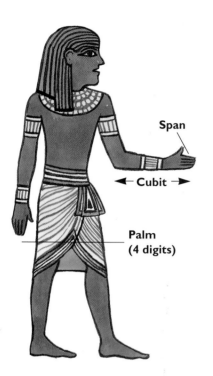

▲ **Many measurements of dimensions were originally based on parts of the body. The ancient Egyptians used the palm, the span, and the cubit.**

▼ *The School of Athens*, **by Raphael. This work is an example of how painters often try to make their paintings appear three dimensional by using perspective and shading.**

the small intestine from an organ called the *pancreas*. Bile from the liver is added after having been collected in the gall bladder. Bile is useful in breaking up fat into small drops, or *globules*, that enzymes can get at more easily. Squeezing movements of the small intestine break up and knead the food, mixing it thoroughly with the intestinal juices and enzymes. At the same time, continuous wavelike movements push the food along. The small intestine is about 21 feet (6 m) long in an adult human.

Millions of tiny, fingerlike projections called *villi* line the small intestine. The nutrients in the digested food pass through the surfaces of the villi and into the blood and *lymph*. (Lymph is an important body fluid that helps "clean up" your body.)

The food finally reaches the end of the small intestine about 6½ hours after a meal. It now enters the *large intestine*. All the nutrients have been taken from the food by this time. What remains is waste matter of indigestible material.

A tubelike organ called the *appendix* is attached to the large intestine. It has no known function (job), but can cause trouble. It can become infected by bacteria and may need to be removed by surgery. This is called an *appendectomy*.

In the large intestine, most of the water is removed from the waste

matter. This reduces the waste to a firm mass, which collects at the end of the large intestine. The waste matter moves out of the large intestine from time to time. It enters the *rectum* and is pushed out of the *anus*. This elimination of waste material is known as *defecation*.

*Carnivores* (meat-eating animals) have much shorter digestive *tracts* (tubes) than *herbivores* (plant-eating animals), who have a lot of roughage to digest. For example, a cow has a small intestine 100 feet (30.5 m) long. Animals like us that eat both plants and meat (*omnivores*) have digestive tracts longer than those of carnivores but shorter than those of herbivores.

▶▶▶▶ **FIND OUT MORE** ◀◀◀◀
Biochemistry; Enzyme; Food; Human Body; Kidney; Liver; Nutrition

## DIMENSION

If someone wants to build a garage for their car, they must be sure that it will be large enough to hold the car. It has to be longer, wider, and higher than the car is. *Length*, *width*, and *height* are called dimensions.

In measuring objects, however, some dimensions may be more important than others. For example, if a farmer wishes to measure a field, only the dimensions of length and width are important. It makes no sense to measure the height of the field. From this, you can see that "two-dimensional" means that only the length and width of the object are to be measured. Two-dimensional objects are flat, like a picture or a page of this book. Three-dimensional objects are solid, and their height or thickness is as important as their length or width.

A property of a two-dimensional figure is its *area*, the space within its boundaries. *Square feet* and *acres* are both common units of area. A two-

dimensional object that is 5 feet wide and 5 feet long has an area of 25 square feet ($5 \times 5 = 25$). A property of a three-dimensional object is its *volume*, the space within its boundaries. The boundaries of a solid object are called *surfaces*. *Cubic inches* and *gallons* are units used to measure volume. Not all measuring units may be familiar to you. The *metric system* uses different units. For example, lengths may be expressed in meters (a meter is about $3\frac{1}{4}$ feet), and areas in square meters or in hectares (a hectare is about $2\frac{1}{2}$ acres). Volumes may be given in liters (a liter is just over two pints).

Mathematicians label figures according to how many dimensions they have. A *solid* figure, such as a cube, has three dimensions. A flat figure, with only two dimensions, is called a *plane* figure, or a *surface*. A straight *line* is a figure with only one dimension, that of length. A *point* is a figure with no dimensions.

▶▶▶▶ **FIND OUT MORE** ◀◀◀◀
Geometry; Measurement; Metric System; Physics; Relativity; Time

## DINOSAUR

Nearly everyone has heard of dinosaurs. But no one has ever seen one of these reptiles. Scientists believe that they all died out about 65 million years ago. Before then, giant

dinosaurs and other reptiles roamed the land. The time in which they lived—about 150 million years in all—is known as the "Age of Reptiles." Scientists call this age the *Mesozoic era*.

We know that dinosaurs existed because *fossil* remains of their bodies have been found: that is, dinosaur bones and teeth that were turned to stone. They have been discovered embedded in rocks in all parts of the world. Also, dinosaur bones and teeth have been found buried in the earth. If you visit a natural history museum, you can see how scientists have put these bones and teeth together to make skeletons. These skeletons help us imagine what dinosaurs looked like. By studying the bones and teeth, scientists have learned how the dinosaurs lived. For example, sharp teeth show that a dinosaur was a meat-eater (*carnivore*). Dull, flattened teeth show that a dinosaur was a plant-eater (*herbivore*).

The word "dinosaur" means "terrible lizard." Many dinosaurs were quite fierce-looking. Although they were not really lizards, some of them did look like lizards. Others looked like alligators; still others, like birds.

▲ Two sworn enemies, Edward Drinker Cope (top) and Othniel Marsh (bottom), made huge collections of dinosaur bones in North America in the late 1800s. Their bitter rivalry to identify new types of dinosaurs has been called the "Bone Wars"!

▶ From its skeleton we know that *Camptosaurus* could rear up on its hind limbs to reach leafy trees, or go down on all fours to walk.

Several thousand kinds of dinosaurs roamed the earth, although they did not all live at the same time, or even in the same parts of the world. Some walked on four legs, while others walked on only their hind legs. Some were plant-eaters, while others were meat-eaters who preyed on the plant eaters. Some roamed the land, while others spent most of their time in water. Our planet was hot and steamy then, and much of the land was marshy.

The earliest dinosaurs were small. One kind looked something like a turkey without feathers. It could run swiftly along the ground on its two large hind legs. It had two smaller forelegs, which it used to grab things. The early dinosaurs gradually developed into many other kinds. Some changed into giants.

*Brachiosaurus*, one of the biggest dinosaurs we know about, was 40 feet (12 m) high and up to 90 feet (27 m) long from nose to tail. It had a tiny head at the end of a very long neck. This dinosaur weighed well over 50 tons (51 metric tons)—more than eight elephants! Brachiosaurs were so heavy that they could not move about easily on land. Only water could support their weight, so they lived mainly in swamps and fed on tender plants found there. Brachiosaurs had to keep eating continually in order to nourish their huge body.

*Apatosaurus*, once known as *Brontosaurus*, was a giant plant-

▼ **A *Triceratops* drives off an attacking *Tyrannosaurus*. The Triceratops was massive, and its bony armor and pointed horns were enough to scare off even the most fearsome meat-eater.**

▲ *Tyrannosaurus rex* **lived in North America. It was the biggest and fiercest meat-eater ever to have lived on Earth. Its head was about 5 feet (1.5 m) long, but its arms were tiny and probably only used to lift it off the ground.**

eater. It looked something like Brachiosaurus but was smaller, growing to a length of 67 feet (20 m) and weighing about 35 tons (35.5 metric tons). Like many other dinosaurs, Apatosaurus was probably very stupid. In spite of its huge body, it had a tiny brain that weighed only one pound (about 0.45 kg).

One of the scariest-looking plant-eating dinosaurs was *Stegosaurus*. A row of bony plates, like armor, ran down its back. It is thought these were used to help control the animal's body temperature. Its heavy tail bore four pointed spikes. Another armored plant-eater was *Triceratops*. It had a bony frill around its neck and three sharp horns for armor. The longest dinosaur was *Diplodocus* at some 88 feet (27 m) long.

Probably the most fearsome dinosaur of all was a meat-eater called *Tyrannosaurus rex*. It was about 20 feet (6 m) high and 47 feet (14 m) long. It had long, powerful hind legs that allowed it to run after and catch other dinosaurs for food. Its head was enormous, and its mouth was full of daggerlike teeth that were 6 inches (15 cm) long. Probably, even the armored dinosaurs fell prey to this fierce creature.

Why did these beasts become

▲ **Silvisaurus was a medium-sized armored dinosaur. It measured about 13 feet (4 m) in length.**

▼ **Hadrosaurus was the first dinosaur skeleton to be named in North America. Many had plain heads (as below), while some species had ridges and crests.**

▼ **Iguanodon lived 120 million years ago in the warm forests of southern England. It was a plant-eater and probably used its thumb claws to fend off attacks.**

▼ **Stegosaurus is sometimes called the most stupid dinosaur because its skull contained a brain the size of a walnut.**

Some scientists now believe that a few of the dinosaurs were warm-blooded (that is, they could control their body temperature). They think that these dinosaurs were the ancestors of the birds. However, this theory has not yet been definitely proved.

▲ Organizations such as the British CND (Campaign for Nuclear Disarmament), shown here demonstrating outside a U.S. air base in England, attempt to influence government decisions about disarmament.

▶ During the Cold War the Soviet Union and the United States took part in an arms race. This cartoon from 1962, shows the Soviet leader, Nikita Khrushchev, arm wrestling with U.S. President John Kennedy. They are sitting on nuclear weapons. It was only after the Cold War ended in 1990, that major disarmament began.

extinct? No one knows for sure, but many scientists now think that about 65 million years ago, a comet hit Earth. The impact was so huge that vast quantities of debris were thrown up into the atmosphere. There they stayed for many years, blocking out the sunlight, destroying plant life, and chilling our planet. The dinosaurs could not find food or stand the cold!

▶▶▶▶ **FIND OUT MORE** ◀◀◀◀
Evolution; Fossil; Reptile

## DIRIGIBLE

SEE AIRSHIP

## DISARMAMENT

Weapons of war are called "armaments." When nations agree to disarm, they agree to reduce the number of their armaments, or even get rid of certain types of weapons altogether. This is called "disarmament." Another term for limited disarmament is "arms control."

During the 1800s, new and more powerful weapons were invented. The strongest nations, or "Great Powers" as they were known, met to try to set limits to the use of such deadly weapons as poison gas. But these meetings, at The Hague (Netherlands) in 1906 and 1907, did not succeed, and poison gas was used during World War I. After this war, Germany, which lost, was forbidden such weapons as tanks and submarines. The Great Powers met in Washington to discuss naval disarmament. The League of Nations held a disarmament conference in 1932. But these talks accomplished little.

After World War II, the United Nations urged the Great Powers to disarm. But the "cold war" between East and West led instead to an arms race, with both sides spending huge amounts of money on armaments. The invention of nuclear weapons posed a new, and much greater, threat to world peace.

Since the 1950s, there have been various attempts at disarmament agreements. The nations have agreed to ban nuclear tests in the atmosphere, and in Antarctica. The United States is a *signatory* (signer with others) to these treaties and to the *nuclear nonproliferation treaty* signed in 1968. During the 1970s and 1980s, the strategic arms limitation talks between the United States and the Soviet Union made slow progress. In 1986, there was an agreement on military maneuvers in Europe. This agreement included important provisions for inspection, to ensure that both sides obeyed the agreement. Talks continued on such questions as the banning of chemical weapons and the introduction of space weapons, following the United States' unveiling of its strategic defense initiative (SDI or "Star Wars") proposals. In December 1987, U.S. President Ronald Reagan and Soviet Union leader Mikhail Gorbachev signed a treaty eliminating all medium- and shorter-range nuclear missiles. This led to a treaty ending the Cold War between West and East in 1990.

After the collapse of the Soviet empire, the United States further reduced its nuclear weapons in 1991, and signed an agreement with Russia, once part of the Soviet Union, in 1992. But many countries in the world still possess nuclear weapons and some, such as Iraq, are acquiring nuclear weapons for the first time.

## DISCRIMINATION

If pupils in your school start a club for stamp collectors, anyone who is not a stamp collector is excluded. We say that the club's members are *discriminating* against non-stamp collectors. That is a harmless form of discrimination, but many kinds are bad. One form of discrimination is by religion. For example, until 1829, Roman Catholics in Britain could not vote.

*Racism*, is discriminating against people on account of their race. In the United States, blacks were discriminated against for many years. Blacks had fewer opportunities than whites. For example, blacks were refused certain jobs or entry to colleges. Another form of discrimination is by sex. In some countries, women cannot vote and are barred from many jobs because of their sex.

▶▶▶▶ **FIND OUT MORE** ◀◀◀◀
Black Americans;
Civil Rights

## DISEASE

A disease, or sickness, is a condition that prevents a living thing from functioning in a normal, healthy way.

If you think of the diseases you know about, you will realize that each one is different from the others. When you are sick, something has gone wrong in your body. The doctor examines you and finds *symptoms* (signs) of disease. The combination of symptoms you have tells the doctor what disease you have. The most common symptoms of disease include fever, chills, pain in some part of the body (such as sore throat, headache, or muscle aches), swelling, rash, coughing, weakness, and loss of weight.

A very important part of medicine is *diagnosing* (finding out) what disease a person has. This special kind of detective work is not always easy to do.

### Kinds of Disease

Doctors *classify* (group) diseases in several ways. For example, sometimes diseases are classified according to the part of the body they affect. There are bone diseases, eye diseases, skin diseases, and many other kinds. But the most important and useful way to group diseases is by their causes.

INFECTIONS. An infection is caused by living things (organisms) that grow inside the body. Most infections are caused by *germs*, living things so tiny they can be seen only with a microscope. There are several different kinds of germs, including bacteria, viruses, and fungi.

▲ **Roman Catholics in England suffered from discrimination for many years. These riots in London in 1780 took place when people showed their strong anti-Catholic feelings.**

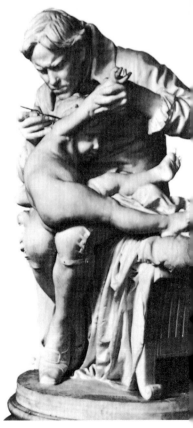

▶ **Edward Jenner, a great British physician, developed a way of treating disease. He called this *vaccination*. He had heard that people who had the mild disease, cowpox, never caught smallpox. Jenner took fluid from a blister of a person with cowpox and injected it into a young boy. Two months later he injected the boy with smallpox. The boy did not get smallpox.**

Doctors now realize that there is a close link between "mind" and "body." They know that if someone is worried or unhappy, this could bring about a physical or mental illness.

▶ Bubonic plague, or the Black Death, killed about 25 million people in Europe in the 1300s. It was an infectious disease, passed to humans by the infected fleas that lived on rats.

▼ A typical European street of the 1300s had filthy open sewers, rats, and garbage everywhere. These conditions helped to spread the Black Death rapidly.

*Bacteria* cause many diseases, including pneumonia, strep throat, tuberculosis, scarlet fever, and whooping cough. Bacterial diseases were once among the most feared of all diseases, but today most diseases caused by bacteria are easy to treat with modern antibiotics. Some bacterial diseases are also prevented by *vaccines*. A *vaccine* consists of dead or weakened disease-causing organisms or parts of germs. These organisms cause the body to develop antibodies to fight that disease.

*Viruses* cause the common cold and many other diseases, including yellow fever, measles, mumps, a type of influenza, and polio myelitis. Many viral diseases can be prevented by vaccines. But viral diseases are hard to treat because antibiotics do not stop most viruses.

*Fungi* cause several diseases. Most, such as athletes' foot, are skin diseases. Fungal diseases are usually not affected by antibiotics, so they are difficult diseases to treat.

Many of these infectious diseases are also *contagious*—they spread from one person to another. An ordinary cold is a familiar example. When one person gets a cold, people who are in close contact with him or her are also very likely to catch it. Cold germs travel on the droplets of moisture expelled when sneezing and by making hand contact with someone with a cold.

Mumps, measles, chicken pox, and other childhood diseases are contagious. Many contagious diseases can be prevented by vaccination. A good example is the successful prevention of smallpox. It has been almost completely eliminated because of worldwide vaccination of children and adults.

Very occasionally a new contagious disease, such as AIDS, appears. Scientists have to study the disease and the way in which it is transmitted. Then they can try to develop a vaccine to eliminate it.

Some infectious diseases are not contagious. The organisms that cause these diseases must be passed from person to person by animal carriers. The germs that cause typhus and bubonic plague, two of our most terrible diseases, are spread by certain lice and fleas. Malaria is another such disease. Malaria germs can be carried only by certain mosquitoes. When there are none of these mosquitoes, the disease cannot spread.

Flea

Black rat

Some infectious diseases, including malaria, are caused by certain *protozoans* (protists), single-celled animals. These diseases occur mostly in the tropics, where these tiny animals are not killed by cold weather.

Still other infectious diseases are caused by organisms much larger than germs—certain kinds of worms. These worms are *parasites*, animals that live on or in *hosts*, plants or other animals. Parasites harm the host on which they live. Worms cause many serious human infections. The tapeworm, for example, attaches itself to the intestine of its human host, where it can grow to be 15 feet (4.6 m) long. A tapeworm drains food that its host needs, and it can cause stomach pains and a feeling of weakness.

NEOPLASMS. A neoplasm is a *tumor*, an abnormal growth of body tissue. "Neoplasm" comes from Greek words meaning "new form" or "new shape."

There are two main kinds of tumors, *benign* and *malignant*. *Malignant* tumors, or cancers, are extremely serious. Malignant tumors are found in plants and in humans, as well as in other animals. A cancer can kill healthy tissue around it, and it can spread throughout the body of the host. Different kinds of cancers grow and spread at different rates. But any cancer will grow and spread until it kills its host, unless it is treated. Treatment may involve use of radiation and chemicals or cutting out the diseased tissue in surgery. *Benign* tumors do not spread, and they do not kill healthy tissue. They are usually treated if doctors aren't sure what kind of tumors they may be or if they cause pain. One way doctors can determine if a tumor is malignant or not is to perform a *biopsy* (the removal and examination of tissues, cells, or fluid from the body). X-rays also help doctors identify the kinds of tumors people may have.

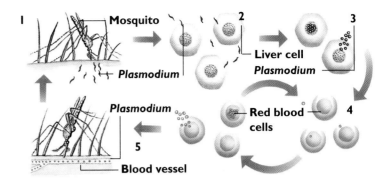

ALLERGIES. An allergy is a strong reaction or resistance to something that touches your body or gets inside it. Some "allergies" are good. Your body often "fights" germs that get into it, and, therefore, can keep you from getting a disease. But when your body fights something that will not harm you, you may become tired, sneeze, or feel itchy. Allergic reactions can be very serious. A person who is allergic to bee stings or peanuts can become very sick, and even die.

GENETIC DISEASES. These diseases are present at birth and are inherited from the genes of one or both parents. For example, some boys and men suffer from the disease called *hemophilia*. The blood of persons with this disease does not clot, so bleeding goes on and on. If you cut yourself, a small scab forms quickly, and the bleeding stops. But when hemophiliacs cut themselves, the cut continues to bleed. Even a tiny cut is very dangerous. Some sons inherit this disease from their mothers, even though their mothers do not show signs of the disease. Other diseases, such as *diabetes*, may also be hereditary. Doctors now think that some cancers also belong to this group of *genetic* diseases.

CONGENITAL DISEASES. Congenital diseases attack unborn babies. They are not inherited but happen when the *embryo* (developing baby in the womb) is disturbed. For example, if a pregnant woman has German measles (rubella)—especially during the first three months of her pregnancy—her unborn baby may

▲ The disease malaria is caused by a parasite called *plasmodium*, passed on by mosquitoes. (1) Following a bite from an infected mosquito, the parasite attacks and reproduces inside the person's liver cells. (2) After several days, new *plasmodia* (3) spread to the blood (4) where they may infect other mosquitoes (5).

**WHERE TO DISCOVER MORE**

Krementz, Jill. *How It Feels to Fight for Your Life.* Boston: Little, Brown & Co., 1989.

▲ We are surrounded by possible sources of disease. Household pests such as flies and mice often carry disease. Close contact between people can allow contagious diseases to spread. Eating food that is not fresh can also cause diseases.

suffer from the effects of the illness. The baby may be born with a defect such as deafness or blindness. Some heart defects, as well as other physical problems, are also congenital.

NUTRITIONAL DISEASES. People who do not eat correctly may develop special diseases. People who always overeat may gain so much weight that they strain the heart, blood vessels, or kidneys. Overweight people get diseases such as diabetes and high blood-pressure more often than people of normal weight. People who do not eat the right food develop *deficiency* diseases. A person who does not drink milk, may not get enough calcium. Without calcium, bones become so weak that they bend into peculiar shapes. If vitamin C is not part of the diet, scurvy may develop, so that cuts heal slowly, skin bruises easily, *capillaries* (tiny blood vessels) break, and gums bleed.

ENVIRONMENTAL DISEASES. Our environment sometimes contains disease-causing elements. For example, coal miners work in an environment in which the air often contains tiny particles of coal dust. The miners breathe these particles into the lungs. This often results in a serious disease called "black lung" from which many miners suffer. We sometimes pollute our environment, causing disease. Thousands of people have become seriously ill from breathing smog, a poisonous mixture of smoke and fog. Being around cigarette smokers is dangerous to a person's health, too.

OTHER TYPES. *Hormonal* diseases occur when the functions of the endocrine glands are disturbed. These glands control body shape, growth, how the body uses food, and how the body adjusts to the world. Dwarfism and giantism are two diseases that occur when people's glands do not work properly. Several other serious diseases are also hormonal diseases.

*Circulatory* diseases happen if blood cannot flow normally. A *clot* (block) in a blood vessel may cause pain. If the clot forms in the heart, a heart attack may result.

*Metabolic* diseases occur when the normal chemical activities of the body are disturbed. Such diseases include diabetes, in which the victim cannot use sugar properly.

*Degeneration* includes diseases of old age, when parts of the body begin to *degenerate* (wear out and break down). Such breakdowns may cause blindness or deafness or attack bones, muscles, or joints.

*Mental illness* includes many problems that affect the way in which a person lives. Some problems are minor, but some mental illnesses may make a person completely unable to live a normal life and may even cause physical illness.

**Prevention and Treatment**

Many diseases can be prevented. The means of prevention depends on how the disease is spread. Diseases carried by animals can be stopped if the animals that spread the diseases are controlled. Nutritional diseases are prevented when people eat properly. And many very serious diseases are prevented when sanitary conditions are improved.

Just as many kinds of diseases exist, there are many cures. Antibiotics cure most bacterial diseases. Other kinds of diseases have other cures.

Germs are everywhere in the world. They are constantly in contact with the human body. Did you ever wonder why people are not sick all the time? The answer to this question is that the best and most wonderful prevention and cure of disease is the human body! The skin keeps out most germs. Eyebrows, eyelashes, and eyelids protect the eyes, and tears wash out anything that slips past these "fences." Tiny hairlike structures that line the breathing passage

▲ This child is being vaccinated against German measles to prevent her from getting the disease. An injection gun is being used instead of a needle.

trap most germs that are breathed in. Saliva and acid in the stomach kill most germs eaten in food. Sneezing and coughing push irritating substances out of the body.

When illness occurs, the body usually cures itself. White blood cells and body proteins called antibodies *may* quickly bring the disease under control and then force it out of the body. This happens when you have a cold. There is no known cure for the common cold. You do not take medicine to cure the cold, although it may help you feel more comfortable. Your body stops the cold. Your body is usually the best "medicine" for disease. Your doctor gives you medicine only when the body's defenses are not enough.

▶▶▶▶ **FIND OUT MORE** ◀◀◀◀

**Causes of Disease** see Bacteria; Fly; Fungus; Genetics; Gland; Heart; Insect; Parasite; Protist; Virus; Vitamins and Minerals; Worm

**Cures and Preventions** see Antigen and Antibody; Immunity; Medicine; Mental Health; Public Health; Sanitation; Surgery

**Diseases** see AIDS; Allergy; Cancer; Childhood Diseases; Cold, Common; Fever; Plant Diseases; Rabies

**Drugs** see Anesthetic; Antibiotic; Antiseptic; Drugs

## 🎭 DISNEY, WALT (1901–1966)

As a young artist, Walt Disney would often work late at night in his studio. As the story is told, he heard some mice in his wastebasket one night. He captured them and kept them in little cages on his desk. One of them was his particular friend. This mouse was to give Disney the idea for his famous cartoon character, Mickey Mouse. Disney received more than 100 awards for his work.

Walter Elias Disney was born in Chicago, but he spent most of his boyhood in Missouri. Disney studied at the Chicago Academy of Fine Arts. He began his career as an artist in Kansas City, Missouri, and made his first cartoon movie there. In 1923, Disney moved to Hollywood and started the Disney Studio.

Many of Disney's cartoons deal with *fantasy* (the world of make-believe). Mickey Mouse first appeared in 1928 in a cartoon called *Steamboat Willie*. Disney's first full-length cartoon, or *animated feature*, *Snow White and the Seven Dwarfs*, was released in 1937. *Fantasia* and *Pinocchio* followed. Some of Disney Studio's other animated features were *Cinderella, Peter Pan, Bambi, Lady and the Tramp, Sleeping Beauty, The Little Mermaid*, and *Aladdin*, the last two done after his death. Disney also made non-cartoon films.

In 1955, Walt Disney opened an amusement park, *Disneyland*, in Anaheim, California. This park was based in part on Disney's movies and cartoon characters. A similar theme park, *Walt Disney World*, opened near Orlando, Florida, in 1971. In 1982, the EPCOT Center was opened in Walt Disney World. It features futuristic technology exhibits. These parks and exhibits are extremely popular, and other countries (Tokyo, Japan, 1983) have opened parks based on Disney. In 1992, the *Euro Disney World* was opened just outside Paris, France.

**WHERE TO DISCOVER MORE**

Eliot, Marc: *Walt Disney: Hollywood's Dark Prince: A Biography.* Carol Publishing Group, 1993.

▲ Walt Disney, creator of some of the best animated cartoons of all time.

▲ Disney's most famous character, Mickey Mouse, shown here in what is usually believed to be his best-ever role—as the Sorcerer's Apprentice in *Fantasia* (1940).

## ☼ DISTILLATION

When a liquid boils, it becomes a gas, or *vapor*. If a vapor is cooled, it *condenses,* or becomes a liquid again. If boiling and condensing take place in an apparatus that contains the boiling liquid and also cools the vapor, the process is called *distillation*.

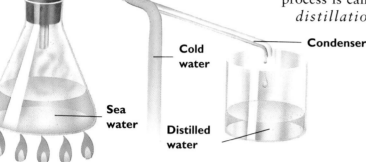

▲ **Distilling fresh water from salt water is the process carried out on a large scale at "desalination plants". In these plants sea water is changed into drinkable, unsalted water. This diagram shows how the process works on a smaller scale.**

The apparatus in which a liquid is distilled is commonly called a *still*.

Distillation is often used to separate two or more liquids that are mixed together. When these liquids are heated together in a simple still, the liquid that boils at the lowest temperature evaporates more quickly than the other liquids. The temperature at which a liquid boils is the *boiling point*. The vapor then passes through a *condenser*. The condenser is cooled. This lowers the temperature of the vapor inside the condenser. The vapor condenses back into a liquid called a *distillate*, which collects in a *receiver*. Mixtures of liquids that have boiling points that differ greatly are distilled by a process called *simple distillation*. *Fractional distillation* is the process by which mixtures of liquids that have close boiling points are distilled into separate portions, or different fractions.

*Destructive distillation* is used to separate liquids, such as wood alcohol, from solid substances (wood). When the solid is heated in a closed container, the liquid that forms boils away as vapor. The vapor is collected and condensed into a liquid again (wood alcohol). A solid substance (charcoal) is left behind in the still.

Distillation has been used for centuries to make perfumes, flavorings, and alcoholic beverages such as whiskey, and to purify water. Fractional distillation is used to make alcoholic beverages and to separate gasoline, kerosene, fuel oil, and other useful products from petroleum.

▶ ▶ ▶ ▶ **FIND OUT MORE** ◀ ◀ ◀ ◀
Alcoholic Beverage; Petroleum

---

### 🗽 DISTRICT OF COLUMBIA

Many students from all parts of the United States make special trips to Washington, D.C., to see the nation's capital. The government buildings, national monuments, and cultural attractions in the nation's capital make the trips exciting. The white-domed Capitol and the White House are among the city's most famous buildings. The Lincoln Memorial, the Washington Monument, and the Jefferson Memorial honor three great Presidents. The Vietnam War Memorial, dedicated in 1982, honors the men and women who were killed in the armed forces in Vietnam. The Smithsonian Institution, a center of scientific learning and the nation's archives, has world-famous collections. Other attractions in Washington, D.C., are the John F. Kennedy

---

### LEARN BY DOING

Heat a kettle of water to boiling. You will see a clear space above the spout and below the cloud of "steam" that is pouring out. This space is actually the steam, or water vapor, which is water in the form of a gas. The cloud of "steam" is not water vapor, but actually a mass of condensed water droplets. Carefully place the bowl of a spoon in the cloud. Droplets of distilled water will form on the spoon, as the steam condenses.

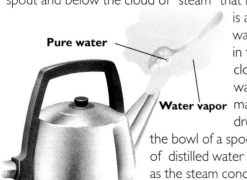

Pure water

Water vapor

## STATE SYMBOLS

◀ The city seal (in use since 1871). Justice is pictured placing a wreath on a statue of George Washington.

◀ The scarlet oak. Its leaves turn a brilliant red in autumn.

▲ The wood thrush is a songbird often found in the eastern United States. Its song sounds like a flute.

▶ The American beauty rose. The District of Columbia adopted this wonderfully fragrant rose as the official state flower on June 6, 1925.

### DISTRICT OF COLUMBIA

**Area**
69 square miles
(178 sq. km)

**Population**
606,900 people

**Principal river**
Potomac (383 miles/
616 km)

**Highest point**
420 feet (128 m)

**Motto**
(Justica omnibus)
"Justice for all"

**Song**
"Washington"

**Famous people**
Duke Ellington,
J. Edgar Hoover, John
Philip Sousa

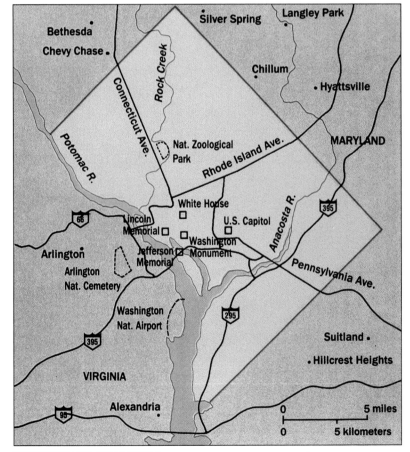

**DISTRICT OF COLUMBIA**

▲ The White House, in Washington, D.C., is the home of the President of the United States. From there he directs the administration of the government.

▼ The Washington Monument was built to pay tribute to the first President of the United States. It stands in a park bordering on the Tidal Basin.

Center for the Performing Arts, which opened in 1971, and the National Gallery of Art. The U.S. Holocaust Museum opened in 1993.

This great city began as a small area of marshy land. Congress had decided in 1790 that the United States should have a brand-new city as its capital. The city would not be in a state. It would be in a district belonging to the nation. Some bad feeling between Northern and Southern states, which later led to the Civil War, was evident even in 1790. So Congress wanted to locate the new district on the border between North and South.

Maryland and Virginia agreed to give land for the district. The district was to be a square, with each side 10 miles (16 km) long. The square would lie on both sides of the Potomac River.

George Washington was President then. He chose Pierre Charles L'Enfant, a French architect, to draw up careful plans for the capital. President Washington spoke of it as "the Federal City." But Congress decided to call it "the City of Washington in the District of Columbia," to honor both President Washington and Christopher Columbus.

President John Adams moved the Federal Government from Philadelphia to the new capital in 1800. Thomas Jefferson was the first President inaugurated there in 1801.

For many years Washington City was a forlorn little cluster of buildings on Capitol Hill. A few miles away was the prosperous port town of Georgetown on the Potomac River. The British and Americans went to war in 1812. Two years later, the British invaded Washington. The White House was burned, and important government buildings were destroyed. President James Madison's wife Dolley rescued the original Declaration of Independence from the flames.

Washington was completely rebuilt immediately after the war. It remained a small, quiet community. Congressmen and other government officials did not like to come to this undeveloped little capital city. They fled to the cultural centers of Baltimore and Philadelphia whenever they could for concerts and plays.

Congress voted in 1846 to return to Virginia the District of Columbia lands south of the Potomac River. It appeared that the city would never need all that land. Besides, slave trading was not allowed in the District of Columbia, and some Virginians wanted slave markets there.

After the Civil War, Washington grew rapidly into a large and beautiful city. Many new government office buildings were built of white or gray stone in the classical style. This style, with its graceful columns and domes, serves as a reminder of ancient Rome and its Senate. Benjamin Banneker, who became chief architect after L'Enfant resigned, saw that the city developed around the original plan of L'Enfant, using his "spokes of a wheel" city plan, with circles at street intersections. Broad, tree-shaded avenues and large parks were also built. Universities, museums, and embassies of foreign countries were established in the city. The lovely area of Georgetown became part of Washington in 1895. Georgetown's picturesque old houses, many dating back to the 1700s, gave charm to the city.

In 1874, Congress took control of Washington's government. City officials were chosen by Congress and the President. The 23rd Amendment to the Constitution, ratified in 1961, gave Washingtonians the right to vote in Presidential elections. City residents sought more national political representation and local self-government. They won a nonvoting delegate to the House of Representatives in 1970, and the right to elect their own mayor and a 13-member city council in 1974. The city also won the right to levy its own taxes.

▶▶▶▶ **FIND OUT MORE** ◀◀◀◀
Banneker, Benjamin; Capitol, United States; Congress, United States; Library of Congress; Smithsonian Institution; United States Government; White House

## DIVING

Have you tried diving from the side of a pool or from a diving board? You can accidentally hit the water with your chest first instead of your head. This is called a "belly flop," and it hurts. But once you get the swing of it, diving is great fun.

Good diving is exciting, especially when it is done from a high platform or diving board. Competitive divers, such as the people who take part in the Olympic Games, are as skillful as acrobats. They practice hard to perfect their timing, coordination, and grace of movement.

There are five basic types of dives used in competitions. In a *forward dive*, divers stand on the diving board, facing straight ahead. (They may begin by taking a few running steps.) They then dive from the board, plunging into the water in a

forward position, head first. In a *back dive*, they start out facing the board and then flip over backward into the water. In a *full gainer*, they start out facing forward, but enter the water in a backward position. A *cutaway* is just the opposite. Divers start out facing the board, but turn in the air and enter the water in a forward position. In a *twisting dive*, the diver twists in the air before plunging into the water.

Divers do some fancy movements in the air as part of these basic dives. In a *pike*, or *jackknife*, divers bend their body at the hips. They keep their knees rigid and touch their ankles with their fingertips. In a *tuck*, they bring their knees up against their chest. In a *layout*, they straighten their body and hold it parallel to the water. An example of the layout position is the *swan dive*, where the diver arches the body up and out when leaving the springboard. These positions are held for only a short time before the diver straightens out and enters the water head-first.

A dive commonly used in swimming competitions is the *racing dive*. It is done at the beginning of a race. The swimmer dives straight into the water from the edge of the pool. He

▲ The pike position is used in dives from springboards and highboards. Legs must be kept together and extended if the diver is to earn high marks in a competition.

▼ This diagram shows a selection of five popular dives often used in competitions. Dives like this require great skill and a lot of practice.

Swan dive          Back dive

Jackknife     Half twist     Half gainer

## DJIBOUTI

**Capital city**
Djibouti (290,000 people)

**Area**
8,494 square miles (22,000 sq. km)

**Population**
528,000 people

**Government**
Single-party republic

**Natural resources**
Coffee

**Export products**
Coffee, cattle, hides, skins

**Unit of money**
Djibouti franc

**Official languages**
Arabic, French

▲ Dorothea Dix, champion of reform in the care of the mentally ill. Her work also helped improve prison conditions.

or she tries to go as far as possible in the air and to skim the surface of the water as the body hits it, the legs already kicking. This way the swimmer can begin to swim at full speed as soon as the body touches the water.

▶▶▶▶ **FIND OUT MORE** ◀◀◀◀
Swimming

## DIVISION

SEE ARITHMETIC

## DIX, DOROTHEA (1802–1887)

In 1841, Dorothea Lynde Dix visited a jail in East Cambridge, Massachusetts, and was horrified to see that mentally ill people were being treated in the same way as criminals. They were chained and often beaten. She visited other jails in Massachusetts and found the same kind of conditions. She pleaded with the state legislature to do something about the problem.

Dorothea Dix was born in Hampden, Maine, and grew up in Massachusetts. She founded a school for girls in Boston in 1821, and was its head for 16 years. She spent almost 40 years of her life campaigning for better treatment of the mentally ill. She traveled throughout the United States, Canada, and Europe, talking to many people and raising money. Her work resulted in the founding of special institutions for the mentally ill in more than 20 U.S. states.

▶▶▶▶ **FIND OUT MORE** ◀◀◀◀
Mental Health

## DJIBOUTI

The small republic of Djibouti lies on the northeast coast of Africa at the southern entrance to the Red Sea. The country, which is the size of Massachusetts, is largely a stony desert with some highlands. Its climate is hot and dry.

In 1862, France gained control of the area and in 1896 named it *French Somaliland*. France renamed it the *Territory of Afars and Issas* in 1967, after the territory's two largest native tribes. The Issa tribe is one of the tribes of the people called the *Somalis*, who also live in nearby Somalia. (See the map with the article on AFRICA.)

The country took the name of its capital and largest city, Djibouti, on attaining independence from France in 1977. Many of neighboring Ethiopia's exports are carried by railroad to the port of Djibouti, where oceangoing vessels dock. Most peo-

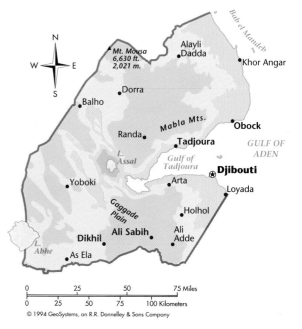

ple beyond the city are nomadic herders of goats and cattle.

▶▶▶▶ **FIND OUT MORE** ◀◀◀◀
Africa; Ethiopia; Somali Republic

# DOG

Dogs are very popular pets. They are loving, loyal, obedient, playful, and intelligent. They can be house pets, working dogs, show dogs, and sporting dogs. The same qualities that make dogs wonderful pets also make them useful working animals. Guard dogs and sentry dogs protect property. They have been used in wartime to carry coded messages. Guide dogs lead and protect people who are blind. Dogs are used by narcotics officials to smell out drugs hidden in packages and luggage. Some dogs herd sheep, goats, or cattle. Dogs can also be trained to save lives in the water or on snowy mountains, and to track down lost people.

Dogs have well-developed senses. They hear and smell better than people can. That is why hunting dogs find game better than the hunter. Whistles pitched so high that people cannot hear them are sometimes used to call dogs. Sharp teeth, powerful jaws, and speed for running away are a dog's natural defenses.

## Types of Dogs

An ancestor of the dog, which probably looked like a wolf, began to live and hunt with people about 12,000 years ago. It was the first *domesticated*, or tame, dog.

It is easy to see how dogs first began their association with primitive peoples: Scavenging packs of dogs would follow the early nomadic tribes and feed off scraps and bones. The dogs, in turn, would provide warning if anything unusual approached. Eventually, both dogs and groups of humans began to hunt together.

The dog of today is the result of centuries of breeding and close association with humans. Foxes, wolves, coyotes, and jackals are among the wild cousins of the dog. Few wild dogs exist today. One that does is the dingo of Australia, which is really a domesticated dog that ran wild. Many dogs are mixed breeds. Some people think that these dogs make the best pets. But other people prefer to own a dog of one breed: a *purebred*. A purebred has a *pedigree* (a list of the dogs in its ancestry), and it can be registered with the American Kennel Club.

*Sporting dogs* are a group of medium-sized to large dogs that are used for hunting game and as pets. Setters, retrievers, spaniels, and pointers are sporting dogs. Most of them are slim, with long legs and a keen sense of smell.

The golden retriever and the Irish setter are probably the best-known sporting dogs. The golden retriever is a medium-sized hunting dog, which is also very popular as a guide dog for the blind. It has a rich golden coat and a very friendly personality. The Irish setter is often used to hunt birds. It has a bright, coppery-red coat. Chesapeake Bay retrievers, English retrievers, German shorthaired and wirehaired pointers, cocker spaniels, and Weimaraners are some other sporting dogs.

**Rolled leather collar**

**Trigger clip**

**Choke chain**

**Decorative collar**

▲ **A selection of different dog collars, both practical and decorative. A choke chain is used for obedience work. A leather lead and collar, with a trigger clip, is suitable for a dog's walk.**

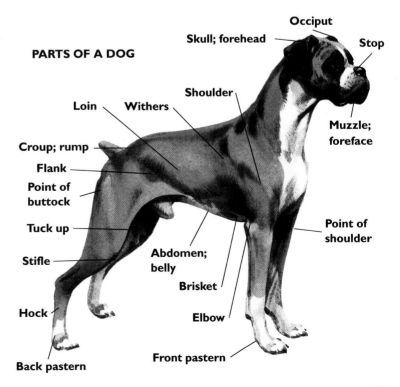

**PARTS OF A DOG**

Occiput

Skull; forehead

Stop

Shoulder

Muzzle; foreface

Loin  Withers

Croup; rump

Flank

Point of buttock

Point of shoulder

Tuck up

Stifle

Abdomen; belly

Brisket

Hock

Elbow

Front pastern

Back pastern

## BREEDS OF DOGS
### ELIGIBLE FOR REGISTRATION IN AMERICAN KENNEL CLUB STUD BOOK

### SPORTING GROUP
Brittanys
Pointers
Pointers, German
  shorthaired
Pointers, German
  wirehaired
Retrievers, Chesapeake
  Bay
Retrievers, curly-coated
Retrievers, flat-coated
Retrievers, golden
Retrievers, Labrador
Retrievers, English
Setters, English
Setters, Gordon
Setters, Irish
Spaniels, American water
Spaniels, clumber
Spaniels, cocker
Spaniels, English cocker
Spaniels, English springer
Spaniels, field
Spaniels, Irish water
Spaniels, Sussex
Spaniels, Welsh springer
Vizslas
Weimaraners
Wirehaired pointing
  Griffons

### HOUND GROUP
Afghan hounds
Basenjis
Basset hounds
Beagles
Black & tan coonhounds
Bloodhounds
Borzois
Dachshunds
Foxhounds, American
Foxhounds, English
Greyhounds
Harriers
Ibizan hounds
Irish wolfhounds
Norwegian elkhounds
Otter hounds
Pharaoh hounds
Rhodesian ridgebacks
Salukis
Scottish deerhounds
Whippets

### WORKING GROUP
Akitas
Alaskan malamutes
Bernese mountain dog
Boxers
Bullmastiffs
Doberman pinschers
Giant schnauzers
Great Danes
Great Pyrenees
Komondorok
Kuvaszok
Mastiffs
Newfoundlands
Portuguese water dogs
Rottweilers
St. Bernards
Samoyeds
Siberian huskies
Standard schnauzers

### TERRIER GROUP
Airedale terriers
American Staffordshire
  terriers
Australian terriers
Bedlington terriers
Border terriers
Bull terriers
Cairn terriers
Dandie Dinmont terriers
Irish terriers
Kerry blue terriers
Lakeland terriers
Manchester terriers
Miniature schnauzers
Norfolk terriers
Norwich terriers
Scottish terriers
Sealyham terriers
Skye terriers
Smooth fox terriers
Soft-coated Wheaten
  terriers
Staffordshire bull
  terriers
Welsh terriers
West Highland white
  terriers
White fox terriers

### TOY GROUP
Affenpinschers
Brussels Griffons
Chihuahuas
English toy spaniels
Italian greyhounds
Japanese Chin
Maltese
Manchester terriers
Miniature pinschers
Papillons
Pekingese
Pomeranians
Poodles (Toy)
Pugs
Shih Tzu
Silky terriers
Yorkshire terriers

### NON-SPORTING GROUP
Bichons frises
Boston terriers
Bulldogs
Chow Chows
Dalmatians
French bulldogs
Keeshonden
Lhasa Apsos
Poodles
Schipperkes
Tibetan spaniels
Tibetan terriers

### HERDING GROUP
Australian cattle dogs
Bearded collies
Belgian malinois
Belgian sheepdogs
Belgian Tervuren
Bouviers des Flandres
Briards
Collies
German shepherd dogs
Old English sheepdogs
Pulik
Shetland sheepdogs
Welsh Corgis, Cardigan
Welsh Corgis, Pembroke

*Working dogs* are many different sizes and shapes. They also have many different abilities. All of them are useful to people in some way, but they make good pets, too. Some working dogs, such as the collie and the Belgian sheepdog, were first bred to herd sheep. The strong, and sometimes fierce, Doberman pinscher and the German shepherd make good guard dogs. Despite their great size, the Great Dane and the Saint Bernard are among the calmest of breeds. Siberian huskies and other working breeds are used as sled dogs in cold climates.

The *hound* breeds are quick, graceful, and lively. They love to romp and play. Many hounds are used in hunting and in dog racing. The basset hound and the dachshund have very short legs and long bodies. Greyhounds and whippets can run faster than other dogs. Police use bloodhounds for tracking because of their keen sense of smell. The saluki is probably the oldest breed of dog. They were the royal dogs of Egypt.

▼ **When two breeds of dog are mated, the puppies that they produce, may have a combination of features from each parent. The puppies are called cross-breeds.**

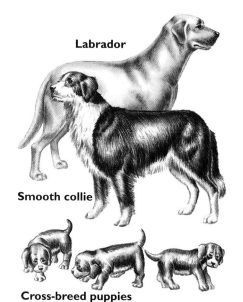

**Labrador**

**Smooth collie**

**Cross-breed puppies**

*Terriers* were first bred to hunt rodents by going down into their underground burrows. Many terriers are wire-haired, with coarse, wavy coats. Most of the terrier breeds are medium or small in size. They can run very fast, and they are frisky. Terriers were first brought to the United States from Britain. Another terrier, the Bedlington, resembles a fluffy white sheep. The Scottish terrier and the Cairn terrier have alert expressions and long whiskers. Skye terriers have long fur, hiding the body and eyes. The Airedale terrier is one of the bravest breeds.

*Nonsporting* dogs are usually pets or show dogs, and they are rarely used in sport or as working dogs. The Dalmatian has a white coat with black spots. It is sometimes a fire-department mascot. Boston terriers are small dogs with pug noses. They are not true terriers. Bulldogs are slightly pigeon-toed and have many wrinkles on their faces. The most popular nonsporting breed is the poodle, which comes in several sizes. It was originally a water retriever. Poodles are intelligent and lively, and they love to show off. They are often used in circus acts.

All *toy dogs* are unusually small in size. They are brave and alert, but some of them are nervous. The smallest poodle is a toy. The Pekingese is a proud little dog, whose body and expression are lion-like. The Yorkshire terrier has long, silky hair and usually weighs less than nine pounds (4 kg). Pomeranians and pugs have courageous, independent characters. The littlest dog of all is the Chihuahua. An adult Chihuahua can sit in the palm of a man's hand. Although they are small, toy dogs often have loud barks.

## Selection, Care, and Training

A female dog carries her young for about two months before giving birth to puppies. Usually four to six puppies are in a litter, but a litter may have only one or many more than six. The puppies are cared for and nursed by the mother for about a month.

The best time to get a puppy is when it is between six and eight weeks old. Make sure that the puppy is healthy. It should have clear, bright eyes; a shiny coat; a cool, moist nose; and an alert personality. Pick the liveliest puppy in the litter. A new puppy should be taken to a veterinarian, who will check its health and give it shots against rabies and distemper.

### WHERE TO DISCOVER MORE

Siegel, Mary-Ellen, and Hermine M. Koplin. *More Than a Friend: Dogs With a Purpose.* New York: Walker & Co., 1984.

Silverstein, Alvin and Virginia. *Dogs: All About Them.* New York: Lothrop, Lee & Shepard Books, 1986.

**Newfoundland**

**Black and tan coonhound**

**American foxhound**

**Boston terrier**

**American cocker spaniel**

▲ **A selection of North American dog breeds. The American Kennel Club (AKC) is the main organization of dog breeders in the United States. There are about 130 breeds of dogs registered with them. The breeds are divided into seven groups: sporting, hound, toy, working, herding, terrier, and nonsporting breeds.**

## ▶ TRAINING A DOG

**1. Heel.** Do not let your dog pull on the lead. If it is not in the right position, gently jerk it back. **2. Sit.** Hold your dog's head up with one hand while pushing its rear down with the other. **3. Down.** Gently slide the dog's forepaws out from under it. **4. and 5. Stay and Come.** Stand in front of your dog to stop it moving until you tell it to come. Gradually increase the distance between you and your dog. **6. Praise.** Pet your dog for every success. Don't ever get irritable or lose your temper.

The great inventor Thomas Edison made a singing doll. He placed a small phonograph inside the doll's body, and the phonograph could be made to play different tunes.

Get a dog license and a collar for your new dog as soon as possible.

Dogs can get sick easily. For this reason, the dog owner must feed his pet a balanced diet, give it a dry and sheltered place to sleep, and brush it regularly. Find out what is the best diet for your dog from a veterinarian or a good book on dog care. Dogs need plenty of water, meat, and dog biscuits. Never give a dog a bone that might splinter. Big dogs need a lot of exercise and space in which to run and walk about.

All dogs need training. Housebreaking (to teach a dog not to soil indoors) is the first training a puppy gets. Put down fresh newspapers and praise it when it uses them. Take your puppy outdoors often, especially after feeding, to encourage clean habits. Do not allow your dog to soil the sidewalk.

A young dog should learn to obey its owner. It should learn to walk on a leash, come when you call, sit, stay, and lie down. After it has mastered the basic commands, it can also learn tricks. Even though dogs are anxious to please, it takes a lot of time to train them. Teach your dog one thing at a time. Never rush it or get impatient. Praise and tidbits of food when it behaves correctly are more effective than punishment when it is bad.

Use the same word or command every time you tell a dog to do something. For example, do not say "down" one time and "lie" another time. After the dog has perfectly mastered one command, it can then learn another one. With patience, a dog can be taught many tricks and become an important member of the household.

### ▶▶▶▶ FIND OUT MORE ◀◀◀◀
Aesop; Carnivore; Coyote; Domesticated Animals; Fox; London, Jack; Mammal; Pet; Wolf

## DOLL

Children all over the world love to play with dolls. Even if the doll is only a stick covered with cloth, it can become a beloved friend and a constant entertainment. Dolls are really toy people.

### Ancient Dolls

Doll-like figures have been found from the most ancient times. But dolls were not made especially for children to play with until the 1700s. Some of these ancient dolls may have been religious or magical figures.

Dolls were buried with rich people in ancient Egypt. Many Egyptian dolls were flat pieces of wood, painted to represent people at work. The Egyptians may have believed that the dolls would serve the spirit of the person buried in the tomb. The dolls were made without legs so that they would not be able to run away. Because of their odd shape, these dolls without legs are called *paddle dolls*.

We know that Greek and Roman children played with dolls. They had clothes for their dolls and tiny (miniature) pieces of furniture. When a Greek or Roman girl got married, she offered her dolls to the gods.

### Crib and Fashion Dolls

A very special kind of doll became popular in Italy during the 1400s. At Christmas time, models were made of the crib, or manger, in which Christ was laid. Dolls representing Mary, Joseph, and the Christ Child were placed at the crib. The Three Kings who followed the star to Bethlehem were also part of the scene. The artists who made these dolls used very hard wax for the heads. The wax could be carved and colored to look like real skin. The costumes were made of silks and velvets in lovely colors. Some churches still have these scenes, called *crèches*, and display them at Christmas.

Today, magazines and newspapers show people the latest clothing styles. *Fashion dolls* were made for the same purpose in the past. In 1391, the queen of England sent to France for dolls dressed in the latest fashions. Women in the American colonies ordered fashion dolls from both England and France.

### Dolls for Children

Many dolls were, however, made just for children to play with. Some were carved from wood or bone. Others were made of clay, leather, or wax. Dolls for wealthy children were often made of two different materials. The head, and often the legs and arms

were made of fine china, or *porcelain*. They were attached to a cloth body stuffed with sawdust or grain.

By the 1600s, doll making had become a very important business in Germany. Carved German wooden and porcelain dolls were sold all over Europe. Some dolls had a solid base to make them stand upright. They were called *stump dolls*. *Pantin* dolls had jointed legs with strings that could be pulled to make them move. Clothes were carved and painted on some dolls. Others were dressed in real clothes like the fashion dolls had been.

After 1826, dolls were made with eyes that opened and closed. Other dolls could say "Mama" and "Papa." A little machine inside some dolls made them walk by themselves. Dolls had usually been models of grown-ups

▲ In ancient Greece, girls played with dolls, mostly made of wood. Before marriage, they offered them to the gods to show they had outgrown childish things.

▼ The dolls pictured here were made in the 1800s, a time when many new kinds of dolls were created using a variety of materials, such as china.

▲ **This dollhouse can be seen in the National Museum of History and Technology, in Washington, D.C. It is a fine example of a typical wealthy American home of the early twentieth century (1900–1914). Each room is decorated and furnished in the style of the time.**

until this time. But dolls that looked like real babies became popular after 1850. By that time, most dolls were being made in factories.

## American Dolls

Most children in the American colonies played with homemade dolls. Some of these dolls were made of corncobs, pinecones, or any material that was around the house. *Rag dolls* were also popular. These dolls were made of cloth stuffed with straw or sawdust. Their features were embroidered or painted on, and

buttons were often used for eyes. A few wealthy children were given beautiful china or wax dolls from Germany and France. Dolls were made in factories in the United States after 1900.

Some American dolls became very famous. "Billiken" was a doll that every little girl wanted in 1910. "Raggedy Ann" and "Raggedy Andy" are two dolls that have been popular for decades. Some dolls were modeled after real people. They were called *character dolls*. The "Shirley Temple doll" was made to look like the popular child movie actress. There are also lifelike baby dolls, dolls modeled after favorite TV and comic heroes, personalized dolls that come with their own name on a birth certificate, and teenage dolls, such as "Barbie," that come with fashionable clothes and accessories. Dolls are now usually made of unbreakable materials like plastic or rubber.

## Paper Dolls

Japanese and Chinese children have had *paper dolls* for hundreds of years. In the 1800s, European printers sold sheets with printed dolls to be cut out and dressed in flat paper clothes. Like the fashion dolls, they showed the latest styles. You can now buy whole books of paper dolls and clothes.

## Doll Collections

Many people collect dolls, especially dolls made long ago. Museums have collections of dolls. One of the most interesting American doll collections can be seen at the Museum of the City of New York. One good way to start a doll collection is to have dolls wearing the national costumes of different countries. But the best collection of dolls is made up of the dolls that you have loved and taken care of for many years.

▶ ▶ ▶ ▶ **FIND OUT MORE** ◀ ◀ ◀ ◀
Toys

---

## LEARN BY DOING

To make your own dolls you may have to use your imagination. But if you look around your house and garden, you will find many objects that can be made into dolls. Cotton swabs, pipecleaners, and hairpins can become arms and legs. Spools, corks, and acorns make bodies and heads. To make a paper doll, draw the figure of a person on stiff paper and cut it out. Then, on thin paper, draw a suit of clothes the right size and shape to fit the figure. Cut out the clothes, leaving little tabs at the shoulders and waist. You can fit the clothes onto your doll by bending the tabs around the back of the figure.

You could make a rag doll too. Stuff the leg of a sock or stocking with cotton or scraps of material. Sew up the open ends and bind the stocking tightly with thread to make a neck and waist. Then make a face for your doll, either by painting or embroidering the features onto the face. You can sew separate pieces of stocking into tubes to make the dolls arms and legs. Stuff them and sew them onto the body. You can use scraps of material to make beautiful clothes for your dolls.

# DOLPHINS AND PORPOISES

A fisherman happily landed a large fish, when a huge wave suddenly swamped his small boat. He was tossed into the water, and he knew he could never swim to shore. Then something touched him. "A shark!" he thought. But before he could panic, he felt himself being lifted to the water's surface. "The gods are good," he thought, and he relaxed as a dolphin gently pushed him toward shore.

Tales such as this are common among seacoast peoples, who since ancient times have regarded the sea-living mammals, called "dolphins," as friendly. To the ancient Greeks, dolphins were the helpers of Poseidon, god of the sea.

Other people scoffed at these legends. Now, scientists taking a closer look at dolphins and their relatives, porpoises, are finding out through their studies, that the old tales were probably based on truth.

## Mammals of the Sea

Dolphins and porpoises are mammals. They breathe air and give birth to living young that they suckle. They belong to the order or group of mammals called *cetaceans,* which includes whales. Dolphins have beaklike mouths. Porpoises have blunt mouths and are smaller than dolphins. But both dolphins and porpoises are toothed whales, and their close relatives include the killer, sperm, and pilot whales.

Cetaceans are mammals that returned to the sea. Their hind legs disappeared and were replaced by a strongly muscled tail-end and a flat tail or *fluke.* The front legs evolved into flippers. One primitive species—

▼ In ancient times, Mediterranean people often portrayed dolphins and porpoises in art, as on this drinking cup.

the boutu or river dolphin of the Amazon and other Southern American rivers—has finger bones that still show clearly in its flippers. Most mammalian hair has also disappeared from the streamlined body of the cetacean.

The nostrils for breathing air have gradually moved to the forehead. In the dolphins and porpoises, the nostrils have become one "blowhole," which leads right to the lungs instead of to the mouth and throat. The river-living dolphins, such as the boutu, must come up for air every 30 seconds, but the ocean dolphins can stay under water for several minutes. When they surface, a great spout of moist, used air is released from the blowhole. More air is taken in, and they dive again.

A dolphin or porpoise baby is born in the water, tail first. The mother and at least one other female dolphin, which acts as

## WHERE TO DISCOVER MORE

Patent, Dorothy Hinshaw. *Dolphins and Porpoises.* New York: Holiday House, 1987.

Rinard, Judith E. *Dolphins: Our Friends in the Sea.* Washington, D.C.: National Geographic Society, 1986.

▼ Bottle-nosed dolphins live in warm or tropical waters. They can leap up to 32 feet (10 m) out of the water. These dolphins always seem to be smiling, due to the shape of their head, and short, rounded beak, or snout.

▲ **The bottle-nosed dolphin grows to a length of about 12 feet (4 m). It is a naturally playful animal, and shows friendliness towards humans.**

**Common dolphin**

**Killer whale**

▲ **Dolphins and porpoises are part of the whale family. They range from 4 to 30 feet long. The killer whale is the largest dolphin.**

"nurse," then rush it to the surface for its first breath of air. Gradually the baby moves to deeper water and can stay under water for longer periods of time. At first mother and baby return to the surface for the baby to suckle its mother's milk. The baby spends a full year feeding on milk and never strays from its mother. Usually only one baby is born at a time.

### Intelligence and Communication

Scientists are discovering that our kinship with dolphins and porpoises is quite close in some ways. We both have language. We are both intelligent. We both try to help friends and neighbors in trouble. And we both get stomach ulcers.

Dolphins carry on conversations with each other. So do porpoises and, probably, other whales. They make a great variety of sounds, mainly clicks and whistles, which are produced by a complex group of air sacs and valves in the head. (They do not have vocal chords like ours.) If one dolphin of a group is caught in a trap, it appears to warn the others, not just of general danger, but specifically what and where the danger is. The dolphins then seem to discuss how to release the trapped one and carry out their plan.

Each animal continually sends out an echo-sounding signal that locates prey, obstacles, and any other objects in the water. When a dolphin is resting, one signal is emitted every 20 seconds. When actively hunting, a dolphin sends out about five signals every second. A very complex brain—perhaps as complex as ours—picks out the specific echo the animal is interested in from the thousands of sounds and echoes always bouncing through the water. Dolphins have no outer ear, just a tiny pinhole behind the eye, but their hearing is superb.

The star performers at marine aquariums and in research work are usually *bottle-nosed dolphins*. These dolphins appear to enjoy human company, although no one can say how they feel about being kept in captivity. Dolphins can learn tricks much more quickly than dogs. But dolphins cannot be taught to do tricks that they do not want to do. When a dolphin does learn a game or trick, the animal seems to understand the purpose of the game, and it may even add some ideas of its own.

The *common dolphin* prefers deep water and does not do well in captivity, which usually is in a fairly shallow pool.

**Common porpoise**

The dolphins often seen leaping around ships are common dolphins.

Dolphins are not always playful. They are among the few animals that will fight sharks. An attacked dolphin tries to get some swimming space, and then charges rapidly from underneath so that its hard beak hits the shark's soft belly. Dolphins are even said to have saved swimmers from sharks, and to have carried drowning people to shore.

▶ ▶ ▶ ▶ **FIND OUT MORE** ◀ ◀ ◀ ◀
Mammal; Whales and Whaling

# DOMESTICATED ANIMALS

People first made regular contact with animals through hunting and fishing. Prehistoric people chased animals, perhaps trapping them in pits or driving them into traps with fire. But gradually our ancient ancestors came to depend on keeping some animals near, both to help with hunting and to supply meat and milk. Those animals, in turn, came to depend on people for food and shelter. The animals were *domesticated,* or tamed.

because smaller animals needing less food were bred more often than larger, harder-to-control animals. Domesticated animals also became gentler. Later, when a species was completely domesticated, it might be bred for size again, the way beef cattle were in the 1800s. Some horses were bred for speed and others for strength. Sheep were bred for thick woolly coats. In some animals, the teeth, horns, and even head shape have changed through domestication, as a result of this *selective breeding.*

▼ This picture from the 1400s shows a farmer plowing with oxen. Oxen are slow-moving animals, but very strong. They were used on farms until the 1800s.

No one knows for sure when and how animals were domesticated. Wild dogs may have been the first, perhaps as long ago as 20,000 years. It may be that people took in some dog puppies, after killing their mothers. The pups grew up alongside the people and helped in the hunt. A partnership began. Keeping young animals as pets may also have been how people began to domesticate animals that they had always hunted. Soon tame dogs were helping to control herds of reindeer, goats, and sheep.

Once a group of wild animals was tamed, their young became even tamer because they depended on people from the time they were born. Over hundreds of years, a domesticated animal often became quite different from its wild relatives. Many of them were smaller, perhaps

The process can happen in reverse, too. Domesticated animals released from captivity turn wild again if they survive. Such animals are called *feral animals.* Within a few generations, feral animals may return to the size and shape of their wild relatives. The dingo is a feral dog that was brought to Australia 12,000 years ago by the aborigines and later returned to the wild. The wild mustangs of the American West are feral horses.

## Reasons for Domestication

The animals that have been domesticated fit into several groups by their use. Some animals fit into more than one group. One group includes animals that are useful for getting rid of pests. The cat, for example, eats mice and other rodents that destroy grain. The Indian mongoose attacks and kills dangerous snakes called

It has been estimated that there are more than 55 million domesticated cats in the United States and 52 million dogs. Cats usually live longer than dogs. There have been cases of cats living for more than 32 years. Most dogs live from 8 to 14 years, and there have been very few cases of dogs living any longer than 20 years.

◄A sheepdog working to round up three sheep. From the earliest times, herdsmen have trained dogs to help them control their flocks.

▼ All types of pet rabbits have been bred from wild rabbits. They now come in different sizes, colors, and even shapes. The tiny dwarf lop-eared rabbit has ears that droop.

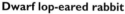

**Wild rabbit**          **Dwarf lop-eared rabbit**

▲ Kittens that are not exposed to live prey, may never learn the killing bite which severs the spinal cord of their prey.

812

cobras. Another group is made up of those that provide milk, meat, and hides, such as cattle, goats, and sheep. A third group contains working animals such as horses, elephants, donkeys, and camels. Cattle come partly into this group because oxen have great strength and can pull heavy loads.

Animals that provide useful products make up another group. The mink is bred for its soft, luxurious fur. More sheep are raised for their wool than for their meat. The Chinese discovered centuries ago that the cocoon fibers of the silkworm moth made a beautiful soft fabric, silk. Honeybees are kept for the sweet honey they produce. And chickens are kept for their eggs and meat.

A final group of domesticated animals are kept purely as pets. Cage birds, such as canaries, parakeets, and finches, have entertained people for centuries. Many cats and dogs are family pets. Goldfish were once plain little pond fish, but they have been bred into creatures of great beauty and variety.

Unfortunately, one result of domesticating animals has been the gradual elimination of their wild rel-atives so that mating between wild and tame animals could not occur. The ancestors of cattle (one of which was probably the aurochs) are now extinct. Truly wild horses are almost extinct and live mainly in zoos. Some exist in Chinocoteague on the Chesapeake Bay. But we have fed and clothed ourselves and made life easier by forming domestic partnerships with animals.

▶ ▶ ▶ ▶ **FIND OUT MORE** ◀ ◀ ◀ ◀
Bee; Camel; Cat; Cattle; Dog; Donkey; Ecology; Elephant; Fur; Goat; Horse; Pet; Poultry; Sheep

## DOMINICA

SEE WEST INDIES

## DOMINICAN REPUBLIC

SEE WEST INDIES

## DOMINOES

Dominoes is a simple, enjoyable game that is played the world over.

A set of dominoes has 28 flat black blocks made of wood or plastic. Each domino has white dots on one of its sides. The side with the dots is called the *face*. The face is divided into two halves. Most of the dominoes have from one to six dots on each half of their faces. But a few have one or both halves blank.

### How to Play
Two to four people can play dominoes. The floor or any table can be the playing surface. At the start of a game, all the dominoes are placed on the table, face down. When two peo-

ple are playing the game, each one selects seven dominoes. In a game with three or four players, each one selects five dominoes. The extra dominoes remain in the center of the table for the time being.

The first player lays one domino face up on the table. The second player looks to see if one of his or her dominoes can match the number of dots on either half of the first player's domino. If this player can match the dots, he or she places that domino next to the first one. The dominoes are placed in a line, with their matching dots together. The blank halves can be matched, too.

If the second player cannot match the first domino, he or she must pick up another one from the extra dominoes on the table. After several plays, the extra dominoes may be all gone. Then, when a player can't make a match, he or she must lose this turn. The winner is the first one who plays all his or her dominoes.

## DONKEY

The donkey is a domesticated ass and is closely related to the horse. It has a rough coat, long ears, and short mane. A donkey stands 4½ feet (1.4 m) high and makes a loud braying sound. A donkey is more sure-footed and more stubborn than a horse and has greater endurance. It may live to be 50 years old—far longer than a horse. Donkeys are used as beasts of burden in many countries.

Donkeys are hard working and especially useful on steep mountain trails. During the days of the Gold Rush in the western United States, prospectors often used donkeys as pack animals.

▼ Most sets of dominoes consist of 28 pieces, which are usually made out of wood, plastic, ivory, or bone. Dominoes were probably invented by the Chinese, and later introduced into Europe in the 1300s.

The *burro*, a small donkey, is usually used as a pack animal. *Dwarf* donkeys, the smallest kind, are kept as pets. A male donkey is called a *jack*, or *jackass*, and a female is called a *jenny*.

Their offspring is known as a *colt*. A *mule* is an animal that has a donkey for a father and a horse for a mother. A *hinny* has a donkey for a mother and a horse for a father. Mules and hinnies are bigger than donkeys. In the past, mules were harnessed in teams to pull plows and wagons. A mule is normally *sterile* (that is, it can not breed).

Few kinds of wild asses are alive today. The *onager* and the *kiang* are Asian wild asses. They are small, with shaggy coats, and short manes and ears. They can run fast across the deserts and plains. African wild asses were the ancestors of the donkey.

▼ Donkeys can carry very heavy loads for their size. They are patient and hardworking, and have been used as pack animals for many centuries.

▶▶▶▶ **FIND OUT MORE** ◀◀◀◀
Domesticated Animals; Horse; Mammal

▼ The pitch of the sound made by a motorcycle seems to get higher as it approaches an observer and lower as it moves away. This is caused by the movement of the source of the waves in relation to the observer.

# DOPPLER EFFECT

Listen to the sound of a train's whistle as it passes a curve or a grade crossing. The whistle's *pitch*, or the sound it makes, seems to go down as the train moves away. But the same

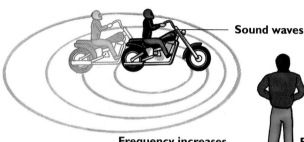
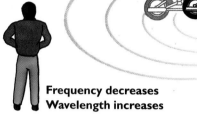

Sound waves

Frequency increases
Wavelength decreases

Frequency decreases
Wavelength increases

whistle doesn't seem to change if the train is stopped. This change in pitch is caused by the *Doppler effect*. It was first described by Christian Johann Doppler, an Austrian physicist, in 1842.

Sound travels through the air in waves, like the waves that spread out from a stone that is thrown into the water. The different pitches that we hear correspond to the distances between these sound waves. These gaps are also called *wavelengths*.

The pitch of the sounds we hear depend on their *frequency*, or the number of waves we hear in a given time. We hear a longer wavelength as a lower pitch because it has a lower frequency, and shorter wavelengths sound higher.

The Doppler effect describes how these wavelengths become shorter as an object approaches an observer. Those of an object traveling away become longer.

Imagine that train whistle again. When the train is stopped, you hear the same note because the sound reaches you at the same wavelength that it had when it was emitted. The sound keeps the same frequency. But as the train moves away, each wave is emitted farther apart, so each wavelength becomes longer. The fre-

quency becomes lower, so the sound of the train whistle seems to become lower. In the same way the train whistle seems to become higher as the train approaches.

Astronomers use their knowledge of the Doppler effect in order to study the light coming from distant stars and galaxies. Like sound, light travels in waves. What we see as different colors are the different frequencies of light waves. Light from objects traveling away from us appears red because the color red has a longer wavelength than the other colors. Astronomers call this change *red shift*.

Because light travels much faster than sound, an object must be traveling extremely fast for its light to appear redder. All objects outside our own solar system appear at least a bit red, so they must be moving away from us.

The most distant objects appear even redder, which means that they are traveling away from us faster. This increasing red shift may be evidence for one theory that the universe was created with a *Big Bang*. That theory says that objects in space have been flying away from each other since an explosion that may have started the universe.

▶▶▶▶ **FIND OUT MORE** ◀◀◀◀
Astronomy; Light; Red Shift; Sound; Universe; Wave

# DOUGLAS, STEPHEN A. (1813–1861)

Stephen Arnold Douglas was a Democratic Senator from Illinois before the Civil War. Nicknamed the "Little Giant," Douglas is best remembered for the seven debates he

To make a red traffic light appear green, you would have to drive towards it at a speed of about 37,282 miles per second (60,000 km/s)! The apparent change in the frequency (color) of the light waves given out by the traffic lights would be caused by the motion of the driver in relation to the traffic lights.

▲ Stephen A. Douglas, the Democratic opponent of Abraham Lincoln.

had with Abraham Lincoln on the question of slavery.

Douglas was born in Brandon, Vermont. He moved to Illinois as a young man and became a lawyer. He was elected to Congress, and in 1847, he became a U.S. Senator. Douglas introduced the Kansas-Nebraska Bill to let people in these territories decide upon slavery by popular vote. This bill turned many people against him.

People who were against slavery formed a new party, the Republican Party, in 1854. When Douglas ran for re-election to the Senate in 1858, the Republicans chose Lincoln to run against him. Lincoln challenged Douglas to debate and Douglas accepted. The debates were held in several cities and towns in Illinois. The two politicians attracted great attention all over the country as they argued over slavery. Lincoln said slavery should not be allowed in new U.S. territories. Douglas said that the territories should decide about slavery for themselves, and he won the election.

In 1860, the northern Democrats nominated Douglas to run for President against Lincoln, the Republican candidate. Douglas lost the election and died the next year.

▶▶▶▶ **FIND OUT MORE** ◀◀◀◀
Lincoln, Abraham; Slavery

## DOUGLASS, FREDERICK
### (about 1817–1895)

Frederick Douglass was born a slave in Tuckahoe, Maryland. The cruelty that he suffered there led him to escape from his owner in 1838. He

fled to Massachusetts, where he became a laborer and taught himself to read and write.

In 1841, Douglass attended a meeting of a Massachusetts *abolitionist* (anti-slavery) group. He gave such an excellent speech that the leaders of the group hired him as a regular speaker. He began to lecture at many meetings, telling of the evils of slavery. In 1845, his friends urged him to go to England, because they feared he might be captured as a runaway slave. Douglass spent two years as a public speaker in England and Ireland. His English friends raised money so that he could return home and buy his freedom. When he returned to the United States in 1847, Douglass began his own anti-slavery newspaper, *The North Star*. It became an important source of news and opinion for slaves, free blacks, and all people who were opposed to slavery in the United States.

During the Civil War, Douglass helped organize two regiments of black Soldiers in Massachusetts to fight for the North. After the war and the freeing of the slaves, he continued to struggle for equal rights for blacks. His leadership was highly respected, and he was appointed to several government posts, including that of U.S. Minister to Haiti.

▶▶▶▶ **FIND OUT MORE** ◀◀◀◀
Abolition; Civil War;
Slavery

▲ **Although Stephen A. Douglas was a short man, his powerful speaking voice and strong build gained him the nickname the "Little Giant."**

▲ **Frederick Douglass, one of the most outstanding civil rights leaders in United States history.**

▲ Sir Arthur Conan Doyle, author of the Sherlock Holmes stories.

▼ Dragonflies are among the world's fastest insects. They can travel through the air at speeds of 19 miles per hour (30 km/h) and can make amazing high-speed turns to snatch smaller insects in mid-air.

## DOYLE, SIR ARTHUR CONAN (1859–1930)

A club exists in Britain and the United States in memory of a detective who lived only in books. The detective is Sherlock Holmes, and the club is the Baker Street Irregulars. Holmes was the creation of Sir Arthur Conan Doyle.

Conan Doyle was born in Edinburgh, Scotland. He became a doctor but turned to writing. In 1887, he published his first Sherlock Holmes story, *A Study in Scarlet*. He wrote many books, including romantic and historical novels and some plays. But he could never get away from Holmes' success. Sherlock Holmes appeared in 68 stories, including the famous *The Hound of the Baskervilles* and *The Sign of Four*. Holmes is a detective who excels in deduction. He draws marvelous conclusions from the smallest bits of evidence. His loyal friend, Dr. Watson, lives with him on Baker Street in London and works on many cases with him. After writing so many Sherlock Holmes stories, Doyle became tired of Holmes and had him killed in a story. Faithful readers everywhere insisted that Sherlock Holmes be brought back, and Doyle gave in to their demands and wrote more stories about the famous fictional detective. Conan Doyle was knighted in 1902.

▶ ▶ ▶ ▶ **FIND OUT MORE** ◀ ◀ ◀ ◀
Detective

## DRAGON

SEE ANIMALS OF MYTH AND LEGEND

## DRAGONFLY

Dragonflies are the tigers of the insect world. Large, swift, skillful fliers, with excellent eyesight (compared to other insects) and strong jaws, dragonflies are superb hunters. They are found near fresh water in almost all parts of the world, especially in South America and Japan.

Dragonflies have long, narrow, red, green, blue, brown, or black bodies. They have two pairs of transparent veined wings. These may be striped or splotched in brilliant colors or may reflect light in rainbow hues. Dragonflies have large, compound eyes that enable them to see in all directions. Their legs are formed for perching, rather than walking. Dragonflies range from 2 inches (5 cm) in length with a 2½-inch (6-cm) wingspan to 5 inches (13 cm), with a 7½-inch (19-cm) wingspan.

Dragonflies feed on a large variety of insects, which they catch in flight. When hunting, the dragonfly forms its legs into a kind of basket and scoops its prey out of the air.

Dragonfly eggs, which are laid in water, hatch wingless larvae, called *nymphs*. They live in water from one

to three years, then become adult dragonflies.

Dragonflies sometimes are called devil's darning needles, snake doctors, and mule killers. These names make them sound like unfriendly insects, but in fact dragonflies are useful to people. They prey on many harmful insect pests, such as mosquitoes. There are two main groups of dragonflies. *True* dragonflies rest with their wings outstretched. *Damsel flies* rest with their wings held upward and do not fly as fast as the true dragonflies.

▶▶▶▶ **FIND OUT MORE** ◀◀◀◀

Insect

## DRAKE, SIR FRANCIS (1540–1596)

This daring English sea captain was such a fierce fighter that the Spaniards called him the "Dragon." Drake left home in Devon, England, as a child to go to sea as a captain's cabin boy. He was captain of his own ship by the time he reached his mid-twenties. He sailed on a slave-trading voyage to the West Indies in 1567. The Spanish attacked the English fleet and seized or sank most of the ships. Drake escaped with his own ship, vowing to get even with the Spanish.

Drake returned to the area five years later with only 73 men and landed in Panama. They captured the Fort of San Lorenzo on the Atlantic and marched across the isthmus to capture the city of Panama on the Pacific Ocean. This was the first of Drake's many acts of piracy against the Spaniards. In Panama, Drake gazed on the Pacific Ocean and vowed he would be the first Englishman to sail upon it.

In 1577, Drake set off from England in his ship, the *Golden Hind*. He sailed around the tip of South America and into the Pacific. He looted Spanish settlements along the Pacific coast of South America.

Drake knew the Spanish would expect him to return to England by the same route. He sailed as far north as the present state of Washington, hoping to find a water passage east across America, but without success. So he went west across the Pacific, circled south of Africa and arrived in England three years after he set out. He was the first Englishman to have circled the Earth. For this feat he was knighted by Queen Elizabeth I.

In 1588, the Spanish determined to crush the English once and for all. They built a great fleet of ships called the "Armada" and set out to invade England. Drake was one of the commanders of the English fleet, which succeeded in routing the Armada and saving England.

Drake died of dysentery on a voyage to the West Indies. He was buried at sea in the harbor of Portobello, a Spanish fortified city on the coast of Panama.

▶▶▶▶ **FIND OUT MORE** ◀◀◀◀
Elizabeth I; Exploration; Magellan, Ferdinand; Spanish Armada

## DRAMA

Making up a play can be great fun. You don't even have to write down the words. With a few friends, choose a situation and the right number of characters (parts, or *roles*, in your play), and start acting. (Pretend you meet an alien in the backyard; you are stranded on a cold, rocky island after a plane crash; you are

The largest prehistoric insect ever found was a dragonfly that lived about 300 million years ago. Fossil remains found in central France showed the dragonfly was as big as a seagull.

◀ **Sir Francis Drake, English sailor (sea captain and later an admiral) and adventurer. He helped to make England a great sea power, and was successful in helping to defeat the Spanish Armada.**

▲ **A costume design for a masque—an elaborate performance of words, music, and dance, which was popular at European courts in the 1600s.**

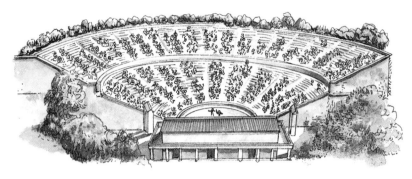

In about 320 B.C., the architect Polykleitos constructed a theater at Epidaurus which could seat more than 13,000 people. Every spectator had an excellent view, and the smallest sound could be heard all over the theater. Greek plays are still performed there today.

In Europe, in the Middle Ages or medieval times, plays were acted out in the streets. The audience looked on as each scene in the story was presented to them on a separate pageant or cart.

lost in the Sahara Desert; or any exciting situation you can imagine.) When you make up and perform a play, or drama, you are sharing in one of the oldest arts. People put on plays long before writing was invented.

You can read a story silently. You can read poems silently, too, but most poems sound better when the words are spoken. You can also read a play, but plays are really meant to be performed. You can understand a song by reading its words, but to really enjoy and understand a song, you have to *hear* it. A play is very similar. The words of a play tell you what the play is about. But words are only the skeleton of a play. The voices and actions of the actors, the scenery, the lighting, and sometimes the music, give a play *body*, that is, make it more interesting and believable.

### Early Drama
Performances—combining words, music, and dancing drama—have been part of religion for thousands of years. The ancient Greeks developed drama as part of their worship of

Dionysus, the god of wine. At first, men danced around a statue of the god and recited an *ode*, or poem of praise. Then a speaker was added. The speaker replied to statements made by the chorus of men. Then another actor was added, and another. Movement became part of the ceremony, and writers began to think of new material to perform.

The Greeks developed the dramatic forms of comedy and tragedy. A *comedy* is amusing and usually has a happy ending. A *tragedy* deals with serious human problems that cause deep suffering. The hero of a tragedy usually comes to a terrible end because of some weakness of his own. The Greeks believed that watching a tragedy caused the release of feelings such as terror and pity, and that the audience felt much calmer after such a play. Greek plays were concerned with religion, with the relationships between people and gods, and with the mysterious forces that affect human life. Greek comedy began with Dionysus, but soon branched out to cover other areas of Greek life. Greek comedies often dealt with everyday affairs, just as comedies do today. Even though they were written thousands of years ago, many Greek plays—both tragedies and comedies—still seem to speak to us about today's world and its problems.

### Drama Develops
In the early Middle Ages, the Roman Catholic Church decreed that drama was sinful. But most people could

not read, and priests discovered that they could use plays to teach Bible stories. These *miracle* plays became so popular that they had to be held out-of-doors to make room for the audience. Then, groups of actors began to travel from town to town to perform these plays. Later, people realized that Bible stories were not the only subject for plays, and new plays were written.

Companies of professional actors built their own theaters where they put on entertainment for the towns-people. Many actors also wrote plays. William Shakespeare, who many people think is the best drama-tist who ever lived, was such an actor. Some of the plays Shakespeare wrote are historical. *Julius Caesar* tells the story of the great Roman statesman. Others, such as *Twelfth Night*, are comedies that joke about Eng-lish life. Still other Shakespearean plays are tragedies. *Mac-beth* tells the story of a great man who is destroyed by his own ambition. His desire to win the throne of Scotland changes him from a good man into an evil one. Dramatists ever since have been influenced by the wonderful plays of Shakespeare.

## Modern Drama

Henrik Ibsen and Anton Chekhov are usually said to be the founders of modern drama. Their plays dealt with everyday life and its problems. Ibsen, a Norwegian, wrote plays on two major themes—that people are important, and that society's purpose is to help people. *An Enemy of the People* tells what happens when peo-ple refuse to accept the truth because they do not like it. Chekhov, a Rus-sian playwright, wrote about people

◄ Molière wrote many plays and ballets to entertain the court of Louis XIV of France. Best known are his comedies which laugh at human failings such as meanness.

who have given in to feelings such as lone-liness. *The Cherry Orchard*, like many of Chekhov's plays, has a very quiet and sad beauty.

Modern dramatists continued to write about life as they saw it. The German dramatist, Bertolt Brecht, combined drama, dance, song, and mime into a "total theater" that pic-tured many kinds of unfairness and cruelty. Modern playwrights devel-oped the *Theater of the Absurd*. This type of drama tends to show how ridiculous human life is. Writers and directors have also experimented with new ways of presenting classic drama to modern audiences.

Most early American plays were imitations of European drama. But in the 1900s, dramatists such as David Belasco, in his play *The Girl of the Golden West*, began to deal

► Theater going was a very popular pastime in Elizabethan England. This picture shows Shakespeare's Globe Theater which was built in London in 1599.

### SOME FAMOUS DRAMATISTS

**Aeschylus,** Greek (about 525–456 B.C.)

**Sophocles,** Greek (496–406 B.C.)

**Terence,** Roman (about 195–159 B.C.)

**William Shakespeare,** English (1564–1616)

**Ben Jonson,** English (1572–1637)

**Moliere,** French (1622–1673)

**William Congreve,** English (1670–1729)

**R. B. Sheridan,** Irish (1751–1816)

**Henrik Ibsen,** Norwegian (1828–1906)

**August Strindberg,** Swedish (1849–1912)

**Oscar Wilde,** Irish (1856–1900)

**George Bernard Shaw,** Irish (1856–1950)

**Anton Chekhov,** Russian (1860–1904)

**Luigi Pirandello,** Italian (1867–1936)

**Eugene O'Neill,** American (1888–1953)

**Bertolt Brecht,** German (1898–1956)

**Samuel Beckett,** Irish (1906–1986)

**Tennessee Williams,** American (1911–1983)

▲ A scene from Arthur Miller's best-known play, *Death of a Salesman*. The play won a Pulitzer Prize in 1949.

▼ *Home Worker* by the German artist Käthe Kolwitz (1867–1945). In this drawing, the weakness and sadness of the figure are emphasized by the use of charcoal, which gives a much harsher effect than pencil.

with American themes in new ways. Eugene O'Neill created dramas that show how people react to the forces that shape their lives. His powerful play *Long Day's Journey into Night*, which deals with the drama of tortured family relationships, won the 1957 Pulitzer Prize. Clifford Odets's plays showed some of the problems of life during the Great Depression in America. Twentieth-century American playwrights such as Arthur Miller, Tennessee Williams, and Edward Albee, have made important contributions to American drama.

##  DRAWING

Have you ever watched very young children scribble on paper? They make lines, circles, and dots. They are beginning to learn how to draw. A drawing is a picture made on a flat surface with the use of lines.

### How Did Drawing Begin?
People have made drawings for thousands of years. Cave dwellers made drawings on the walls of their caves. They drew those things that were important to their lives, especially the animals they hunted.

The early Egyptians also made drawings. Many of their drawings were made on the stone walls of tombs and temples. Egyptian writing developed from drawing. So did the writing of the Chinese and Japanese. Instead of letters, they use a picture to represent a whole word.

Through the centuries, artists have expressed themselves through different styles of drawing. Sometimes artists want to show their feelings about a subject. They want to create a mood. To do this, they may be more interested in colors and shapes, rather than making something look like a photograph.

Drawing is important today in many occupations. Painters and sculptors make drawings of what they wish to create. Engineers and architects draw pictures of the buildings, machines, bridges, airplanes, and other things they build. Computers can help with these drawings! This is known as CAD, or Computer Assisted Design. Commercial artists make drawings for newspaper and magazine advertisements. They also make pictures for posters and signs. Other artists draw cartoons and comics.

## The Importance of Drawing

The study of drawing trains the student in three important skills: observing, memorizing, and hand-and-eye coordination. The drawing of a visible object is really the recording of an impression received through the eye. The object must be looked at carefully. Then it must be remembered or memorized in the mind as

▲ **Try out your own drawing skills by sketching (with pencil or charcoal) or painting a portrait of a friend or a member of your family.**

the eye is moved to the paper. Next, the memorized image must be transferred to the movement of the hand.

When viewing a scene or an object, the areas close to you seem larger than the areas farther away. This is called *perspective.* When you draw a scene, the objects that are nearby should be drawn larger than the objects that are farther away. The more distant an object, the smaller it should be drawn.

FREEHAND DRAWING. When someone draws without the aid of

---

## LEARN BY DOING

How to draw a picture: first, choose a subject to draw. Carefully examine the object or scene you wish to make a picture of. Suppose you want to draw your cat. Look at it. Stroke its fur. Feel its warm body, and carefully touch its sharp claws. The more ways you can experience something, the better the drawing will be. Make several pictures.

You can use many *media* to draw pictures. Try crayons, felt-tip pens, brushes, pencils, chalk, and ballpoint pens. Large sheets of paper are usually best, including drawing paper, construction paper, wrapping paper, and shirt cardboards.

**Colored felt-tip pens**

**Pen and ink**

Experiment with each material to see what you can do with it. Take a crayon, and jab the paper. Use short, long, or thick strokes. Pull the crayon over the paper, push the crayon. Don't be afraid to rip the wrapping off the crayons. Use them on their sides. Notice how pressing down hard on the crayon makes the color stronger and darker. Place the paper over objects such as sandpaper, leaves, coins, or alphabet blocks. Rub on the paper over the object with the side of the crayon. These drawings are called *rubbings.* The marks made by rubbing show different textures.

Start by drawing simple objects—a cup, a chair, a favorite toy. Can you draw a picture of a place you enjoy visiting—like the zoo? Your grandmother's house? The ice cream store? Can you make a scene showing something you and your friends enjoy doing—such as riding bikes or playing in the park? Can you draw a picture of a make-believe or faraway place— maybe a magic kingdom or the planet Mars?

▲ The boy in this picture is making a *silhouette* portrait of the girl. A silhouette is a shape colored black, like a shadow. Artists use silhouettes to add interest and depth to their paintings.

Scientists have found out that four out of five dreams are in color. But people describe most dreams as being in black and white. It seems that as dreams fade from our memory they lose their color.

some mechanical device, such as a ruler, it is called *freehand drawing*. Some of the greatest artists in the world, such as Leonardo da Vinci and Michelangelo, made many different drawings of each of their paintings before they ever put a brush to canvas. In drawing from any object or model, the first thing to do is observe, and sketch in, the main lines. The more important details are added next, and the minor details are last. Lightness of touch and sureness of line are important qualities. Taste and imagination are both used in deciding what to show and what to omit. Only practice, trial-and-error, and patience will tell the artist the most effective methods for self-expression.

▶▶▶▶ **FIND OUT MORE** ◀◀◀◀
Abstract Art; Art; Art History; Comics; Dimension

## DREAM

You are walking along a beach. A wave casts a fish at your feet. You reach down to pick up the fish, and it turns into a pile of dimes. A huge wave towers above you. You try to run, but your feet are like lead. The wave crashes down upon you, and you think you are drowning. Then, suddenly, you wake up in your bed,

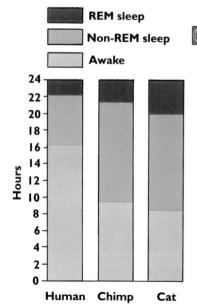

**REM sleep**
**Non-REM sleep**
**Awake**

◀ These graphs compare the length and type of sleep for humans, chimpanzees and cats. Note the different periods of REM (rapid eye movement) sleep, when dreaming occurs, in each case.

frightened, but relieved to know that you were only dreaming.

A *dream* is an activity of the mind that takes place when you are asleep. Many dreams are pleasant. A *nightmare* is a bad or frightening dream. Many of the things that happen in dreams could happen when you are awake. Others could not.

You dream many times each night, especially in the last few hours of sleep. You probably have awakened many mornings and have said that you did not dream. You did, but you could not remember your dreams. The average dream lasts about 20 minutes.

Humans aren't the only animals to dream. You can sometimes tell if a dog is dreaming by watching its legs which may start to twitch and move as if it was chasing something. Some dogs whine and growl as the excitement of the dream-chase becomes greater. Some people talk, or even walk, in their sleep.

It is still not fully understood why we dream. There are various theories on this subject. One reason may be that, while we dream, the brain's ability to deal with tasks such as learning and memory are restored. It is also believed that dreams help reveal a person's hidden feelings.

People far back in history have felt that dreams have meanings. In the Bible, Joseph told the meaning of Pharaoh's dream. People all over the world used to ask those who dealt in magic to say what dreams meant. People believed that dreams could tell the future, but this is not so.

Sigmund Freud, a famous doctor, discovered that dreams can be the key to understanding certain mental disorders, called *neuroses*. Freud's treatment of neuroses, called *psychoanalysis*, is still a major tool of *psychiatry*, the study of the mind.

▶▶▶▶ **FIND OUT MORE** ◀◀◀◀
Freud, Sigmund; Mental Health; Psychology and Psychiatry; Sleep

## DRESS

SEE CLOTHING; FASHION

## ⚙ DREW, CHARLES (1904–1950)

Charles Richard Drew, a black American physician and professor of surgery, developed ways to prepare large quantities of blood for transfusion to people who urgently need blood. He was born in Washington, D.C., and studied at McGill University School of Medicine in Montreal, Canada. He was awarded a scholarship in surgery at Columbia University in 1938. Blood preservation soon became his special field of study.

When World War II began, the British urgently needed blood for their wounded soldiers and civilians. Drew was chosen to head a project called "Blood for Britain." His problem was to find a way to store and preserve blood on a large scale. The method then used in hospitals was to remove the red cells from blood and use only the remaining fluid, called *plasma*, for transfusion. But hospitals at that time were only able to separate red cells in small amounts. Drew learned that the British had used an ordinary cream separator (a centrifuge used by farmers to separate cream from milk) to remove red blood cells. Drew designed large equipment similar to the centrifuge to produce plasma.

After the United States entered the war, Drew was appointed director of the first American Red Cross Blood Bank supplying plasma to the U.S. armed services. His work helped to save the lives of thousands of wounded servicemen and led to the setting up of bloodbanks all over the world. In 1944, he was awarded the Spingarn Medal for his work.

▶▶▶▶ **FIND OUT MORE** ◀◀◀◀
Blood

## 🏛 DRILLING RIG

The oil that we use to make gasoline for cars and the gas we burn as fuel both come from deep underground. The oil and gas *deposits* are trapped beneath layers of hard rock. To reach them, engineers have to bore holes, or *shafts*, down through the rock. The shaft may be several miles deep.

A drilling rig is used to bore the shaft. It is a high tower containing machinery that drives a long steel pipe into the ground. At the bottom end of the pipe is a drill, with hard teeth that grind away the rock. When the shaft reaches the deposit below, the oil or gas flows up the shaft to the surface. Sometimes pumps are needed to force the oil or gas up the shaft. One rig may drill several shafts.

Many deposits of oil and gas lie offshore, beneath the seabed. To reach them, drilling rigs are towed out to sea and positioned above the deposit. Some rigs have very long legs that stand on the seabed. Others float in the water. Offshore drilling rigs are huge. They carry all the machinery needed for drilling shafts and handling the oil or gas which is taken away by pipelines or ships. They also contain accommodations for all the engineers who work on the rig.

▶ **The drill derrick is a tower that supports the drill pipes. It lowers them as the drill is gradually lengthened, by adding extra sections of pipe, or raises them in sections when the drill bit needs to be changed.**

▲ **Charles Richard Drew, American doctor, famous for his research on blood preservation and the organization of blood banks.**

Drill derrick

Monkey board

Kelly

Oil bearing rocks

Diamond drill bit

Soft-formation metal drill bit

The record for driving in reverse is held by James Hargis and Charles Creighton of Missouri. They drove a Ford automobile in reverse from New York City to Los Angeles in 1930, and did not stop the engine during the entire trip. The pair then drove back to New York, also in reverse, to complete a 7,180 mile (11,555 km) round trip.

▼ To be a good driver, a person must be able to drive safely in all weather conditions. Driving in snow and ice requires particular skill and care.

## ⚙ DRIVING

A driver must do several things before setting off on a journey. First, he or she must adjust the seat to be able to see well and comfortably reach the pedals on the floor. Then the mirrors (rearview and side) must be adjusted to give a clear view of the road behind. Next, everyone in the car must *fasten his or her seat belt*. When the road is clear, the driver can move off.

Driving seems so easy. But good drivers know that making a car move correctly takes training and skill. Driving can be easy and safe, if the driver knows what to do. But driving can be dangerous, if the driver is not skilled and careful.

A driver must know the driving laws. Each state and country has its own driving laws. Many of these laws are the same. But there are also many differences. For instance, in Britain, people drive on the left side of the road. But people drive on the right side in almost every other country. In some countries, you can drive as fast as you like. But in the United States there are posted speed limits on streets and highways.

Nobody can learn everything about driving from a book. Many high schools have driver education courses. Students start out in the classroom, where they learn the rules and techniques of good driving. Later they can begin to practice driving in a car. Some states require learners to get a *learner's permit* first. This allows the learner to practice driving, accompanied by a licensed adult driver. Some students practice with their driver education teacher. Other young people may learn in the family car with a parent as the teacher, or with a professional instructor in a car equipped with dual control brakes.

To obtain a driver's license, the learner must be of his or her state's legal driving age. Most states require the driver to pass an eyesight test and a written examination on the rules of driving, as well as a practical test of driving on the road.

### The Parts of a Motor Vehicle

Two or three pedals are on the floor in front of the driver's seat. The pedal on the right is the *accelerator*, or gas pedal. The accelerator is connected to the *carburetor*. When the driver pushes this pedal, more gas flows into the engine, and the engine runs faster. A spring pushes the pedal back when the driver relaxes his or her foot. The *brake* pedal is to the left of the accelerator. When the driver pushes the brake pedal, strong clamps tighten inside the wheels. This makes the car slow down and stop. Both the brake pedal and the accelerator should always be pushed with the right foot.

Many cars have *automatic transmissions*. The transmission carries the power from the engine (in varying amounts) to the steering axle. Cars with *manual transmissions* have a third pedal on the floor. It is the *clutch* pedal. A clutch is two plates that cut the transmission in half. One half connects to the engine. The other half connects to the gears. The gears are toothed wheels that mesh with each other when they turn and cause

▲ **Clear, easily-read instruments and easy-to-use controls are essential in a car, and every driver should know what each instrument/control is for.**

movement of the engine parts. The driver pushes the clutch pedal with his or her left foot and uses the shift lever to put the transmission into first *gear.* Then the driver releases the clutch pedal. The two plates come together, the gear starts to spin, and the car moves. The driver shifts into second gear between 10 and 15 miles an hour (15 and 25 km/h). The driver shifts into third gear between 20 and 25 miles an hour (32 and 40 km/h). Each time the driver shifts, the clutch pedal is used. The clutch must be released slowly and smoothly. Otherwise the car jumps and jerks.

Driving is easier in a car with an automatic transmission. Once the shift lever has been moved into the position marked "drive," the driver need do no more shifting unless he or she wants to back up, or needs extra power at slow speeds. Then the lever is moved to the "reverse" or "low" position, and "park" when stopped.

## Watch the Road Signs

An alert driver watches for road signs. The shape of the sign has meaning. A *stop* sign has eight sides and is usually bright red. A *warning* sign is diamond-shaped. The message on the sign tells what to look for ahead. A *yield* sign is a triangle with one corner pointing down, meaning that the driver must let cars on the cross street go first. An *information* sign is a tall rectangle. This sign gives speed limits or other information the driver needs.

Good drivers learn certain ways to make driving safer. They slow down before a curve, then speed up slowly through the curve. The car then holds the road better. If the car skids on ice or water, good drivers turn the wheel in the same direction the car is skidding. This stops the car from spinning around. They do not drive too closely behind another car (tailgate), but allow enough space to be able to brake quickly but safely if the car ahead were to stop suddenly.

Most important of all: a person must drive carefully, just the way he or she wants other people to drive, and have consideration for all other road users, including pedestrians.

▶ ▶ ▶ ▶ **FIND OUT MORE** ◀ ◀ ◀ ◀
Automobile; Engine; Gear

**The fastest automobile journey around the world—a distance of 24,901 miles (40,075 km)—took 39 days 23 hours and 35 minutes. The three men and three women in two cars passed through six continents and 25 countries.**

◀ **Every driver must observe and obey all road signs. Here is a selection of several traffic signs, that you might see.**

## DROMEDARY

SEE CAMEL

Fertile

Semiarid    Arid

▲ If an area of land constantly affected by drought is inefficiently irrigated or over-grazed, the long-term effects can be devastating. The land can become arid and desert-like.

▲ A barren, dry landscape can actually drive away rain, so the drought gets worse. Planting trees is one way of fighting drought, because forests help make rain and prevent the area from becoming a desert.

# DROUGHT

A *drought* is a long period of time with little or no rain. Droughts cause crops to dry up and livestock to die of thirst. The United States Weather Service says that there is a drought in an area when 21 or more days go by during which rainfall is three-tenths or less of the average amount for that place and season. The American Midwest was struck by drought in the 1930s. The land was so dry that huge dust storms were created, and the afflicted area earned the nickname "the Dustbowl."

There are two main types of drought, *seasonal* and *contingent*. *Seasonal drought* takes place every year in tropical countries where there is a rainy and a dry season. This type of drought can be overcome by storing water behind dams in the rainy season. The stored water is then used during the dry season to irrigate crops and water livestock. South and Southeast Asia and parts of Latin America and Africa have seasonal droughts. Sub-Saharan and northeast Africa (Ethiopia and Somalia in particular) have suffered more severe, long-lasting droughts in recent times.

*Contingent drought* takes place when rainfall is less than the average over a long period. No one knows what causes contingent droughts. They seem to appear in an area regularly, every so many years. In the United States, for example, the northeast seems to have a serious drought every 11 years and a less serious one about halfway between.

Shifting ocean currents that pass near the shores of continents, wind patterns in the upper atmosphere, and slight changes in the amount of sunlight that reaches Earth, are all factors that have something to do with causing droughts.

▶▶▶▶ **FIND OUT MORE** ◀◀◀◀
Dam; Rain and Snow; Weather

# DRUG

Have you ever had an operation in the hospital? If so, you may remember that you were given a painkiller. This might have been a *general anesthetic,* so that you slept right through the operation, or a *local anesthetic,* which just "killed the pain" in the part of the body where the doctor was operating.

Anesthetics are a kind of drug. Doctors use many other kinds. A drug is any substance that changes the way in which our bodies work. Even some of our everyday foods have drugs in them. For example, coffee contains caffeine, a drug that makes your heart beat faster and excites your brain and nervous system. Some people drink strong coffee to keep themselves awake late at night, or if they have had to go without sleep.

## Where Do Drugs Come From?
One day in 1928, a Scottish scientist called Alexander Fleming was working with germs called bacteria in the laboratory. He was about to throw away a dish of bacteria he no longer wanted. Then he noticed specks of mold in it. Mold was not unusual. What was unusual was that all the germs near the specks of mold had died.

Fleming found that in the mold there was a substance, which he called "penicillin," that killed many types of bacteria but was harmless to our bodies. He had discovered the first *antibiotic*.

Many other drugs are found in plants and animals. Some of these drugs have been known since ancient times. Quinine, a famous drug doctors once used to cure malaria, was taken from the bark of a South American tree, the cinchona. The leaves of foxgloves contain a powerful poison used to make the drug digitalis, which, when used in small amounts, helps a person's heart beat properly after a heart attack. The deadly nightshade, although very poisonous, contains the drug atropine that helps cure some types of ulcers. The curare used by South American jungle peoples as a poison on weapons is (in small quantities) an important medical drug. It comes from plants.

Some drugs are even found inside ourselves! Insulin is found in an organ of the body called the pancreas. If your pancreas does not produce enough insulin, your body is not able to use the sugar in your food properly. You have a disorder called *diabetes*. As part of your treatment you may take insulin to help your body's own supplies.

Insulin is one example of a *hormone*. Many other hormone drugs are used. Some work like insulin by helping the body out. Others, while found naturally in our bodies in small amounts, are injected in very large amounts for a special purpose. *Steroids* are hormone drugs of this type. They are often used in the treatment of asthma.

Many of the drugs we use, however, are not found in nature. They must be made in laboratories. *Barbiturates*, which are used as sedatives (they help people relax), are entirely man-made.

The modern science of *genetic*

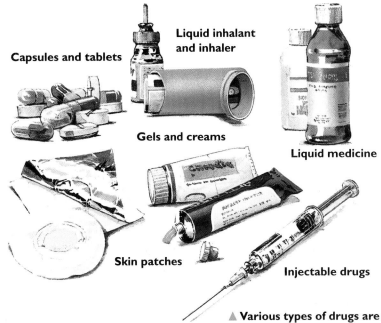

*Various types of drugs are used to treat illnesses and diseases. They are introduced into the body in various ways: swallowing, inhaling, or injecting through the skin.*

*engineering* is producing all sorts of new drugs from living creatures, usually yeasts and bacteria. The possibilities of these are exciting, but there may be dangers, too. Such drugs must be tested very carefully before being widely used.

All drugs made in the laboratory have to be tested for safety and *efficacy* (does the drug always do what it is said to do?). Only when the Food and Drug Administration (FDA), a branch of the U.S. Government, agrees that a new drug is safe and useful, can it be tried on people. Even after they have been fully tested and licensed for sale, many drugs can be bought only if prescribed by a doctor.

*Today, drugs are made in factories. An automatic pill-packing production line accurately puts the right number of pills into each passing container.*

## DRUGS AND THEIR DANGERS

**Marijuana ("cannabis," "pot," "weed")** is harmful to the lungs when smoked as a cigarette ("joint"). It can cause cancer of the lungs. If taken during pregnancy, the drug can affect the unborn child.

**Hallucinogens ("psychodelics"** such as LSD) cause the taker to lose some control over his or her thoughts and actions. Long-term use causes anxiety and depression. Heavy users sometimes develop brain damage.

**Cocaine (coke)** can be a poison. Deaths have occurred as a result of injecting, swallowing, or even "snorting" cocaine in large doses.

**Crack,** a derivative of cocaine, is usually smoked. It can accelerate the heart rate to dangerous levels.

**Narcotics (opium** and drugs made from opium such as morphine, heroin, and codeine). Heroin ("junk," "smack") accounts for 90 percent of narcotic abuse in the United States. Addicts often suffer from abscesses, swollen veins, and congestion of the lungs.

**Alcohol** taken in large quantities over a long period of time, can damage the liver and heart. On average, heavy users shorten their life span by about 10 years.

▶ A man in Yemen smoking a *hookah* pipe. Some drugs, such as tobacco, are inhaled as smoke.

## Side Effects

Many drugs can produce side effects. In other words, as well as helping our bodies, they may cause other changes. Some side effects are harmless; others are not. Quinine, for example, can make people feel dizzy, vomit, and go deaf! That is why safer, alternative drugs are now used.

Any drug can be dangerous if a person takes too much of it. Barbiturates are used much less now than they were a few years ago because some people died from taking too many of them. Another danger from drugs is that some of them (including barbiturates) are addictive (they create a physical need for a drug), leading to drug abuse.

▶ ▶ ▶ **FIND OUT MORE** ◀ ◀ ◀
Anesthetics; Antibiotic; Drug Abuse;
Fleming, Sir Alexander; Genetics;
Hormone

## DRUG ABUSE

All drugs have an effect on the body, but some also have an effect on the brain. Many of these are called *drugs of abuse*. This means that they are

taken for reasons other than medical treatment. They are called drugs of abuse because they can harm or abuse, the body.

People take drugs because drugs make them feel good for a short time, or help them forget the problems of everyday life. *Tranquilizers* are drugs prescribed by doctors to people who are very anxious and need to be calmed. If some people who take tranquilizers or other drugs find that they cannot do without the drugs, they have become *addicted*.

Drugs cause addiction in two ways. The effects of taking them may be so pleasant that the user finds it difficult to do without them. In the other type of addiction, the body is affected so it becomes *dependent* and must have regular doses of the drug. This eventually damages the body and can even cause death.

Drugs like heroin are particularly dangerous, because addicts often take them by injection. Addicts often use old or dirty syringes, with the risk of infection and disease. This practice can also spread liver disease and AIDS (Acquired Immune Deficiency Syndrome) among drug addicts. Heroin is just as hazardous when taken in other ways. Other common drugs are cannabis (marijuana) and cocaine. Tranquilizers, heroin, and cannabis make the user sleepy and relaxed. But cocaine and *amphetamines* (pep pills or speed) cause excitement. LSD (Lysergic acid diethylamide) can have an *hallucinatory* effect, causing visions and distortions of what the user sees and hears.

Addicts need more and more of a drug to recreate the effect of the first dose. But then they need still more to prevent discomfort as the effects wear off. Because they are illegal, drugs are very expensive, so addicts may be forced to steal in order to get money to buy them.

When people decide to stop taking drugs *(withdraw)*, they usually need help. For many drugs, withdrawal feels like being ill. The illness feeling wears off after a while, but the craving for drugs may last for years. Former addicts need help from doctors and counselors to encourage them to keep off drugs. Public health education programs warn people of the risks of drug abuse, and advise addicts on how to get help. One way governments fight the drug problem is by trying to stop the growing of crops of the plants from which drugs are made. Another is to use dogs trained to sniff out illegal drugs being brought into the country.

▶ ▶ ▶ ▶ **FIND OUT MORE** ◀ ◀ ◀ ◀
Addiction; Alcohol; Narcotics

## DRUMS

SEE PERCUSSION INSTRUMENTS

## DUCKS AND GEESE

Ducks, geese, and swans are related to each other. They are web-footed, swimming birds found all over the world. They can swim without sinking because they have special oil glands that coat their feathers and make them waterproof. Underneath their regular long feathers, they have short, fluffy feathers called *down*. Tame ducks and geese are raised on poultry farms. Both wild and tame ducks and geese are good to eat. There are fewer species of swans than of ducks and geese. Swans are large, graceful birds, sometimes seen on ponds and rivers.

### Ducks

A male duck is called a *drake*. The female is a *duck*. Baby ducks are *ducklings*.

North America's many ducks are divided into two main groups: *puddle ducks* and *diving ducks*. You can tell which kind of duck you may be watching by where it lives.

PUDDLE DUCKS. Puddle ducks usually live around rivers, marshes, and shallow streams. When they are on water, they usually feed by dipping their heads beneath the surface. They can dive, but they don't often go completely underwater. These ducks also feed on croplands. Puddle ducks ride higher in the water than diving ducks. They also take off directly upward as they rise in flight. They usually have bright-colored wing patches.

The most common puddle duck in North America is the

*mallard*. The drake has a large, glossy green head. The duck, which is nearly as large as the drake, is a spotted brown color. Both have orange or orange-red feet. The brightly colored feet of the mallard often show when they are swimming. Mallards can withstand cold weather. Some pass the winter as far north as they can find unfrozen

The total cost of drug abuse in the United States may be about $100 billion a year. This includes time lost from work because of illness caused by drug-taking and hospitalization.

Pintail

male

female

male

Common goldeneye

Canada goose

female

Shoveler

Mallard

male

female

male

▲ Ducks and geese are migratory birds. They nest in the north and travel south in the winter. Some will travel huge distances, even from Alaska to Texas.

▲ A male mandarin duck. This handsomely marked species is often seen on park lakes and ponds.

water. Mallards feed in flocks. A flock leaves the water early in the morning to feed for awhile in a nearby field and returns in the afternoon for a second feeding.

One of North America's most beautiful puddle ducks is the *wood duck*. It has a crested head and an unusually long tail for a duck. Wood ducks live throughout the nation in the summer, but they are most often seen in the Mississippi River area. This duck likes forest streams and ponds. It often perches in trees and can fly through thickly wooded areas with speed and ease.

Other puddle ducks are the *widgeon, black, gadwall, shoveler, teal, and pintail.*

DIVING DUCKS. Diving ducks find their food by diving underwater. They make their homes on large, deep lakes, coastal inlets, and bays. Their wing patches are not nearly so bright as those of the pud-

over North America in summer. It spends the winter fairly far north in tidal waters.

Other diving ducks are the *scaup,* the *scoter,* and the *goldeneye.*

Ducks are mainly plant-eaters. They browse on wild celery, cereal grains, pond grasses such as wild rice and foxtail, and pond weeds. They also eat insects, snails, shellfish, and worms. A few ducks, such as the *mergansers* or *sheldrakes,* feed mostly on fish. Wood ducks eat acorns, berries, and grapes.

Mallards nest near water in areas well protected by dense reeds and grasses. The nest itself is lined with dead grasses or *reeds.* Covering the lining is a layer of down. A nest may hold more than a dozen olive-green eggs. Other ducks nest on small, well-protected islands. Some ducks hide their nests in a grassy clump. Still other ducks build nests away from the water. Most ducks conceal their nests, but the *pintail* often nests out on the open prairie. Some ducks,

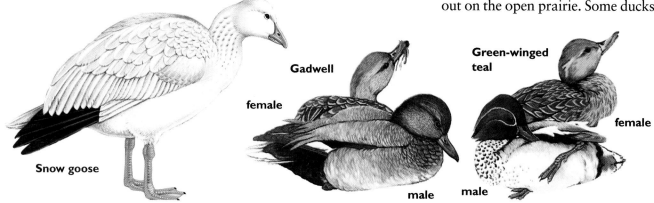

Gadwell

female

Snow goose

Green-winged teal

female

male

male

▲ The plumage colors of ducks and geese often act as camouflage. The snow goose, pictured above, is well suited to its Arctic home.

dle ducks. Most diving ducks run along the water flapping their wings wildly before taking to the air and really flying. They also have a much more rapid wingbeat than puddle ducks, because they have smaller wings.

The *canvasback,* is a large diving duck, with a wedge-shaped, reddish-brown head and neck. It usually lives in the central part of the United States and can be found as far north as Alaska. The *redhead* is similar to the canvasback. It is found all

called *tree ducks,* make their nests in trees.

### Geese

Geese have larger bodies and longer necks than ducks. Among these birds, perhaps the best known is the *Canada goose* of North America. It is one of 13 species that live on this continent. The Canada goose is easily identified. It has a long, black neck. The head is black, except for a white marking below the chin. Both the male, called the *gander,* and the female, called the *goose*, have these markings. Canada geese take one mate for life. The gander helps the goose in rearing the young. The babies, called *goslings*, hatch from creamy-white eggs, usually five in a nest. Most nests are on the ground. These geese eat water plants, insects, and grain. Canada geese nest in northern North America. They fly south in autumn when the weather turns cold. You may have seen the large, beautiful V-shaped formation of a flock of migrating Canada geese.

The kinds of geese raised on farms are called the *Emden*, the *Toulouse*, and the *African*.

## Swans

These elegant, long-necked, plump birds are larger than ducks or geese. All of them have white feathers, except the black swan of Australia and the black-necked swan of South America. Various species are found throughout the world. The best known one in North America is the *whistling swan*. It lives in northern Canada during the summer and goes south for the winter.

The female whistling swan, called a pen, lays five to seven eggs in a large nest made of water plants. She lines the nest with down, as many ducks and geese do. The gray-brown babies are called *cygnets*. They become white by the time they are a year old. Hans Christian Andersen's fairy tale "The Ugly Duckling" is about a cygnet who thinks it is just an ugly duckling, until it grows up to be a beautiful swan. The male swan is called a *cob*.

Another famous swan is the *trumpeter*. This close relative of the whistling swan weighs as much as 40 pounds (18 kg). It is the heaviest North American flying bird. Most swans in parks and zoos are *mute swans*. They were introduced to North America from Europe, where they are seen on lakes, rivers, and ornamental ponds.

## Flyways

Many ducks, geese, and swans *migrate*. They live in different places in summer than they do in winter. Each spring and fall, they fly from one feeding ground to the other along certain routes. They travel the same way each year. These routes are called *flyways*. Land has been reserved in many places along these routes for the birds to rest. Conservationists are trying to get more land for this purpose, especially marshes, where the birds can find food and safety. They also want to stop people from hunting along flyways.

▶ ▶ ▶ ▶ **FIND OUT MORE** ◀ ◀ ◀ ◀
Bird; Migration; Poultry; Water Birds

▲ **The Canada goose is the best known of all North American geese. Flocks of these birds can be seen migrating across the continent.**

▼ **Swans are excellent parents. The adult birds keep a close eye on the young, called cygnets. This is a mute swan, surrounded by her cygnets.**

► The end of a pistol duel
between French soldiers
fought about the beginning
of the nineteenth century.
Each duelist had a "second"
to ensure fair play.

► Alexandre Dumas the
Elder, the author of *The
Three Musketeers.*

▼ A scene from *The Three
Musketeers*, an exciting
adventure story set in
seventeenth-century
France at the time of King
Louis XIII.

## DUEL

Years ago when two men were very angry with each other, they sometimes fought a *duel*. Dueling has been against the law in most countries since the late 1890s. Today, if people hurt or kill other people in duels, they can be put on trial for murder.

If a man felt he had been insulted, accused of cheating, or called a coward by someone, he challenged the other person to a fight. The challenged person chose the weapons (usually swords or pistols) and decided where and when to meet. Duelers sometimes fought in a forest clearing early in the morning, so that they would not be discovered by law officers. Each man brought along a witness, called a *second,* and sometimes brought a doctor, too.

Certain rules were followed in dueling. When the men used pistols, they stood back to back and marched a certain number of steps in opposite directions. Upon a signal, such as the dropping of a handkerchief, they turned quickly, faced each other, and fired. Swords were also used in duels, and so, in some countries, were various kinds of knives. In many countries a duel was regarded as over when one man was hurt, but in other countries it was only over when one was killed. Sometimes both men were hurt.

Several famous Americans who lived in the early 1800s fought duels. Aaron Burr killed Alexander Hamilton in a pistol duel in 1804, because Burr believed Hamilton had caused his defeat in an election. Andrew Jackson killed Charles Dickinson in 1806 in a pistol duel, following an argument about a horse race.

During the late 1800s, dueling was common among German army officers. The duelers fought with swords, and to be scarred was regarded as a mark of honor. The government tried to ban dueling, but it continued in secret before it finally died out.

## DUMAS FAMILY

Two French writers, father and son, were famous in the 1800s. The father was Alexandre Dumas the Elder (usually known as Dumas) and the son was Alexandre Dumas the Younger. Dumas the Elder is most famous for writing *The Three Musketeers* and *The Count of Monte*

*Cristo. The Three Musketeers* tells of the rollicking adventures of a young swordsman, D'Artagnan, and his three musketeer comrades in the service of King Louis XIII in 17th-century France. *The Count of Monte Cristo* is about a nobleman, wrongly imprisoned, who sets out to punish the people who put him in prison.

Dumas the Elder was born in Villers-Cotterêts, France. His father was a general in Napoleon Bonaparte's army. He wrote hundreds of books—novels, plays, histories, and memoirs often with the help of hired writers. Though he earned a fortune from his books, he spent it carelessly and died nearly penniless.

Alexandre Dumas the Younger, also known as Dumas *fils* (French for "son"), was born in Paris. He too wrote many books. His greatest success, however, was in writing plays. His *The Lady of the Camellias,* often misnamed just *Camille,* is a drama of a tragic love affair. It was first performed in 1852, and became a sensation. Giuseppe Verdi based his opera *La Traviata* on this story.

## DUNCAN, ISADORA (1878–1927)

The exciting, natural, free movement of modern dance began with Isadora Duncan. As a child, Isadora loved skipping, leaping, and just walking barefoot. As a grown woman, Isadora rebelled against the stiff, unchanging forms of ballet.

Isadora Duncan was born in San Francisco, California. The Duncans were poor, but Isadora's mother, a music teacher, helped her children understand and enjoy music, poetry, and art. Isadora loved to dance and had some instruction. But she did not like the strict rules she was taught.

She went to Europe, where she studied ancient Greek art and dance. She felt this was the key to her own free, expressive dancing. She danced, barefoot, and wore flowing robes or tunics, not tight costumes. She did not use scenery. Her dancing enchanted many people, but shocked others.

Duncan taught her methods to other dancers and set up dance schools. Her unconventional method of dance helped establish the art of modern dance.

Duncan's life ended in tragedy. Her two children were drowned, and

Isadora Duncan herself was killed in a tragic car accident.

▶ ▶ ▶ ▶ **FIND OUT MORE** ◀ ◀ ◀ ◀
Ballet; Dance

## ☼ DURYEA, CHARLES (1861–1938) AND FRANK (1869–1967)

Inventors in the United States were making cars by 1890. These early American automobiles used steam or electricity for power. Charles and Frank Duryea saw a way to make improvements. Their plan required a gasoline engine small enough to fit in a buggy. But gasoline engines were heavy and unreliable.

Charles and Frank built a small engine and drove the first gasoline-powered American car in 1893. Charles solved one problem by inventing the spray carburetor. This controlled the gasoline going into each engine cylinder, which made the engine run smoother. Frank drove a Duryea car in America's first automobile race in Chicago two years later and won the race. The brothers established the Duryea Motor Wagon Company in 1895.

▶ ▶ ▶ ▶ **FIND OUT MORE** ◀ ◀ ◀ ◀
Automobile; Engine

## ⊕ DUST

Have you ever helped clean, or dust, furniture? It seems to be a daily chore, because dust is always with us. Dust is made up of very tiny, solid particles that float in the air. Billions of tons of dust exist in the Earth's atmosphere.

Dust is made of many things—bits of dry soil and rock, animal and plant remains, and salt from sea spray. Bacteria spores, pollen, and tiny fibers may be found with dust. Grinding, sawing, polishing, and

▲ Isadora Duncan, American dance pioneer, who caused a sensation dancing barefoot in loose tunics or Grecian-style robes. Her free flowing dance movements and style helped launch modern dance.

▲ Charles Duryea in the winning car of the first gasoline-powered automobile race in the United States. The race took place from Chicago to Evanston, Illinois.

833

scraping create it, and smoke adds tons more.

Some dust is good to our environment. Volcanic dust and dirt can enrich the soil. Dust helps form droplets that become rain and snow. But most dust is harmful because it adds to air pollution, causes hazy days, causes certain diseases, and helps wear out machinery.

▶▶▶▶ **FIND OUT MORE** ◀◀◀◀
Air Pollution

## DUTCH AND FLEMISH ART

The Netherlands of the 1600s had recently freed itself of Spanish rule. The Dutch fleet ruled the seas. Wealth came from trade with the East Indies. In this economic climate, art flourished. For most of the 17th century, many talented painters lived and worked in Holland. Dutch art became famous. Much of that fame is due to the wealth and power of those 100 great years.

Most Dutch were Protestants. They believed in having plain churches with no paintings or sculpture in them. So Dutch artists found no market for their work in churches, as artists did in Italy and Spain. But many people in this newly rich country wanted portraits painted. One of the great portrait painters was Frans Hals (about 1580–1666). His parents had left the southern Netherlands and settled in the rich city of Haarlem. Using a quick brush-stroke technique, Hals managed to catch the look of a moment in time in his pictures. As Hals became older, his paintings were no longer fashionable, and he became very poor in his old age.

The greatest Dutch painter was Rembrandt van Rijn (1606–1669). His paintings, etchings, and drawings are masterpieces. He enjoyed a very successful career in Amsterdam. But in his later years, he was much less popular. Rembrandt often painted portraits of himself, in various hats and costumes; there are 60 of these self-portraits. Rembrandt bought a house in the Jewish section of Amsterdam, and he became fascinated with the Jewish people—their appearance, customs, and traditions which he captured on canvas.

Still-life paintings—pictures of objects such as fruit and flowers—were enormously popular among Dutch and Flemish painters of the mid–1600s. Jan de Heem (1606–about 1683) was one of the greatest Dutch still-life painters. In a painting called *The Vase of Flowers* (pictured on page 835), de Heem included more than 20 species of flowers from a Dutch garden, apparently casually stuck in a vase. However, careful organization underlies the arrangement. See how the stalk of wheat draws your eye into the picture, then bends and goes off onto another diagonal, and how the three tulips and candytuft in the center make an obvious horizontal line.

▲ **In the mid-1930s, a series of terrible dust storms swept across the American Great Plains. The area became known as the Dust Bowl. Hundreds of millions of tons of dry topsoil were carried off by the winds, destroying the land.**

▼ *Laughing Gypsy* **by Frans Hals. Hals's style of painting was famous for showing lively expressions and poses. His subjects really came to life on the canvas.**

▲ **A self-portrait by Rembrandt. As an artist, Rembrandt displayed an incredible talent for painting a wide range of subjects.**

This painting, *Interior with Lady Reading a Letter*, is by the Dutch painter Jan Vermeer (1632–1675). Vermeer was a master of "domestic" scenes, showing people engaged in simple, everyday tasks.

▼ *The Vase of Flowers* by Jan de Heem is a typical example of a Dutch still-life painting.

## Flemish Art

Flanders, the land of the Flemings, is today part of Belgium. The Flemings were close to the Dutch in location, and yet very different in art. They kept the Roman Catholic faith, when the Dutch became Protestant. So the Flemish continued to paint religious art. But some Flemish painters were so-called *genre* painters. (Genre is French for "branch" or "kind.") Genre painters painted scenes from everyday life. Pieter Bruegel the Elder (about 1525–1569) was one of the greatest genre painters. We know almost nothing of Bruegel except that he lived in Antwerp and Brussels, where he did most of his work. He painted scenes of everyday life and religious subjects. The power of his paintings capture the feel of what it was like to live in the 1500s.

▶ ▶ ▶ ▶ **FIND OUT MORE** ◀ ◀ ◀ ◀
Art History; Bruegel, Pieter; Hals, Frans; Rembrandt Van Rijn

## DWARF

SEE GIANT

## ☼ DYE

Look at the clothes on people around you. Many of them are brightly colored. Most clothes are made of colored cloth. The cloth is colored by substances called *dyes*. The three kinds of dyes are *natural*, *mineral*, and *synthetic*.

*Natural dyes* are made from plants or animals. Saffron flowers have provided a yellow dye since they were used to color the wrappings of Egyptian mummies 4,000 years ago. Tyrian, or royal, purple was an expensive dye made from a murex snail of the Mediterranean Sea. The deep-blue dye, indigo, was made from a plant. Carmine, a scarlet dye, came from the dried bodies of female cochineal insects of

▲ **William Perkin accidentally discovered how to make the first artificial dye, a mauve color, when he was only 18. He was trying to make the drug quinine. His discovery made possible the many dye colors made today.**

## LEARN BY DOING

Try dyeing some old pieces of cotton cloth with natural dyes. For red, try beetroot, cherries, or red cabbage. For green, try spinach, and for brown, try onion skins, tea, or coffee. Take the leaves or fruit of plants and cover with boiling water. Let stand for fifteen minutes.

Then pour the liquid through a filter into a jar. Dye the cotton by soaking it in the liquid for several hours.

Mexico and Central America.

*Mineral dyes* are made from materials which are dug from the earth and are rarely used today. Ochre, a yellow mineral dye, comes from one kind of iron ore mixed with a certain kind of clay.

*Synthetic dyes* are man-made chemical substances. Most are made from coal tar *(aniline dyes)*, a material that remains when soft coal is distilled. The first synthetic dye, called "mauvene", was made by accident in 1856 by William Henry Perkin, an English chemist, who was only eighteen years old. He was trying to find a way to make the drug quinine. The introduction of synthetic dyes was disastrous for farmers who grew natural dye plants such as madder and indigo, and many of them went out of business. More than 10,000 synthetic dyes have been made since this first discovery.

Fabrics and other materials, such as paper and leather, may be dyed simply by soaking them in dye dissolved in water. Dyes can also be printed onto fabrics. The soaking method usually does not produce a dye that is *fast*, or permanent. A non-fast dye may wash out or bleach out in sunlight. To make a dye fast, it is often necessary to fix it in the material. Fixing is done by combining the dye with a chemical called a *mordant* or *dye assistant*. The dye assistant binds the dye to the fibers of the material.

▶ ▶ ▶ ▶ **FIND OUT MORE** ◀ ◀ ◀ ◀
Coal; Synthetic; Textile

## DYLAN, BOB (1941– )

The songs of the folksinger Bob Dylan are enjoyed by people all over the world, and have been praised by literature experts as fine examples of modern poetry. Bob Dylan's real name is Robert Zimmerman, and he was born in Duluth, Minnesota. He took the name Dylan from the Welsh poet Dylan Thomas, whose writing he admired.

As a teenager, Bob Dylan traveled around the country, doing odd jobs and singing. His great idol was the folksinger Woody Guthrie. Dylan started singing in Greenwich Village, in New York City, and in the 1960s achieved fame as a singer of "protest" songs. Dylan's songs, such as "Blowin' in the Wind" and "The Times They Are A'Changin'," were played and sung by young people during the civil rights movement, and by other people around the world.

Since the 1960s, Bob Dylan has continued to write and record songs, in different styles, and on varying themes. He has also acted in several motion pictures. Musicians from around the world paid tribute to Bob Dylan at a special concert in New York City in 1992. The concert celebrated his 30-year singing career.

▶ ▶ ▶ ▶ **FIND OUT MORE** ◀ ◀ ◀ ◀
Folk Song; Popular Music

## DYNAMITE

SEE EXPLOSIVES

▼ **Bob Dylan, American folk and rock singer.**

## EAGLE

SEE BIRDS OF PREY

## EAR

The ear is the organ not only of hearing but also of balance and position. The ear of humans and other mammals has three principal parts to it: the *outer ear,* the *middle ear,* and the *inner ear.* All three parts play a special role in hearing.

The *outer ear* is the only visible part. It is the skin and cartilage that grow on the side of the head. It

air hit the eardrum, they cause it to *vibrate* (shake rapidly back and forth).

The *middle ear* is a small, air-filled chamber. It contains three little bones named because of their shapes—the *hammer,* the *anvil,* and the *stirrup.* These bones work together to carry the vibrations from the eardrum into

▽ **This picture of the human ear shows the three main parts. The outer ear collects sounds from the air. The middle ear carries the vibrations of the sounds across to the inner ear, where they trigger off nerve impulses that then travel to the brain.**

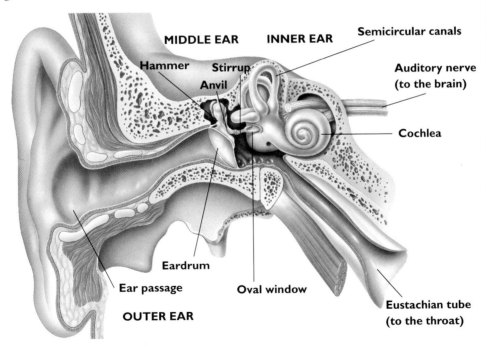

**MIDDLE EAR**     **INNER EAR**     Semicircular canals

Hammer     Stirrup     Auditory nerve (to the brain)

Anvil

Cochlea

Eardrum

Ear passage     Oval window

**OUTER EAR**     Eustachian tube (to the throat)

includes the outer ear canal, which leads into the head. At the end of the canal is the *eardrum,* a taut membrane something like the head of a drum. The eardrum separates the outer ear from the middle ear. The function of the outer ear is to collect sound waves and carry them to the eardrum. When sound waves in the

the inner ear. The hammer touches the eardrum, the anvil touches the hammer, and the stirrup touches the anvil. The eardrum vibrates in response to sounds, and its vibrations cause the ear bones to move. This movement is carried to the inner ear through an opening called the *oval window.*

**DEVELOPMENT OF THE LETTER E**

**The Egyptian E** c. 3000 B.C.

**The Phoenician E** c. 1000 B.C.

**The Greek E** c. 600 B.C.

**The Roman E** c. A.D. 600

## INNER EAR OF THE FENNEC FOX

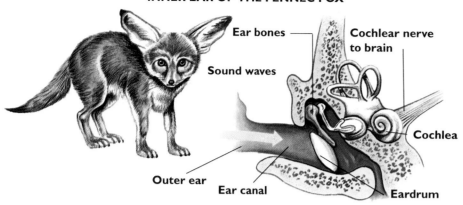

Ear bones

Cochlear nerve to brain

Sound waves

Cochlea

Outer ear

Ear canal

Eardrum

▲ **A fennec fox has huge ears. The ears are like this so that the fox can hear its prey of worms and insects, which are moving about in the desert sands, where the fox lives and hunts by night.**

**The wax we get in our ears is made by special glands. This wax is important because it prevents dust and other foreign material from reaching the eardrum. Sometimes too much wax is made by the glands and our hearing becomes impaired. Our ears are delicate instruments; don't try to poke the wax out yourself. If the wax doesn't come out naturally, it should be removed by your doctor.**

The chamber of the middle ear is connected to the throat by a narrow tube that leads to the nose. The tube keeps the air pressure in the middle ear chamber the same as the air pressure outside. People's ears get plugged up and may hurt when they ride into a railroad tunnel, or when they are in an airplane coming down for a landing. This happens because the pressure inside the ear is greater than it is outside. The tube quickly corrects this, and the pain goes away. You can help equalize the pressure by swallowing, by yawning, by gently blowing your nose, or by chewing gum. If the pressure difference were not corrected, your eardrum could soon burst, like a balloon with too much air in it.

The *inner ear* is a fluid-filled spiral passage that looks like a snail shell. A membrane winds down this passage, almost but not quite dividing it into two complete parts. This membrane contains rows of special cells called *hair cells*, which are connected to the

*auditory* (hearing) nerves, leading to the brain.

The rapid back-and-forth movements of the earbones in the middle ear are transmitted through the oval window to the fluid in the inner ear. The fluid moves, pushing the membrane that runs through the spiral passage and moving the hair cells on the membrane. The vibration of the hair cells causes the auditory nerves to send impulses to the brain, which interprets them into the sounds we hear and recognize.

In the inner ear is another organ, called the *semicircular canals*, which gives us our sense of balance. These canals form approximate right angles with each other. Two are placed vertically, or up-and-down, and one is placed horizontally, or side-to-side. The canals are lined with sensitive hairs and filled with fluid. When the head and body move, the fluid also moves, but not quite so quickly. As the movement bends the hairs in the canals, nerves send messages to the brain. If you spin very quickly and stop suddenly, the fluid continues to move for a short time. The nerve cells send confusing messages to your brain, and you suddenly feel dizzy, The dizziness ends when the fluid in the semicircular canals stops moving.

Without the semicircular canals, simple tasks like walking would be extremely difficult, if not impossible. And the canals also provide a sense of position, or *orientation*. Without this, you would even have difficulty knowing whether you were standing up, or lying down.

The ear is a sensitive organ that can be easily damaged, for example by using cotton swabs. Never use small, sharp objects to clean out wax either. The ear may also be damaged by extremely loud noise, resulting in hearing loss.

▶▶▶▶ **FIND OUT MORE** ◀◀◀◀

Brain; Hearing; Nervous System; Sense Organ; Special Education

Human          Bat          Cricket          Frog

## ANIMAL HEARING

Different types of animals hear at different frequencies. For example, humans can hear sounds at frequencies up to 20 kilohertz (kHz), while bats can hear up to 120 kHz, crickets up to 100 kHz and frogs up to 50 kHz, depending on the species.

## EARHART, AMELIA (1898–1937)

Amelia Earhart believed women should be given the same chances as men in any job. But she also believed that women should earn their right to work by doing their jobs as well as or better than men. As a young girl, she saved newspaper stories about various women who had succeeded in difficult professions.

Amelia Earhart was born in Atchison, Kansas. She attended Columbia University but left to go into one of the toughest new professions—aviation. She studied navigation, weather, and how a plane flies and eventually became a professional pilot.

Earhart was the first woman to cross the Atlantic Ocean in an airplane, flying as a passenger in 1928. She wrote a book about it and later married her publisher, George Putnam. In 1932, Amelia Earhart became the first woman to fly alone across the Atlantic and received the Distinguished Flying Cross for this achievement. In 1935, she made the first solo flight from Hawaii to California. She also set a speed record flying from Mexico City to New Jersey. The Harmon Trophy, one of the highest U.S. aviation awards, was given to her.

In 1937, she and her copilot, Fred Noonan, were lost in their plane over the Pacific. They were trying to make the first flight around the world at the equator. Neither they nor their plane were ever found. In recent years, people claimed to have found Earhart's plane wreckage and articles of clothing belonging to her, but these claims remain unconfirmed.

## EARP, WYATT (1848–1929)

Stories are often told about famous people. Sometimes these stories leave out things that happened and add things that did not happen. Some stories are more *legendary* (made up) than *factual* (true). The story of Wyatt Earp is a good example of this.

The legendary Wyatt Earp was a hero of the American West. He was a deputy marshal in Tombstone, Arizona. The stories say he was a brave, honest man who fought against outlaws and brought law and order to the frontier. The stories praise his most famous gunfight—the gunfight at the O.K. Corral on October 26, 1881—in which Wyatt Earp, his two brothers, and Doc Holliday shot it out with the Clanton gang.

Wyatt Earp really was a marshal. But he was also a boaster, a bully, and a cheat at cards. He used his marshal's badge to take advantage of other people. He had many enemies. He killed his enemies and then said that they had been breaking the law. This is what many believe really happened at the O.K. Corral.

▶▶▶▶ **FIND OUT MORE** ◀◀◀◀
Outlaw; Pioneer Life; Westward Movement

## EARTH

The Earth, the planet on which we live, is the third planet from the sun. It is a ball of rock and iron a little

▲ Amelia Earhart, the famous American pilot who broke several world flying records, and whose work opened aviation to women.

◀ The famous "Gunfight at the O.K. Corral." Wyatt Earp, his two brothers, Virgil and Morgan, and the town dentist, Doc Holliday, killed four members of the Clanton gang, who were suspected cattle rustlers.

▲ Wyatt Earp, chief deputy marshal of the American West, whose exploits became legendary.

## EARTH FACTS

**Age:** About 4.6 billion years

**Diameter:** From Pole to Pole 7,900 miles (12,713 km). Through the equator 7,926 miles (12,756 km)

**Circumference:** Around the Poles 24,860 miles (40,007 km). Around the equator 24,900 miles (40,070 km)

**Land Area:** 57,400,000 square miles (149,000,000 sq. km); 29 percent of total

**Water area:** 139,500,000 square miles (361,000,000 sq. km); 71 percent of total

**Volume:** 259,000 million cubic miles (1,082,620 million cubic km)

**Mass (weight):** 6,592 million million million tons (5,980 million million million metric tons)

**Density:** 5.52 (5.52 × weight of water of equal volume)

**Average height (land):** 2,757 feet (840 m) above sea level

**Average depth (ocean):** 12,450 feet (3,795 m) below sea level

**Deepest point (ocean):** Marianas Trench 36,198 feet (11,033 m) below sea level

**Highest point (land):** Mount Everest 29,028 feet (8,848 m)

more than 7,900 miles (12,713 km) through the middle. The Earth is slightly flattened at the North and South poles. The distance from the North Pole to the equator is a little longer than from the equator to the South Pole. Also, the Earth bulges at the equator. But if you were far out in space and could see the whole Earth, it would look like a perfect ball. The flattening and bulging are too small to see.

### On Earth's Surface

The tallest mountain on Earth, Mount Everest, rises a little more than $5^1/_2$ miles (8.8 km) above the level of the sea. This is a very small rise when compared to the size of the whole Earth. If you were in a space ship near the moon, you would not be able to see Mount Everest at all. You might be able to see the huge continent of Asia, but even that would look very small from so far away.

Water covers nearly three-fourths of the Earth's surface. Almost all of this water makes up the oceans. Some parts of the oceans are 7 miles (11 km) deep, but the average depth is 2.4 miles (3.8 km). Although the

oceans seem to be vast and deep, they are only a thin film of water on the Earth's surface.

An envelope of gases, called the *atmosphere*, or air, surrounds the Earth. Oxygen, nitrogen, and carbon dioxide are some of the gases found in the atmosphere. People, animals, and plants need the gases to live.

A little over one-fourth of the Earth's surface is land. Sand or soil covers much of it. The part of the soil in which crops grow is rarely more than 20 inches (50 cm) deep. The materials beneath the soil are usually not many feet deep, but many extend several hundred feet down to solid rock. About one-fifth of the land, including Antarctica and parts of Canada, Alaska, Siberia, and Greenland, is always covered by ice.

The very thin coverings of air, soil, and water—from the bottom of the sea to the top of the thickest part of the atmosphere—compose a very narrow band on and above the Earth's surface. All living things exist within this region, called the *biosphere*.

### Under the Surface

Three thick layers of material—called the *crust*, the *mantle*, and the *core*—lie under the Earth's thin surface. The outermost layer of the Earth is a *crust* of rock. The crust is only 4 miles (6 km) thick in some places under the ocean. Beneath the continents, it may be 35 miles (56 km) thick. The average thickness is 20 miles (32 km).

▶ **Inside the Earth. At the center is a solid *inner core*, surrounded by a liquid *outer core*. The middle layer is the *mantle*. The outer layer is the *rocky crust*.**

The crust changes constantly. The crust and the very top part of Earth's next layer, the *mantle*, are divided into huge sections, called *plates*. The dividing lines between plates are areas of earthquake activity. The plates slide across the mantle, very slowly. The movement of the plates causes what scientists called *continental drift*—very slow movement, about an inch (2.5 cm) every year, of Earth's continents.

The movement of the plates, over hundreds of millions of years, has also built up Earth's mountains in two ways. The plates sometimes crash into each other. The Himalaya Mountains of Asia were formed when the plate carrying India and the plate carrying Asia collided. Other mountains have been formed when a plate slid into a deep trench in the ocean floor. The slipping of the plate disturbs Earth's surface. In places, layers of the rock that forms Earth's crust pile up, and mountains are born. The Rocky, Coastal, Cascade, and Sierra Nevada mountain ranges were all formed in this way.

At the same time that mountains are rising, they are being worn down by the action of running water, blowing wind, and freezing and heating. This wearing away is called *erosion*. Even the highest mountains are eroded, if given enough time. Many times in the long history of the Earth, whole mountain chains have been worn down to sea level.

Below the crust is the *mantle*. Like the crust, the mantle is made up of rock. The temperature of the mantle is so great—from 2,000°F

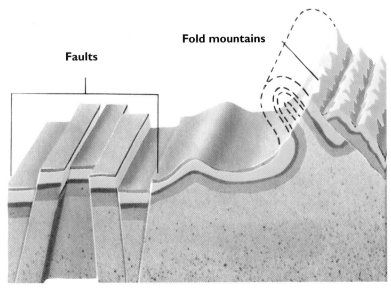

**Faults**

**Fold mountains**

(1,100°C) near the crust to 4,000°F (2,200°C) at its lowest boundary—that the rock of the mantle is not completely rigid. The rock of the mantle can move when great force is applied to it for a long time. The tremendous pressure caused by the weight of the Earth's surface works with the high temperatures of the mantle to keep the rock from becoming firm. The mantle extends 1,800 miles (2,900 km) toward the center of the Earth, ending where the Earth's core begins.

The Earth's *core* is divided into two sections. The *outer core* is 1,400 miles (2,240 km) thick, and it probably is made up of molten iron. The *inner core* is a sphere 1,540 miles (2,440 km) in diameter. It is probably made up of solid iron, nickel, and sulfur or silicon. Scientists really do not know very much about Earth's mantle and core. What they do know, they have learned by studying how earthquake energy moves through the Earth.

▲ **Fold mountains are thrown up when huge forces from the collision of the Earth's crustal plates buckle rock layers into giant wrinkles. Other kinds of mountains are formed when faults in the Earth's crust appear.**

If the Earth were the size of a basketball lying on a table before you, the highest land masses such as the Himalayas would be no higher than a coat of paint on the ball. The deepest ocean trenches would be almost invisible scratches in the paint.

◄ **The different layers of the Earth are known collectively as the *geosphere*. Each layer is of a different thickness and is made up of a different composition of substances. The crust varies in its thickness beneath the oceans and the continents.**

**Crust**

**Mantle**

**Outer core**

**Core**

◄A spectacular photograph of the Earth taken from 250,000 miles (400,000 km) away by the crew of the Apollo 10 spacecraft. The west coast of North America can be seen through the cloud "swirls" that cover the surface.

## Measuring the Earth

The ancient Greeks knew the shape of the Earth. They understood that an eclipse of the moon is caused by the Earth's shadow on the moon. They saw that the shadow was *always* circular as the sun moved in its path around the Earth. (Most Greeks thought the sun moved around the Earth, not the Earth around the sun.) They reasoned that only a sphere could always cast a circular shadow. Therefore, the shape of the Earth must be spherical.

In the third century B.C., a Greek named Eratosthenes figured out the distance around the Earth. He had been told that at the town of Syene (now called Aswan) in Egypt, the sun

could be seen reflected from water in a deep well at noon on June 21. This meant the sun was directly overhead. At noon on the same day, Eratosthenes measured the angle of sunlight falling on Alexandria, a city at the mouth of the Nile River. He knew the distance from Alexandria to Syene. With these pieces of information, he calculated the distance around the Earth to be 24,500 miles (39,428 km). Today we know that the Earth's circumference at the equator is almost 24,900 miles (40,070 km). Around the poles, the distance of the circumference is some 40 miles (63 km) less.

In 1810, an English scientist, Henry Cavendish, "weighed" the Earth in an experiment based on the force of gravitation. He then made a calculation based on the experiment.

**Water 71%**

**Land 29%**

More than two-thirds of the Earth's surface is covered by water. The land area makes up only 29 percent.

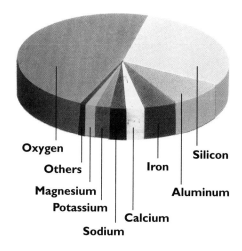

Oxygen  Silicon
Others  Iron
Magnesium  Aluminum
Potassium  Calcium
Sodium

▲ This diagram shows the elements that make up the Earth. Oxygen is the most common element in the Earth's crust—nearly 50 percent by weight. Silicon is the next most common element—about 28 percent by weight.

---

## LEARN BY DOING

Prove to yourself how the Greeks reasoned. Get an egg, a small juice can, a ball, and a flashlight. Shine the flashlight on the wall. Can you hold the egg in a position that will cause it to have a circular shadow? When you have found this position, move the source of light. What happens to the shape of the shadow? Next, use the can instead of the egg. Finally, use the ball. Can you find a position in which the ball will NOT cast a circular shadow?

He found that the Earth weighs 6,592 million million million tons (5,980 million million million metric tons). Scientists today, with the most modern equipment, find that Cavendish's answer was very accurate.

▶▶▶▶ **FIND OUT MORE** ◀◀◀◀

## EARTH HISTORY

Earth history is the study of the creation and formation of the Earth. Today, scientists think that the sun, the Earth, and the other planets in our solar system were formed about five billion years ago. Many scientists believe that they were made from the shrinking and clumping together of a vast cloud of dust and gas in space. They think that the clump that formed the Earth was cold. The sun was cooler than it is today, but it was still very hot.

The Earth and its atmosphere formed a sphere hundreds of times larger than it is today. The atmosphere was tens of thousands of miles deep. Ninety-nine percent of it was made up of the gases hydrogen and helium, the two lightest elements.

The much larger sun-clump shrank, slowly at first, then faster and

**FLAT EARTH?**

Until about 500 years ago, many people thought that the Earth was flat. They feared that if a ship sailed too far to the east or the west, it would topple over the edge of the Earth into space. Then the early voyages of discovery showed that the Earth was in fact round.

▼ **Even after the young Earth cooled, volcanoes erupted on its surface. The lava that gushed out cooled to form rocks. The released gases helped to form Earth's primitive atmosphere.**

faster. As this sun-clump became smaller, it heated up. It took about 80 million years to shrink to its present size. Toward the end of this time, the sun flared up, becoming brighter and hotter than it is today. During this flare-up, which lasted several million years, the sun poured out tremendous amounts of heat and light.

**QUIZ**

1. What percentage of the Earth's surface is covered by land?
2. What is the biosphere?
3. What are the different layers of the Earth called?
4. Name three of the elements that the Earth is made of.
5. How long does it take the Earth to make one full rotation (turn) on its axis? To make one full orbit around the sun?

*(Answers on page 896)*

The Mohole Project was an attempt to drill through the Earth's crust to reach the mantle. The plan was to start drilling in one of the deep ocean trenches since the crust is thinnest under the oceans. The Mohole Project was never completed, however. The Moho (short for Mohorovicic Discontinuity) is the scientific name for the "join" between the Earth's crust and mantle.

THE MOLTEN EARTH. The Earth shrank and became warmer, too. Atomic reactions, called *radioactivity*, took place within the Earth. These produced large amounts of heat. As a result, the Earth melted. Heavy materials, such as iron, sank to the center. The lighter materials, those that eventually formed rocks, floated to the surface. The lightest of these probably clumped together in one large mass with an area equal to the area of all the continents today. The planet began to cool and the outer 20 miles (32 km) formed a crust of solid rock. The melting and cooling took about a billion years.

As the Earth melted and then cooled, gases were given off. Some of these gases, mainly nitrogen and carbon dioxide, formed a new atmosphere. Much water vapor existed, too. The vapor formed an unbroken canopy of clouds, hundreds of miles thick, around the Earth. Violent lightning bolts hammered at the planet, and the rumble of thunder never ended. Although torrents of rain fell, the Earth remained dry. Any raindrops that reached the hot, rocky surface boiled upward in steam, rejoining the clouds from which they had first come.

THE OCEAN AND THE CONTINENTS. The Earth finally cooled enough so that rain could remain on its surface. Rainwater formed streams and rivers and ran to the low-lying areas. This water collected in pools, and the pools joined, eventually forming one huge ocean that covered nearly three-fourths of the planet. The only land that remained above water was made up of the lightest rock, which had floated highest on the surface when the Earth was molten.

As the ocean grew, the cloud canopy became thinner and thinner.

> Although the Earth is between 4 and 5 billion years old, no rocks as old as this have ever been found anywhere on Earth. It is thought that the Earth's original rocks have all been worn away. Rock samples found at Granite Falls, Minnesota, have been dated at about 3,800,000,000 years old.

**1,500 million years ago**

**1 billion years ago**

**500 million years ago**

**4.6 billion years ago**

▲ The Earth is thought to have been formed about 4.6 billion years ago. A cloud of gas and dust began to condense under the attraction of gravitational forces to form a solid sphere. After millions of years the rock crust and the oceans and the atmosphere formed. About 200 million years ago there was a single land mass. It later split into smaller land masses, which, after millions of years of drift, formed the continents we know today.

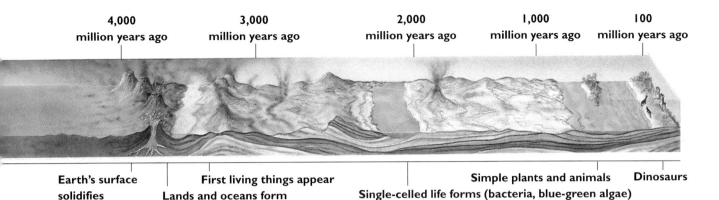

4,000 million years ago    3,000 million years ago    2,000 million years ago    1,000 million years ago    100 million years ago

Earth's surface solidifies    First living things appear    Simple plants and animals    Dinosaurs
Lands and oceans form    Single-celled life forms (bacteria, blue-green algae)

It eventually broke up, and sunlight reached the Earth. Weather and seasons began. This happened more than four billion years ago.

## Recording Earth's History

We know of human history largely from written records. The Earth has kept records, too, in its rocks and fossils. Scientists have hunted for these records and learned to read Earth's "language." Each time a new discovery is made and trans-

and the beginning of the next. Each era lasts many millions of years.

Each era is also divided into *periods*, and each period lasts a long time. The *Carboniferous* period lasted about 75 million years.

The most recent era, the *Cenozoic*, is still going on. Scientists have more information about this era than any other, so its periods have been divided into *epochs*. These time periods together make up *geologic time*, which is measured by

▲ When the Earth formed, it was very hot. Steam and gases hung above the land and water. There were no living things. Fossils show that life forms appeared 3,500 million years ago. For 2,500 million years they were small and simple. Larger organisms appeared less than 1,000 million years ago.

200 million years ago

100 million years ago

Today

lated, we learn a little more about the history of our planet.

Scientists have divided Earth's very long history into sections. The longest ones are called *eras*. At several times in Earth's history, widespread and rapid folding of Earth's crust has built huge mountain chains. Each time of mountain building is called a *revolution*. A revolution marks the end of one era

changes in the Earth's surface.

Scientists use two kinds of records to make up these divisions. One comes from the rocks and soil and how they are arranged. The other comes from fossils, the remains or traces of long-dead plants and animals. These records tell a fascinating story about the Earth. In the chart of Earth's history, you can see the major changes in the Earth.

In 1984, ancient rocks were found in the Northwest Territories of Canada. Scientists believe they are 3,900 million years old. Even older rocks were discovered in the desert in Chile in 1991. They are iron fragments from a meteorite which hit the Earth about 3,500 million years ago. The meteorite probably broke off an asteroid formed at about the same time as the Earth. That makes its rock fragments about 4,500 million years old— the oldest rocks found on Earth.

## HISTORY OF THE EARTH

**Millions of years**

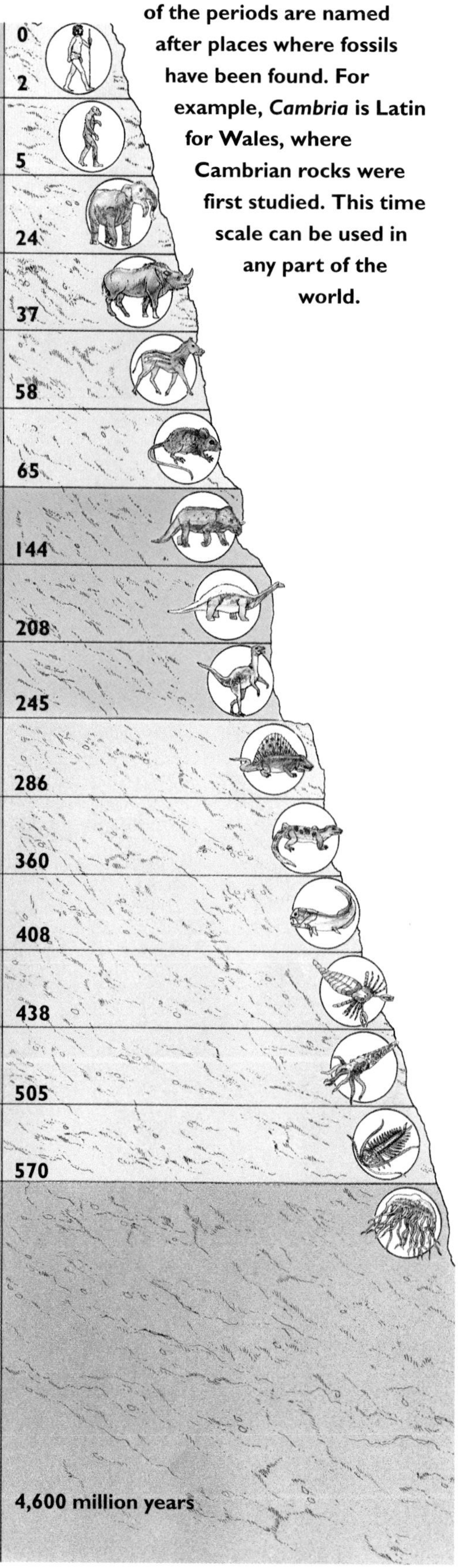

▼ The history of Earth is divided into geological periods. These mark the main stages in the history of life. Many of the periods are named after places where fossils have been found. For example, *Cambria* is Latin for Wales, where Cambrian rocks were first studied. This time scale can be used in any part of the world.

| | Period | Description | Millions of years |
|---|---|---|---|
| **CENOZOIC 65–0.01** | **Pleistocene** | The Great Ice Ages. First modern humans appear. | 0 — 2 |
| | **Pliocene** | *Australopithecus* appears. First cattle and sheep. | 5 |
| | **Miocene** | Many new mammals appear. First mice, rats, and apes. | 24 |
| | **Oligocene** | First deer, monkeys, pigs, and rhinoceroses. | 37 |
| | **Eocene** | First dogs, cats, rabbits, elephants, and horses. | 58 |
| | **Paleocene** | Mammals spread rapidly. First owls, shrews, and hedgehogs. | 65 |
| **MESOZOIC 245–65** | **Cretaceous** | Dinosaurs die out. First snakes, modern mammals. | 144 |
| | **Jurassic** | Dinosaurs rule the land. First birds appear. | 208 |
| | **Triassic** | First dinosaurs, mammals, turtles, crocodiles, and frogs. | 245 |
| **PALEOZOIC 570–245** | **Permian** | First sail-backed reptiles. Many sea and land animals die out. | 286 |
| | **Carboniferous** | First reptiles. Great coal swamp forests. | 360 |
| | **Devonian** | First amphibians, insects, and spiders. | 408 |
| | **Silurian** | Giant sea scorpians. First land plants. | 438 |
| | **Ordovician** | First nautiloids. Corals and trilobites common. | 505 |
| | **Cambrian** | First fishes, trilobites, corals, and shellfish. | 570 |
| **PRECAMBRIAN 4600–570** | **Precambrian** | 700 first jellyfish and worms. Life begins in the sea. | |

**4,600 million years**

---

### RECENT EARTH HISTORY

The most recent era of the Earth's history is called the Cenozoic Era. It began about 65 million years ago. It is divided into these epochs:

**Paleocone Epoch, 65 million years ago**
**Eocene Epoch, 60 million years ago**
**Oligocene Epoch, 35 million years ago**
**Miocene Epoch, 25 million years ago**
**Pliocene Epoch, 5 million years ago**
**Pleistocene Epoch, 2 million years ago**

Throughout these epochs, the animals that we know today were evolving from primitive ancestors. These primitive animals died out and were replaced by more advanced species.

The Cenozoic Era is the age of the mammals, which by the time the Cenozoic Era began, had taken over from the reptiles as the most dominant animals on Earth.

During the Pleistocene Epoch, the Earth experienced the most recent of its several Ice Ages. Canada and much of Europe were covered by ice sheets. Animal life included woolly mammoths, cave bears, giant sloths, and saber-tooth cats. Human beings also appeared during this time, and began their increasing influence on the Earth's history.

▶▶▶▶ **FIND OUT MORE** ◀◀◀◀
**Anthropology** see Anthropology; Human Being; Stone Age
**Astronomy** see Astronomy; Comets; Earth; Moon; Solar System; Sun
**Atmosphere** see Atmosphere; Cloud; Sky; Weather
**Biology** see Algae; Amphibian; Animal Kingdom; Bacteria; Darwin, Charles; Dinosaur; Ecology; Evolution; Fossil; Life; Plant Kingdom; Protist; Reptile
**Chemistry and Physics** see Element; Gas; Hydrogen; Nitrogen; Oxygen; Radiation; Radioactivity
**Earth** see Continent; Erosion; Mineral; Ocean; Soil
**Geology** see Canyon; Earthquake; Geology; Glacier; Ice Age; River; Volcano

# EARTHQUAKE

One day in October 1992, the people of Cairo, Egypt felt the ground shake several times. Each tremor was a little stronger than the one before. A rumbling sound seemed to approach the city. The rumble increased to a roar, as if a huge train were rushing through a tunnel under the streets. The ground rose and fell in waves. After the main shocks came a brief pause, followed by renewed shaking, the aftershock.

People were thrown off their feet by the shaking of the earth. Apartment buildings fell into crumbled heaps of rubbish. Many buildings in Egypt's capital were damaged. Thousands of people were injured or killed by falling buildings. Cracks, called *fissures*, opened in the ground.

The shaking of the earth was an *earthquake*, a sudden violent movement of part of the Earth's crust. The sudden movement is caused by the breaking of rocks that are under great pressure. The pressure comes from the slow movement of the giant rigid plates that make up the Earth's crust, colliding with, sliding past, or moving away from each other. Pressure on one or more layers of rock goes on for many years, becoming stronger as time passes. The pressure finally becomes more than the rock can withstand. The rock breaks and snaps back, shaking the earth.

The tremors caused by earthquakes are recorded and measured with a *seismograph*. A seismograph often consists of a large weight that hangs from a framework resting on a fixed base in the earth (rock). When

**Sideway movement**

**Spring**
**Pen**
**Seismograph**
**Weight**
**Drum**
**Vertical movement**

an earthquake causes tremors in the earth, the base of the seismograph moves. But the weight remains still. The amount of movement the base makes is recorded and traced on a chart. This chart, or *seismogram*, provides a record of the earth's movement.

Sometimes earthquakes under the ocean cause landslides that can create very large waves, called *seismic sea waves* or *tsunamis*. They are often incorrectly called tidal waves.

Not all earthquakes cause damage or injury. About 150,000 occur each year, but only about 100 are really destructive. Nowhere on Earth is entirely free of earthquakes. But some places are much more at risk because they lie on the edge of the

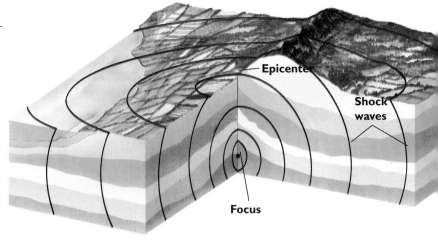

Epicenter
Shock waves
Focus

▲ The epicenter of an earthquake is the point on the Earth's surface immediately above the focus point—the place where movement of the crust has caused shock waves.

◄ A seismograph is a very sensitive instrument which is used to record the *magnitude* (size) of an earthquake in terms of the shock waves it produces. The blue arrows show the direction of the movement (horizontal and vertical) caused by the shock waves. The Richter Scale is used to grade the strength of an earthquake.

▼ Regions in the world where most earthquakes occur, lie along the edges of crustal plates, the edges of continents, and along chains of islands.

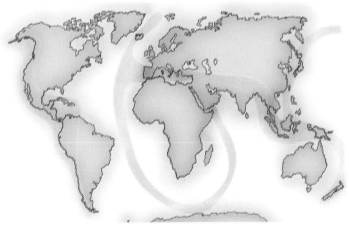

It has been calculated that every single day some 250 earthquakes take place all over the world. Most of them occur beneath the seas. Of those that happen on land, very few cause any damage. The shock waves from a large earthquake can travel right through the Earth from one side to the other. It takes the waves about 21 minutes to do this.

▶ **Worms may come to the surface, especially to breed. If they feel vibrations or touch, they rapidly withdraw back into their burrows.**

▼ **An earthworm's body is made up of many segments. More than 3,000 species of worm are found throughout the world.**

earth's plates. San Francisco, California, is in a high risk area and has had a number of serious earthquakes in living memory. A recent one, in 1989, killed 67 people.

▶▶▶▶ **FIND OUT MORE** ◀◀◀◀
Continental Drift; Earth; Earth History; Geology; Mountain

## EARTHWORM

Earthworms are creatures that are usually easy to find in moist garden soil or around lawns. Their reddish-brown bodies are made up of many ringlike parts, or segments. Little bristles attached to the segments help the worms move through the earth. An earthworm is damp and clammy to the touch. This is because its body has a slimy coating to keep it from drying out. The pointed end that looks like a tail is really its head. If the first few segments of the worm's head are cut off, new head segments grow back. The earthworm can also grow back a new tail if its tail is

cut off. This is called *regeneration*.

Earthworms mate at night. The worm lays its eggs in a cocoon after mating. This cocoon is produced by the worm's body. The young worms that hatch from the cocoon are small but fully developed. They reach their

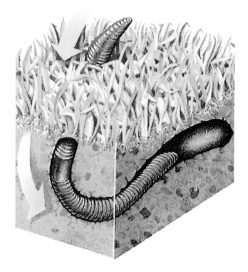

full length, up to 10 inches (25 cm), in a few months.

Earthworms are very helpful to farmers and gardeners. They help keep the soil good for growing plants. One way they do this is by hollowing out many little tunnels underground. This keeps the soil loose, making spaces for air and rainwater to come into the soil. Earthworms also turn the soil over and break it up by eating it. As an earthworm tunnels, it eats the soil that is in its path. The soil is finely ground up in the worm's digestive system. Only the plant matter in the soil is digested. The rest is cast out of the worm's body in little piles, called *castings*, on top of the ground.

Earthworms prefer damp soil. They become inactive if the soil dries out too much. In the United States, earthworms are most common in eastern states.

▶▶▶▶ **FIND OUT MORE** ◀◀◀◀
Animal Kingdom; Worm

### LEARN BY DOING

Earthworms usually stay underground by day, but if a hard rain floods their burrows, they come up to the surface to breathe. Just after a rainstorm is a good time to hunt for earthworms. If you want to keep one to watch for a while, put it in a box with plenty of damp dirt. Remember, it must burrow. Do not leave it in the sun or on a radiator, because strong light or heat can kill it. Put leaves and grass on the dirt.

# EASTER

The most important Christian holiday of the year is Easter. Christians believe that on the first Easter, Jesus Christ rose from the dead.

In most countries, Easter comes in early spring. In A.D 325, a church council decided that Easter should be celebrated on the first Sunday after the first full moon after the spring equinox (March 21). Therefore, Easter comes on a different Sunday each year between March 22, and April 25.

The week before Easter is called *Holy Week*. It begins with *Passion* or *Palm Sunday*, which celebrates the day Jesus rode into Jerusalem on a donkey and the people scattered palm leaves before him. Christ's Last Supper is celebrated on *Maundy* or *Holy Thursday*. His death on the cross (Crucifixion) is commemorated by Christians on *Good Friday*.

On Easter Sunday, many people dress up in new spring clothes and go to church. Many churches have special sunrise services. White lilies, known as Easter Lilies, decorate the altars of churches. Some children receive Easter baskets on this day. Children are often told that Easter baskets are brought by the Easter Bunny. This legend probably comes from an old German folk tale. Easter baskets contain candy and colorful decorated eggs. Eggs are associated with Easter because they, like the holiday, are a symbol of new life.

▶ ▶ ▶ ▶ **FIND OUT MORE** ◀ ◀ ◀ ◀
Christianity; Jesus Christ

# ECHIDNA

SEE SPINY ANTEATER

# ECHINODERM

Echinoderms are small *invertebrates* (animals without backbones) that live on the bottom of the sea. The word *echinoderm* means "spiny-skinned." Most of the animals called echinoderms have many small spines or stiff little points growing from their skin. The best-known echinoderms are starfish. Other common echinoderms are sea urchins, sea cucumbers, brittle stars, sand dollars, and sea lilies.

If you look at a starfish, you can see that its main body is in the center and that it has five arms that stick out like a five pointed star. Other echinoderms also have body parts

**Sunstar**

**Cushion starlet**

grouped around a center part, although the pattern is not always easy to see from the outside.

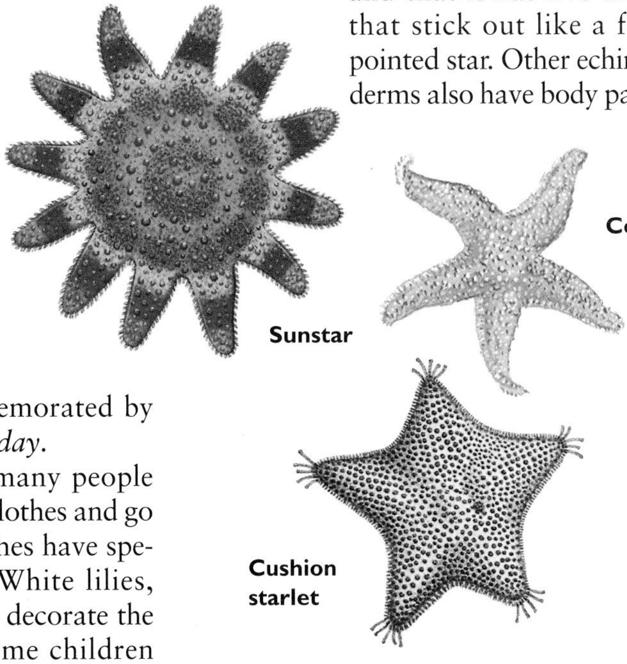

### Major Echinoderms

STARFISH. Starfish live on the bottom of the sea in bays and shallow water. Some are only as big as a 25-cent coin. Others are 3 feet (almost 1 m) across. Most starfish have five arms, although some have seven arms or more. If a starfish loses an arm, it can grow another arm to take its place. If some kinds of starfish are cut into pieces, a new starfish will grow from each arm. This process is called *regeneration*.

▲ **An old Easter greeting card. For thousands of years the egg has been a symbol of new life.**

**Echinoderms are a very ancient order of animal. Fossils of the creatures have been found in rocks dating back 600 million years.**

**Common starfish**

◀ **Starfish are part of the Echinoderm group of animals. They usually have five arms. The sunstar (pictured here) however, usually has between eight and fifteen arms. Starfish can regenerate a new arm if they lose one.**

**Starfish, measuring more than 4 feet (120 cm) from arm tip to arm tip, have been dredged up from deep in the ocean bed.**

▲ The undersides of a starfish's arms are covered with tiny tube-feet ending in suckers. The starfish uses these suckers to pull open the shellfish, such as mussels, on which it feeds.

▼ A selection of other common animals that belong to the echinoderm family.

A starfish creeps along the bottom of the sea in a peculiar way. It has many hollow, tubelike feet on the underside of its arms. To take a step, the starfish lets water into the tube feet of one of its arms. The water makes the arm stretch out. Suckers on the ends of the tube feet hold onto rocks on the sea bottom. That is one step. The starfish then lets water into the tube feet of another arm. The second arm stretches out, and the starfish takes another step. The starfish moves each of its five arms in turn. When it has to, the starfish can move pretty fast.

A starfish also eats in a peculiar way. A starfish's mouth is under its body. It eats by moving on top of its food, opening its mouth, and then letting its stomach come out of its mouth until the stomach covers the food and digests it. Starfish especially like to eat clams and oysters. The soft inside of each clam or oyster is protected by two hard shells. To get at an oyster, the starfish covers the shells with its arms. The suckers on the bottom of the arms hold tight to the shells of the oyster. The starfish then pulls the shells apart with its powerful arms.

BRITTLE STAR. Brittle stars live at the bottom of the ocean where the water is very deep and cold. A brittle star looks more like a spider than a starfish. It has very long, thin arms, with which it can move very fast. If one of the arms breaks off, another arm grows in its place.

SEA URCHIN. Sea urchins look like round balls covered with long, sharp spines that appear something like the quills on a porcupine. The spines protect the sea urchin against its enemies. Some kinds of sea urchins have poison in the tips of their spines. So if you see a sea urchin, be careful not to touch it.

SEA CUCUMBER. A sea cucumber has a sausage-shaped body and a cluster of sticky tentacles, or feelers, surrounding its mouth. The sea cucumber is a sluggish creature. It usually waits for its food to come to it. It catches tiny sea animals with its tentacles. Some sea cucumbers can throw out sticky threads to ensnare an enemy. Others have poison in their bodies and are left alone by hungry fish. The Chinese like to eat dried sea cucumber, which they call *trepang*.

Ophiothrix fragilis (Brittle star)

Edible sea urchin

Violet heart urchin

Rock Urchin

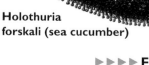

Holothuria forskali (sea cucumber)

► ► ► ► **FIND OUT MORE** ◄ ◄ ◄ ◄
Animal Defenses; Animal Kingdom; Nature Study; Ocean

## ECHO

SEE SOUND

## ECLIPSE

Nearly 2,600 years ago, warring soldiers from the ancient countries of Media and Lydia faced each other across an open plain. Both sides expected victory. But the soldiers from Lydia had a secret weapon. The weapon was a prediction from an astronomer named Thales. Thales predicted that the sun would darken that day.

The battle began. Soldiers fought bravely for hours. Both armies were strong, and neither army was winning. A black shadow suddenly crawled across the sun. Soldiers from Lydia cried out with joy and attacked harder. But the soldiers from Media felt great fear. Why did the sun turn black? They dropped their weapons and ran away, and the battle ended. Lydia won because Thales predicted a *solar eclipse* and warned the soldiers that darkness would occur during the day.

A *solar eclipse* happens when the moon moves directly between the Earth and the sun. The moon blocks out light from the sun for a short time. The moon's shadow falls on Earth. As the moon moves in its orbit, the shadow moves across the Earth. The shadow is small, so only a small part of Earth sees the eclipse.

The center of the shadow is a dark circle called the *umbra*. It is only about 167 miles (269 km) across. Inside the umbra, the eclipse is complete—the moon completely hides

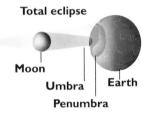

**Sun**

the sun. Around the umbra is a circle of lesser shadow about 2,000 miles (3,200 km) across. This big circle is the *penumbra*. Inside the penumbra, the eclipse is not seen as complete. Part of the sun is still visible. Solar eclipses do not last very long, never longer than 7½ minutes.

Never look directly at a solar eclipse. The sun's rays are so bright, even during an eclipse, that you can be blinded. The brightness makes it very difficult to see what happens, anyway. Instead, watch the eclipse on television. Special equipment, including telescopes and filters, makes it much easier to see the eclipse. And an expert astronomer will explain exactly what is happening and what you should watch for.

A *lunar eclipse* happens when the moon passes through the Earth's shadow. The shadow is not completely black, and the moon usually turns a copper color. A total eclipse of the moon may last for more than one hour. It takes an hour for the moon to move into the shadow and another hour for the moon to move out of it.

*Partial eclipses* can also happen, when the moon moves through an edge of the shadow instead of going through the middle.

▶ ▶ ▶ ▶ **FIND OUT MORE** ◀ ◀ ◀ ◀
Astronomy; Moon; Sun

> A total solar eclipse will be visible only once in about 360 years from any one place on Earth.

▼ During a solar eclipse the moon casts a very small "umbra" on the Earth. This is the only place where a solar eclipse is total. In the "penumbra", observers can see a partial eclipse.

**Total eclipse**

**Moon**

**Umbra** **Earth**

**Penumbra**

**Partial eclipse**

▼ During a total solar eclipse, the moon is seen as a dark ball. The bright glare comes from the sun's corona, or outer atmosphere.

First energy level
Producer

Grass

Second energy level
Primary consumer

Rabbits

Third energy level
Secondary consumer

Fox

## ECOLOGY

*Ecology* is a science that studies how all living things depend on each other, and on their *environment* (surroundings). Wherever you live, you could study the animals and plants that live there and find out about the ecology of the area. Even if you live in a city, you could make a study of the life in your local park.

If you live by a lake, for example, you could make an *ecological* study of the lake and the surrounding area. By watching the lake, you may find out what types of fish live there. You may find bass, perch, and pickerel. You may see many kinds of plants, including reeds and water lilies, growing in the water. Or minnows and other tiny fish that are found in lakes in large numbers. If you had a microscope you would be able to see even smaller living things in the water, including amoebas and hydras.

You may notice that larger creatures, such as birds, squirrels, and deer come to the lake to drink. These types of animals probably live in the woods nearby, along with foxes and

▲ In a food chain at the first level, producers such as green plants are eaten by herbivores or primary consumers. These primary consumers are, in turn, eaten by carnivores, or secondary consumers. Each organism in the food chain feeds on, and obtains energy from, the previous level.

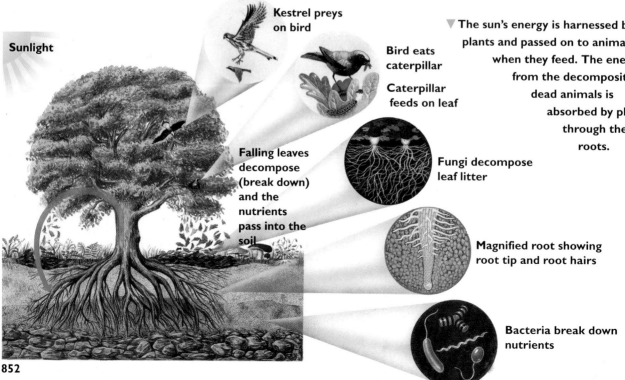

Sunlight

Kestrel preys on bird

Bird eats caterpillar

Caterpillar feeds on leaf

Falling leaves decompose (break down) and the nutrients pass into the soil

Fungi decompose leaf litter

Magnified root showing root tip and root hairs

▼ The sun's energy is harnessed by plants and passed on to animals when they feed. The energy from the decomposition of dead animals is absorbed by plants through their roots.

Bacteria break down nutrients

rabbits. You may discover other creatures, such as blacksnakes, living in a meadow nearby. If you read about blacksnakes, you will discover that they feed on field mice and pests that eat farmer's grain. If you look around, you may find mice living in the meadow, as well as many insects like grasshoppers and butterflies.

The longer you watch the lake and the land around it, the more you will see how all the *organisms* (living things) that make their homes there depend on each other. The areas of the lake, the woods, and the meadows are called *habitats*. *Habitats* are areas where certain organisms usually live. The deer and other animals need the woods and the lake water. And the fish, too, depend on the lake. The snake could not live in the meadow if no mice were nearby. The mice need grain and seeds from farms and gardens.

All the creatures of the lake, woods, and meadow live together in a *community*, just as the people of a town form a community. No living thing exists alone. Every living thing is surrounded by air, water, or soil. And every living thing takes what it needs from its environment and leaves what it does not need.

Many things help make up an environment—climate, atmosphere, soil, land shape, height above sea level, the kinds of plants that grow, the number of people around. Animals and plants survive in environments that are suited to them. Palm trees do not grow in the Arctic, where it is cold. They do not grow in every warm place, either, but only where the right soil and water conditions exist. Birds that nest in trees do not live on grassy plains or high up on mountains, where no trees grow.

The lake, woods, and meadow and all the organisms in them make up an *ecosystem*—all the organisms of a community, plus all the surrounding things that are not living and never were alive. Ecosystems do

not stay as they are forever. They change with time, going through a process of *succession*. The lake may not always stay as a lake. It may gradually dry up and, in the future, the whole area may be covered by small trees. Eventually a forest may exist where the lake is now.

### Ways Living Things Interact

Living things depend on one another in many ways. Lions are predators or *carnivores*. They kill other animals for food. Small carnivores, such as spiders, prey on flies and other small insects. Larger carnivores, such as eagles, wolves, and leopards, eat larger kinds of prey.

Many other animals, including rabbits, deer, sheep, cattle, and horses, are *herbivores*. They feed on plants. From the leaves and other parts of plants, they obtain the

▲ Ecologists study how communities of animals and plants interact with one another and with the non-living elements in their environments. The different roles each of the species plays in its environment is also of importance to studies by ecologists.

---

### LEARN BY DOING

Make a square frame from four even lengths of wood, and divide it into smaller squares by attaching pieces of string across the frame, horizontally and vertically. Put it down at random several times in different fields or gardens. List the plants and insects you find in each square of the frame. Use a field guide to try and identify what you find.

▼ Egyptian plover birds feed by picking parasites from Nile crocodiles. This action is beneficial to both the crocodile and the plover bird.

free ride (the shark is a faster, stronger swimmer). Second, scraps from the shark's dinner float by the remora, which quickly gobbles them up.

Another kind of relationship is called *mutualism* (from the Latin word for "trade" or "exchange"). Squirrels, chipmunks, and other animals that store acorns for winter

energy they need to live and grow.

Animals that feed on both plants and animals are called *omnivores*. People are omnivores since they eat both animals and plants. Another omnivore is the badger, which eats small animals as well as roots, leaves and fruits.

Another kind of dependence exists between parasites and their hosts. A *parasite* is a living thing that lives in or on another living thing (its *host*), and takes food directly from its host. Smut, a fungus that lives on corn, is a parasite. So are blood-sucking ticks and fleas. Tapeworms attach themselves to the intestines of humans. A parasite usually does not kill its host, but it does make the host weak.

Another kind of relationship between living things is *commensalism*, which comes from Latin words meaning "eating at the same table." The remora is a small fish with a kind of suction cup on its head. The remora uses this cup to attach itself to a shark. This has no affect on the shark, but it is good for the remora in two ways. First, the remora gets a

food share a mutualistic relationship with oak trees. These trees provide food for the animals. And each year a few of the acorns that the animals bury are not found. These acorns sprout, and new oak trees grow.

Living things may also be involved in *competition*. This may occur between two plants or animals of the same *species* (kind). Two frogs, for example, cannot catch and eat the same insect—one frog must trap another insect or go hungry. Two maple trees cannot grow in the same square foot of ground. The strong tree survives, and the other dies.

Competition also goes on between species. Green plants cannot live without sunlight. In thick forests, trees block all sunlight, so that none reaches the forest floor. Grass and other flowering plants cannot grow on such a forest floor. Another example of competition exists between bluebirds and starlings. Bluebirds and starlings nest in empty woodpecker holes. In areas where both live, they must compete for available space.

The introduction of animals from foreign lands to a new land can have harmful effects on the balanced ecology of a region. These introduced animals usually arrive without the natural enemies that controlled their numbers. This happened when, in 1850, three pairs of European rabbits were turned loose in Australia. With no natural enemies, the rabbits multiplied so quickly that farmers had to erect rabbit-proof fencing to protect their fields and grazing ranges from the millions of pests. Only the introduction of a disease that was fatal to rabbits halted the plague.

## The Food Web

Have you ever thought about how the fish you eat for dinner got to your table? The story probably starts with green algae, tiny one-celled plants that are eaten by very small herbivorous fish. These very small fish are in turn eaten by bigger carnivorous fish, which are eaten by even bigger fish, until finally one of these big carnivores is caught and made into a tasty meal for a human being.

But the way in which living things feed on each other is not really so simple. If you trace a spider web with your finger, you will find that, sooner or later, you return to the spot you started from. It is that way with food, too. You probably already know that green plants use the sun's energy to produce food from water and other substances in the soil, together with the gas, carbon dioxide, from the air. Another gas, oxygen, which all living things use when they breathe, is produced as a waste product. Animals depend upon green plants for their life-giving oxygen. They also depend upon green plants for their food. For example, in the meadow and woods by the lake, rabbits, mice, and grasshoppers (and other animals, too) eat the plants. Snakes and foxes then eat these animals.

The next part of the food web leads back to the beginning, green plants. Who provides fertilizer for wild plants? Animals and other plants. Animals all produce waste. And all animals and plants die. Bacteria that live in soil *decompose* (break down) the bodies of dead organisms and the waste products of living organisms. Bacteria return necessary chemicals to the soil, growing plants use the chemicals, and the food web goes on.

This food web is just one example of the *balance of nature*. Each part of nature needs every other part in order to exist. If one part of nature dies out or becomes too strong, every other part of nature is eventually affected by the change.

## What Makes Ecology Important?

The world has been in constant change since it was formed. Not all changes are harmful. For example your body is changing all the time. Your heart beats faster when you run

The sensible use of ecology can help to stop pollution. London's Thames River, for example, was one of the most polluted rivers in Europe in the 1950s. No fish could live in it. Then a campaign to clean up the river began. Factories were no longer allowed to pour waste into it. Raw sewage was treated before flowing into the river. Now, for the first time in over a hundred years, there are salmon in the Thames.

▼ An ocean food web. The sun's energy is absorbed by the tiny plants near the sea's surface. These are then eaten by plant-eating animals, and the energy is passed on. The plant-eaters are in turn eaten by the meat-eating animals. The source of energy is passed down the food chain through these links.

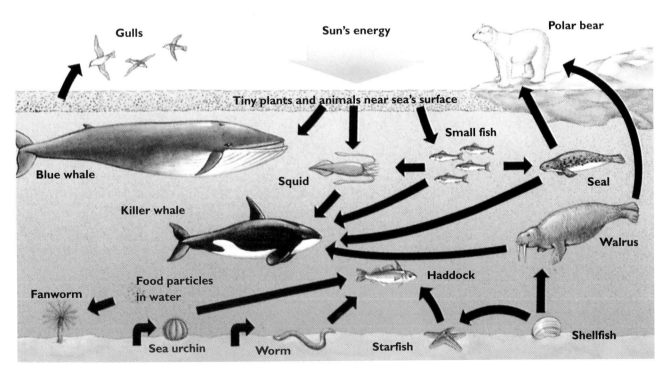

► **Human activities can have unforeseen effects on the natural balance between predators and prey. On the Kaibab plateau in Arizona, people began hunting coyotes and pumas, which preyed upon the local deer population. The deer population rose drastically, but their food ran out, and so thousands died of starvation.**

**WHERE TO DISCOVER MORE**

Norsgaard, Ernestine Jaediker. *Nature's Great Balancing Act.* New York: Cobblehill Books, 1990.
Landau, Elaine. *Tropical Rain Forests Around the World.* Chicago: Franklin Watts, 1990.

At the height of German inflation in the 1920s, a U.S. dollar was worth four quintillion (4,000,000,000,000,000,000) marks.

than it does when you sleep. If your heartbeat did not change, you would probably collapse every time you ran.

Changes in the world are not all bad, either. But human inventions and discoveries are causing rapid changes in some ways that are not healthy. The air is being filled with poisons. Waterways that were once clean and filled with living things are becoming sewers where almost nothing can live. We must learn to *adapt* to our environment. To *adapt* means to change or adjust in order to fit in with the environment or surroundings.

Ecologists can help us understand the ways in which all living things fit together. And they can help find ways to use inventions and discoveries without making the world sick.

► ► ► ► **FIND OUT MORE** ◄ ◄ ◄ ◄
**Animal and Plant Life** see
Agriculture; Algae; Animal Defenses; Animal Distribution; Animal Homes; Birds of the Past; City Wildlife; Desert; Food Web; Hibernation; Jungle; Marine Life; Parasite; Plant Distribution; Polar Life; Prairie; Rare Animals; Swamps and Marshes
**Conservation** see Community; Conservation; Erosion; Forest Fire; Lumber and Lumbering; National Park; Natural Resources; Park; Soil; Water Supply; Wilderness Area

## ECONOMICS

Can you buy everything you want with your allowance? Probably not. You have to choose what you can *afford* to buy out of all the things you *want* to buy. If you decide that you want or need many things, you must figure out how to earn or save the money to pay for them. Just as you have to make these decisions with the money you earn or receive as an allowance, your parents must figure out how they can buy the things your family wants and needs. (Cars, television sets, and even food can be very expensive.)

A nation has the same problem. Its people want many things, such as food, clothes, houses, cars, and furniture. Each nation must find a way to make or buy as many of these things as possible and a way to distribute and sell them to people. The field of economics studies the way a nation handles the problems of making, distributing, and buying what all its people want.

### What is Economics?
Economics is a social science that is affected by three basic things: *natural resources*, *labor*, and *capital*. *Natural resources* are things on or in the Earth, such as water, trees, and minerals. *Labor* is the effort of people who work to turn natural resources into products, or who perform services. The word *capital* can mean one of two things. Capital can be the money needed to build factories and stores and to buy machines and tools. Capital can also be anything made or produced by people that is used to produce something else—like the machines and tools themselves.

Three of the processes studied by economists are *production*, *distribution*, and *exchange*. A factory that makes furniture is engaged in *production*. The furniture is usually sold to a wholesale company that in turn sells it to many different retail stores.

The furniture has to be delivered from the factory to the wholesale company, and from there it goes to the retail stores. In the retail stores, salesclerks will sell it to people who want furniture. The delivering and selling are called *distribution*.

At each step, a number of people must be paid for their work in getting the furniture to the customers who finally buy it. This means that some money goes to the factory workers who made the furniture, some to the workers who loaded it onto trucks, some to the truck driver, some to warehouse workers, some to the wholesale company that sells it to the retail stores, some to the retail store, and some to the clerks who sell it to the customers. Since money is exchanged for work in all these steps, they are types of *exchange*.

After everyone is paid in the furniture industry, as in all industries, there should be money left over. This money is *profit*. Everyone involved in the process of making, delivering, and selling the furniture expects to

make a profit. But perhaps the factories or the stores do not sell all their furniture. Maybe the *supply* of furniture was greater than the *demand* for (or desire to buy) furniture. Or perhaps the price they asked for the furniture was too low to pay everyone for their work. Then they have had a *loss*. They have less money in the bank. They may have to borrow money or even sell their factory.

Production, distribution, and exchange are affected by many other things besides salaries and profit. For example, the United States must buy such goods as coffee, tea, and sugar from other countries. Other countries in turn buy wheat, steel, and other goods from the United States. This *international trade* affects shipping, banking, communications, marketing, and other services.

International trade is an extension of domestic trade and domestic *competition*. In competition, nations and business rivals, such as those in the automobile industry, try to outsell each other. Car manufacturers offer deals to car buyers. They compete with each other in order to get more business—and more profit—than their rivals. Most American companies make small cars to compete

▲ Bartering is known the world over wherever people have no forms of money in common. Here, in the 1800s, goods considered to be of equal value (a crayfish and a piece of cloth) are being swapped by a New Zealand Maori warrior and a traveler. The traveler's money is of no value to the Maori.

Inflation was so high during the Revolutionary War that the price of beef rose by 30,000 percent!

◄ Inflation reduces the real value of money. In Germany during the 1920s inflation was so bad that banknotes became almost worthless. The huge stacks of notes seen here, the wages for a small railroad company, amounted to only one-fourth of their face value.

▲ This one billion mark (German currency) note was issued in Cologne in 1928. Because of the high level of inflation at the time, its real value was a lot less than its face value. In fact, each note was worth less than a penny.

▼ The Tokyo stock exchange. The buying and selling of shares of stock is a basic part of the capitalist economic system, in which land, resources, and industries are owned by private individuals and companies, rather than by governments.

with those imported from foreign countries. Such competition can result in lower prices of cars. Prices could be very high without competition. If only one company made all automobiles, a buyer would have no choice about prices. Such a company would have a *monopoly*. The Federal Government has passed laws to prevent monopolies. But in a private enterprise system, a policy of *laissez faire*, meaning no government interference, is important too.

Many other factors are involved in economics. Some goods may be hard to get. When there is more money available than usual, prices tend to rise, because people can afford to pay the higher costs. This is called *inflation*.

Poor management, demand for goods, rates of interest charged by banks for borrowing money, strikes by workers—all of these factors and more affect the daily lives of people in some way.

## Socialism and Communism

The economic processes described above occur under *capitalism*, the system used in the United States. Another kind of economic system is *socialism*. Under democratic socialism, a government may own and manage big industries such as electric

power, gas, coal, transportation, and communications. These state-owned industries are all run so that everyone shares their benefits. Other businesses are left in private ownership, and small businesses and private homes are still owned by individuals. In the past, Britain, Sweden, and Israel, among other countries, have had democratic socialist governments and adopted socialist measures. In some countries (although now very few), socialism is closer to *communism*. China is the world's largest communist country. The communist system seeks to do away with all ownership of property by individuals. Not only factories and large industries, but even homes and farms are owned by the government for the benefit of all the people. Prices and wages are controlled.

Whether a nation's economic system is capitalist, socialist, or communist, all economic systems are based on the fact that people must have food, clothing, and housing. There must be workers to produce, distribute, and sell the goods, and consumers to buy and use the goods. Therefore, workers and consumers form the basis of economics.

▶▶▶▶ **FIND OUT MORE** ◀◀◀◀
**Business Management and Organization** see Advertising; Corporation; Stores and Shops
**Economic Systems** see Capitalism; Communism; Socialism
**Factors of Production** see Agriculture; Automation; Manufacturing; Natural Resources; Public Utility; Supply and Demand
**Finance** see Accounting and Bookkeeping; Banks and Banking; Insurance; Stocks and Bonds; Tax
**History** see Child Labor; Depression; Feudalism; Industrial Revolution; Marx, Karl; Social Security
**International Economics** see European Community; International Trade

# ECUADOR

The small country of Ecuador lies on the Pacific coast of South America. To its north is Colombia, and to its south and east is Peru. Ecuador is about the same size as Nevada, but has about ten times as many people. Most of them are Native South Americans or part Native, and many speak only the Quechua language. About 10 percent of the people are Europeans, and about 10 percent are black or part black. Many people in Ecuador are very poor—especially the Natives.

The equator crosses the country. "Ecuador" is the Spanish word for equator. Two ranges of the Andes Mountains form a broad highland zone running north to south through Ecuador, separating it into three regions.

The humid coastal lowlands are the richest agricultural area. Here coffee, bananas, and cacao are grown for export. Ecuador's largest city and chief port, Guayaquil, is found there.

More than half the people live in the cool high valleys of the central highlands. They raise cattle, sheep, and llamas. Grain, potatoes, fruits, and vegetables are grown in valleys surrounded by tall, snowcapped volcanic peaks, such as Chimborazo. Ecuador's capital city, Quito, lies in the highlands. Quito is very close to the equator but at an elevation of 9,250 feet (2,819 m). Therefore, it has spring-like weather all year, with an average temperature of 57°F (14°C). Quito is the country's educational and cultural center. It has many old buildings from the Spanish colonial period.

The hot, low plains east of the Andes are mostly thick tropical jungle, through which flow tributaries of the Amazon River. Among the few people who live here is the Jívaro tribe, who were once head hunters. Large deposits of oil have been found in this region and oil is now Ecuador's chief export product.

Ecuador was part of an ancient Indian kingdom when the Inca tribe conquered it in about 1470. Francisco Pizarro led the Spanish expedition that overthrew the Inca Empire in 1533. A Venezuelan general, Antonio José de Sucre, helped Ecuador win freedom in 1822. Ecuador became a republic in 1830.

The Galápagos Islands, lying 600 miles (965 km) off the Pacific coast of South America, belong to Ecuador. They are famous for the giant land turtles and other animals found there.

▶▶▶▶ **FIND OUT MORE** ◀◀◀◀
Darwin, Charles; Galápagos Islands; Pizarro, Francisco; South America

## ECUADOR

**Capital city**
Quito (1,234,000)

**Area**
109,484 square miles
(283,561 sq. km)

**Population**
10,782,000 people

**Government**
Multi-party republic

**Natural resources**
Oil and natural gas, silver, gold, copper, iron, lead, zinc, lumber

**Export products**
Oil, bananas, cacao, coffee, shrimps, fish products

**Unit of money**
Sucre

**Official language**
Spanish

PACIFIC OCEAN

Esmeraldas
Esmeraldas R.
Tulcán
Guayllabamba R.
Ibarra
Putumayo R.
Santo Domingo de los Colorados
Quito ☆
Aguarico R.
Bay of Manta
Chone
Napo R.
Nuevo Rocafuerte
Manta
Quevedo
Latacunga
Curaray R.
Ambato
Portoviejo
Chimborazo 20,702 ft. 6,310 m.
Jipijapa
Riobamba
Pindoyacu R.
Bay of Santa Elena
Babahoyo
Pastaza R.
Macas
La Libertad
Milagro
Guayaquil
ANDES MTS.
Puná I.
Cuenca
Gulf of Guayaquil
Machala
Zamora R.
Santa Rosa
Daule
Loja

N W E S

0 — 100 — 200 Miles
0 — 100 — 200 — 300 Kilometers
© 1994 GeoSystems, an R.R. Donnelley & Sons Company

▶ **A narrow street in Ambato, a town in central Ecuador. The men are wearing ponchos, warm blanket-like cloaks.**

# EDISON, THOMAS ALVA (1847–1931)

What would we do without electric light bulbs, disc players, and motion picture cameras—things we take for granted? They were all invented by Thomas Alva Edison (the disc player developed from Edison's phonograph). In all, he produced more than 1,000 inventions. Few individuals have had such a direct effect on the lives of people everywhere.

Edison was born in Milan, Ohio. He spent only three months in school. His teachers could not under-

▲ **Thomas Alva Edison was perhaps the most successful inventor of all time.**

Telephone

Phonograph

Radio receiver

Electric light

Kinetoscope

▲ **Thomas Edison showed his skill at improving other inventions as well as devising his own. His work improved the performance of the telephone and the radio receiver. The phonograph, electric light, and kinetoscope were his own original creations.**

It was Edison who said: "Genius is one percent inspiration and ninety-nine percent perspiration."

stand why he questioned everything he was told. So his mother decided to educate him herself. He soon developed a keen interest in science. Edison took a job as a newsboy on a train when he was 12. He bought a small printing press and printed a weekly newspaper in a baggage car. When he was 16, he became a telegraph operator and began to experiment with electrical instruments. His first major invention was an improved version of the stock ticker, a machine used by stock-brokers to record the purchase and sale of stocks.

Edison set up a laboratory at Menlo Park, New Jersey, in 1876. He

improved the telephone so that it could carry a voice over a long distance. He invented the phonograph and developed one of the first motion picture cameras. But Edison's greatest experiments were with electric light. A type of electric bulb, called an *arc light*, was already in use. But it was so bright that it could not be used indoors. Edison invented an *incandescent* light bulb, which contains a special wire, or *filament*. When electricity heats the filament, light is given off. The light bulbs people use in their homes today are similar. By 1887, the inventor outgrew his laboratory in Menlo Park, and he moved to one in West Orange, New Jersey.

Edison worked with amazing concentration. He always made sure that his inventions would be workable and useful. He often lived in his laboratory, taking only a few hours of sleep. By the end of his life, "The Wizard of Menlo Park" had been honored all over the world.

▶▶▶▶ **FIND OUT MORE** ◀◀◀◀
Invention; Lighting; Recording; Telephone

# EDUCATION

Education is not just going to school. It is the lifelong learning that takes place as you deal with experiences of all kinds, make decisions, form opinions, and develop relationships with others. Education begins long before you start school! Everyone receives some kind of education just by learning from life. "Schooling," or the instruction and learning that take place in a series of schools over a period of years, is usually called "formal education."

In Stone Age times, children learned only the tasks needed for providing food, clothing, and shelter. Education in ancient times was centered around the home. A boy simply learned to do exactly the same work as his father. He learned by working with his father and other men. A girl learned all necessary skills she would need as an adult from her mother and the other women in the family.

Methods for writing were first invented in Sumer, Babylonia, and Egypt. The first schools were founded to teach boys how to become *scribes* (writers). Egyptian students learned to copy passages from literature on paper called papyrus. Boys in Babylonia learned to write by pressing a wedge-shaped stick into a wet clay tablet. The tablets dried and hardened. Many tablets have been found with this form of writing, called *cuneiform*. Both Egyptian and Babylonian priests gave more advanced training in professions such as medicine, architecture, or the priesthood. All education was practical.

### Greek and Roman Schools

The ancient Greeks developed a broader idea of education. In Athens, for example, all adult men who were not slaves had to be able both to defend the city in wartime and to take part in its government. The Athenians believed that the best way to produce good citizens was to educate boys so that they developed many talents—not just the skills they needed for a single profession.

Boys in Athens began school at the age of seven. Their classes were divided between gymnastics and "music." Music included reading, writing, and the study of literature. The boys copied poems and quotations from Greek literature on a wax tablet with a pointed stick. They then read what they had copied and the teacher, who was sometimes a slave, explained it to them. They also learned to play musical instruments called *lyres* and to sing.

Boys often did dances to express in movement the meaning of a poem. Gymnastics included running, jumping, wrestling, and throwing the *discus* (a circular plate of stone or metal) and the *javelin* (a spear). The boys also did calisthenics and played ball. The Athenians believed that everyone should have "a sound mind in a sound body."

Mothers and fathers in early Rome had complete responsibility for educating their children. But government-controlled grammar schools were later established throughout the Roman Empire. These schools taught Greek and Latin. More advanced schools specialized in *rhetoric*, the art of public speaking.

### The Middle Ages

The only European schools for several centuries after the fall of the Roman Empire were run by the Christian church in monasteries and cathedral towns. Their chief purpose was to train men to become priests and monks. Girls were educated at home.

Young men of noble families were trained to become knights. They became pages at the castle of a noble. They waited on the lord and lady of the castle and were taught social and military skills and sometimes how to

▼ Greek schoolboys were taught to read and write. They also learned music and poetry. Girls, however, were not educated, so most grew up unable to read and write.

Many people think that young children learn more quickly than adults. This is not really true. In many cases a person can remember and memorize school subjects much better at the age of 20 than he or she could at the age of 10.

◄ Many monasteries had schools and large libraries where trained monks copied books by hand. Some of the more learned monks wrote new books as well. These copies and new manuscripts were the basis for much of the learning of the time.

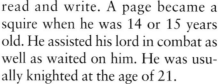

▶ Jewish boys went to schools where they were taught by the rabbis. They kept their Jewish traditions alive by learning to read, write, and speak Hebrew.

---

Boys and girls in Colonial America had very different educations. Six- and seven-year-olds would learn the alphabet at the same school. After that boys would continue their "book learning" in the hope of attending college. Girls would stay at home to be taught domestic skills such as cooking and weaving.

---

▲ In the Renaissance, the "age of learning," the ideal person was the "Universal Man or Woman." This was someone who was educated to be skillful in a wide range of subjects. These included science, travel, music and literature, as well as philosophy and the arts.

862

read and write. A page became a squire when he was 14 or 15 years old. He assisted his lord in combat as well as waited on him. He was usually knighted at the age of 21.

The first European universities were founded toward the end of the Middle Ages. They taught grammar, rhetoric, logic, music, arithmetic, geometry, and astronomy. Advanced degrees were given in medicine, law, and religious studies.

Practical craft education was controlled by the guilds in the town. A guild was an organization of workers in a particular craft, such as weaving, woodcarving, or shoemaking. A boy learned his trade by becoming an *apprentice* to a master craftsman. He worked in the master's shop in exchange for training in the craft. The master also provided the apprentice with clothes, food, and a place to sleep. When he was older, the apprentice became a *journeyman* and worked for daily wages.

### Renaissance and Reformation

The Renaissance was a period of "rebirth" of learning. It began in Italy in the 1300s and then spread to other parts of Europe. The Renaissance was marked by a new interest in the arts, literature, and the culture of Greece and Rome. Renaissance educators adopted the Greek ideal of a well rounded education. They were especially interested in the scientific study of man and the world of nature. This was very different from education during the Middle Ages, which had emphasized the study of religious ideas.

The Renaissance was followed by the Reformation—the period in which Protestant churches were

founded. Protestants believed that everyone should be able to read the Bible. They were in favor of a basic education for everyone. They founded many new schools and reorganized many old ones. The Roman Catholic Church also began to make education available to more people at this time.

### Free Public Schools

The Protestant reformer Martin Luther (1483–1546) recommended that there be free public schools for everyone. But it was not until the 1800s that this started to become a common practice. The United States was a leader in public education. Americans believed that equal opportunity for all was possible only through a free public school system. Many schools had only one room in which students of all grades were taught. *Coeducation* (education of boys and girls together) in public schools also became widespread in the 1800s. By the time of the Civil War, most states had public elementary schools, and several hundred public high schools had been built. Many states also started state universities that charged their students low tuition fees or none at all.

### Modern American Education

Today, most children in the United States must go to school until they are at least 16. One student in three goes on to higher (college) education. More than 55 million students attend public and private elementary schools, junior high schools, high schools, and colleges. Schools organize programs to help each student develop his or her talents. Courses are offered in physical education, art, and music, as well as languages, sciences, and social studies. Courses in industrial arts and business skills prepare students who want to go into those fields when they finish high school.

Colleges and universities offer more advanced academic courses and degree programs, and universities have graduate schools for professions such as medicine, law, engineering, teaching, or architecture. Many states have special agricultural colleges. Technical schools offer training beyond the high school level in such skills as mechanics, drafting, cabinet-making, and operating computers. Many schools have adult education courses for people who are working but want to take courses in the evening.

### Education for All

In some poorer countries in Africa, Asia, and South America, not every child is able to attend school, nor are there many colleges. Also, girls may not have the same educational opportunities as boys. These problems are being tackled by governments that realize the importance of providing a good education for all their citizens.

▶▶▶▶ **FIND OUT MORE** ◀◀◀◀
**Educators** see Bethune, Mary Mcleod; Mann, Horace; Washington, Booker T.; Willard, Emma Hart
**Learning** see Literacy; Psychology;
**Schools** see Colleges and Universities; School
**Types of Education** see Industrial Arts; Physical Education; Special Education

## EDWARD, KINGS OF ENGLAND AND BRITAIN

Three Edwards had ruled as Anglo-Saxon kings of England before the Normans of France took over the country. They were Edward the Elder, who ruled from 901 to 924; Edward the Martyr, who ruled from 975 to 978; and Edward the Confessor, who ruled from 1042 to 1066. Eight other Edwards have also been English kings.

Edward I (1239–1307) was one of England's greatest kings. He gave Parliament the right to pass some important laws and vote on taxes. He conquered Wales and built many great castles. He also won some battles against Scotland.

Edward II (1284–1327) was named first Prince of Wales by his father, Edward I. He was not a strong king. He was beaten by the Scottish leader, Robert Bruce, at the Battle of Bannockburn in 1314. He was

▲ In the modern schoolroom, teachers and students enjoy a relaxed and stimulating class, which encourages work and where learning is fun.

▼ Edward I of England in Parliament in 1274. The Church taught that kings were appointed by God and that it was everyone's duty to obey them.

▲ At the Battle of Bannockburn, a Scottish army of about 7000, led by Robert the Bruce, defeated Edward II's English force that was three times the size.

▶ The Prince of Wales, later King Edward VII, is seen here in 1900 taking his first trip in an automobile.

▼ The Duke and Duchess of Windsor, formerly King Edward VIII and Mrs. Wallis Simpson. They married in 1937, and moved abroad, living mainly in France.

thrown into prison by his enemies, who included his wife. His son was made king. Eight months later Edward II was murdered.

Edward III (1312–1377) became king at about age 15, when his father, Edward II, was put in prison. Edward III was a great warrior but not a great ruler. He fought the Scots, and his claim to the French throne started the Hundred Years' War with France. A plague, called the Black Death, killed thousands during his reign.

Edward IV (1442–1483) became king during the Wars of the Roses, which were between the York and Lancaster families. Edward was a York and was crowned after he defeated the Lancastrians in the Bat-

tle of Mortimer's Cross in 1461, ending the civil war. England and France fought a war in 1475 that ended with King Louis XI of France agreeing to pay a tribute each year to England in return for peace.

Edward V (1470–1483) became king at age 13 on the death of his father, Edward IV. But he was never crowned, and he never ruled. He and his brother, Richard, were held in the Tower of London, and never seen again. Historians believe that the boys were murdered, probably by their uncle, Richard, Duke of Gloucester. The uncle then became King Richard III.

Edward VI (1537–1553) was the son of Henry VIII and Jane Seymour. He became king when he was nine. He was sickly and died at age 16. His half sister, Mary, then became queen. His other half sister, Elizabeth, followed Mary as queen.

Edward VII (1841–1910) was Queen Victoria's oldest son. He was 60 when his mother died and he became king. He was a popular king who enjoyed sports, especially yachting and horse racing. Edward traveled widely and tried to keep peace in Europe. He was called "Edward the Peace Maker."

Edward VIII (1894–1972) reigned only 325 days in 1936 and was never crowned. He *abdicated* (gave up) his right to the throne to marry an American divorcee, Wallis

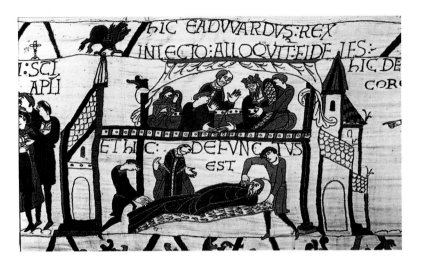

Warfield Simpson. He was given the title Duke of Windsor by his brother, George VI, who became king. He was governor of the Bahamas from 1940 to 1945.

► ► ► **FIND OUT MORE** ◄ ◄ ◄
Edward the Confessor;
Elizabeth I; English History; Mary,
Queens of England;
Richard, Kings of England

# EDWARD THE CONFESSOR (about 1004–1066)

Edward the Confessor was born in England. But he lived in Normandy, a part of France, until he became king of England in 1042, after his half brother, Hardecanute, died.

Edward was a weak king. He allowed his father-in-law, Godwin, Earl of the West Saxons, to make most of his decisions for him. Edward also put several of his Norman friends in important government and church positions. But England had peace during his reign. Some people believed Edward was so good that the sick could be cured by touching him.

Edward was a religious man. He founded Westminster Abbey. He was given the title of "Confessor" nearly 100 years after his death, when Pope Alexander III named him a saint.

Edward had no children. At first he promised that William, Duke of Normandy, should be king after him but Harold, the son of Earl Godwin, later said that Edward, as he lay dying, had promised him the throne. William invaded England with a Norman army to claim the throne. Harold was killed at the Battle of Hastings in 1066, and William, called "the Conqueror," became king.

► ► ► **FIND OUT MORE** ◄ ◄ ◄
English History; Saint;
Westminster Abbey

# EEL

Eels are snakelike fish with small fins and slimy skin. The 16 species of eel include the giant conger, the tropical moray, and the electric eel, which lives in the Amazon region of South America. The electric eel can emit a powerful electric charge.

The common eel lives along the Atlantic coasts of North America and Europe. Common eels breed in the Sargasso Sea, south of Bermuda in the Atlantic Ocean. The eggs hatch there as larvae, which are carried northward by the ocean currents.

The larvae develop into transparent "glass eels," which look like small leaves. They begin to look like eels by the time they reach the shore. These small eels are called *elvers*. Female elvers then swim up rivers and even waterfalls to reach lakes and ponds. Males stay in the sea.

▲ A panel from the Bayeux Tapestry showing the deathbed of Edward the Confessor when he is said to have named Harold as his successor.

▼ Eels look like snakes, but are actually fish. The common eel lives in lakes and rivers, but returns to the sea to breed. The conger eel and the greater sand eel both live in the sea.

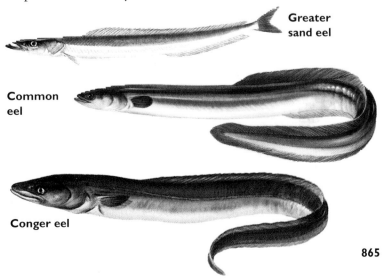

Greater sand eel

Common eel

Conger eel

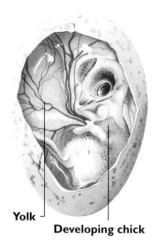

Yolk
Developing chick

▲ **A hen's chick starts to hatch out of its egg about 21 days after the egg has been laid. By this stage its feathers and claws are fully formed.**

▼ **Many birds' eggs are colored for protection. Speckles make many eggs hard to see.**

Common crow
Guira cuckoo
Kiwi
Great bustard
Golden plover
Osprey
American robin
Coot
Emu

It takes 7 to 10 years for elvers to develop into adult eels. Mature females grow to 3 to 4 feet (90 to 120 cm). Males are only 1½ feet (45 cm) long.

Breeding involves a long journey back to the Sargasso Sea, and adult eels begin to leave in the fall. Many must swim thousands of miles, and some eels have been known to crawl across land on this long journey. Eels breed only once and remain in the Sargasso Sea.

▶▶▶▶ **FIND OUT MORE** ◀◀◀◀
Fish

## EGG

Did you know that you developed from an egg? All female animals, except single-celled animals, produce eggs from which their young grow. The eggs of most mammals are developed and protected in the female's body. The young are completely formed before they are born, or pass out of the mother's body.

The eggs most people are familiar with are chicken eggs, which the female lays before the young are developed. Within the newly laid egg is a cell called a *germ cell*, and a supply of food material. If a male sex cell has united with the germ cell during mating, the egg is *fertilized*. The egg must be *incubated*, or kept warm and protected. Some animals (chickens, for instance) keep their eggs warm by sitting on them. Others (reptiles, for instance) bury them in warm places. The single fertilized germ cell divides into millions of cells to form all the parts of the young animal. When it is fully formed, the animal *hatches* from the egg by breaking or tearing the shell around it to get out.

Millions of different kinds of animals produce eggs, including fish, birds, amphibians, reptiles, and insects. The size, shape, and development of eggs vary according to the kind of animal that produces them and the conditions under which they develop. The number of eggs an animal produces at one time varies with the eggs' chances for survival. For example, since fish eggs are often eaten by other animals, many fish lay millions of eggs at one time. The table shows the average number of eggs that certain kinds of female animals produce at one time. There are many variations in the numbers listed in the table because the number of eggs laid depends on the species of animal.

| ANIMAL | NUMBER OF EGGS |
|---|---|
| California condor | 1 (every two years) |
| Pigeon | 2 (twice a year) |
| Hen | 200–350 (every year) |
| Housefly | 600–1,000 (within its 12-day life span) |
| Spider | 10–2,000 (at a time) |
| Snake | 20–30 (every year) |
| Turtle | 2–200 (at a time) |
| Frog | 6,000–25,000 (at a time) |
| Human | 1 (every month) |

### LEARN BY DOING

Eggs that are incubated and develop outside of the mother's body contain everything the *embryo* (developing animal) will need to grow. Break a chicken's egg into a saucer. The large yellow body is the *yolk*. The light-colored, pinhead-sized dot on the yolk is the germ cell. The yolk is the nourishment, or food, for the embryo that will develop from the germ cell. The thick transparent liquid surrounding the yolk is the egg white, or *albumen*. The albumen provides water and a soft cushion for the developing embryo.

▶▶▶▶ **FIND OUT MORE** ◀◀◀◀
Bird; Embryo; Insect; Mammal;
Reproduction; Reptile

# EGYPT

Egypt lies in the northeast corner of the continent of Africa. Its official name is the Arab Republic of Egypt.

Egypt's northern boundary is the Mediterranean Sea. To the east lie Israel and 1,200 miles (1,930 km) of the Red Sea coast. Libya lies to the west and Sudan to the south. Most of Egypt is a hot, dry desert, but the Nile River gives the country some fertile farmland. The Aswan Dam, finished in 1970, added more than one million acres (4,000 sq. km) of farm land through irrigation schemes.

Egypt is primarily an agricultural country. People raise cotton, wheat, barley, rice, citrus fruits, dates, and sugarcane. But industry is growing. There are now textile and steel mills; automotive, fertilizer, and cement plants; glass factories and petroleum refineries. East of the Nile River valley lies the Suez Canal, which connects the Mediterranean and Red seas. Most Egyptians live along the Nile or near the Suez Canal. Cairo, Egypt's capital, is the largest city in Africa.

Nobody knows where the Egyptian people came from, but written records of their history go back 6,000 years. Most Egyptians consider themselves Arabs but there are also large numbers of Greeks, Syrians, Turks, and Armenians. A few are Europeans. Most Egyptians are Muslims. In rural areas almost all the people are peasants called *fellahin*, who make up approximately half the population.

King Farouk governed Egypt between 1936 and 1952, when military officers overthrew him. Gamal Abdel Nasser was president from 1954 to 1970. He was succeeded by Anwar Sadat, who was assassinated in 1981. Muhammad Hosni Mubarak then became president.

Egypt and other Arab nations opposed the creation of Israel in 1948 in what was then Palestine. They said that Israel was Arab land and that the Palestinans should have it as their homeland. In 1967, Egypt closed the Gulf of Aqaba to Israeli shipping. The Six-Day Arab-Israeli War then broke out and ended in a crushing defeat for Egypt, Syria, and Jordan. Israel had gained control of the Sinai Peninsula. Another full-scale Arab-Israeli war in 1973 ended in a negotiated ceasefire. In 1979, Egypt signed a peace treaty with

## EGYPT

**Capital city**
Cairo (6,325,000 people)

**Area**
386,662 square miles (1,001,449 sq. km)

**Population**
53,170,000 people

**Government**
Republic

**Natural resources**
Petroleum, natural gas, phosphates, iron ore, salt, other minerals, hydro-electric power

**Export products**
Cotton, oil, textiles

**Unit of money**
Egyptian pound

**Official language**
Arabic

MEDITERRANEAN SEA

Marsa Matruh
*Libyan Plateau* Al Alamayn
Alexandria
Al Mahalla al Kubra
Damietta
Port Said
Al Arish
Tanta
Al Mansurah
*Suez Canal*
Shibin al Kawm
Ismailia
*Qattara Depression*
Al Jizah
Cairo
PYRAMIDS OF GIZA
MEMPHIS
Suez
*Sinai Peninsula*
Siwah
Al Fayyum
Bani Suwayf
*Mt. Catherine 8,668 ft. 2,642 m.*
*Gulf of Suez*
*Gulf of Aqaba*
Al Minya
At Tur
*Arabian*
Al Ghurdaqah
*Western*
Asyut
N
*Desert*
Suhaj
Qina
W E
*Red Desert*
VALLEY OF THE KINGS
THEBES
Luxor
S
Mut
Al Kharijah
*RED SEA*
Baris
Aswan
ASWAN HIGH DAM
*L. Nasser*
SAHARA

0       100       200       300 Miles
0   100   200   300   400 Kilometers
© 1994 GeoSystems, an R.R. Donnelley & Sons Company

Israel. Much of the Sinai area was returned to Egypt. This agreement was disliked by other Middle East Arab states, leaving Egypt isolated from its Arab neighbors.

▶▶▶▶ **FIND OUT MORE** ◀◀◀◀
Africa; Cairo; Egypt, Ancient; Israel;
Middle East; Nasser,
Gamal Abdel; Nile River;
Red Sea; Sahara Desert; Suez Canal

## EGYPT, ANCIENT

Ancient Egypt was one of the greatest civilizations that ever existed. Its magnificent history began over 5,000 years ago and lasted for almost 3,000 years. Those ancient historians whose writings have survived tell us much about ancient Egypt's civilization. What the historians say is also proved by the remains and mighty ruins, such as the pyramids, the Egyptians left behind. They have been preserved by the hot, dry air of the desert.

People have lived in the Nile River Valley since before 5000 B.C. They settled mainly in two areas, the Nile Valley, which became Upper Egypt, and the Nile Delta (mouth of the river), or Lower Egypt. Egypt's greatness began when these two lands were joined under a single king.

### The Egyptian dynasties

The kingdom of Egypt first came into being when a king named Menes united Upper and Lower Egypt into one nation in about 2920 B.C. He founded the city of Memphis as his capital. Menes started the first Egyptian *dynasty* (a line of rulers in the same family). Kings in Egypt were called *pharaohs*, which means "great house." Egypt's first pyramid was built during the reign of a king named Djoser. The period that scholars call "The Old Kingdom" (2575–2134 B.C.) saw the construction of the pyramids at Giza. Pyramids were immense *tombs* (burial places) for the kings of Egypt. They were made of huge blocks of stone built up in

▲ A statue of an Egyptian scribe. Scribes were important people in Egypt. They copied and made documents using brushes and ink on sheets of papyrus. Before papyrus they had used clay tablets. Their training took up to twelve years. Scribes became civil servants, teachers, or librarians.

▶ Pyramid builders at work. Cargoes of stone were carried up the Nile by boat to the building site. Masons rough-cut the stones into blocks, which were smoothed and finished when they were in position. Other gangs of men dragged the stones up ramps on wooden rollers to the work level.

steps and rising to a point at the top. The pyramids of Giza may still be seen today. The base of the largest pyramid, the "Great Pyramid" covers 13 acres. The "Great Sphinx," a giant stone figure with the body of a lion and a human head, lies near the pyramids. The Egyptians developed a brilliant civilization during this time. They created impressive paintings and sculpture. They made studies of the stars and planets and invented a calendar with a 365 day year. The accurate measurements used for building the pyramids show that they were skilled in mathematics and engineering. The Egyptians also developed new ideas about medicine and surgery. Five dynasties ruled during the period of the Old Kingdom. After the end of this period, Egypt was weakened by constant battles for power among nobles, priests, and pharaohs.

"The Middle Kingdom" lasted from about 2040 B.C. to about 1640 B.C. Three dynasties (14th–12th) ruled during this time. The 12th dynasty was founded by Amenemhet I in 1991 B.C. This dynasty brought prosperity and growth to Egypt once again. Architecture, art, and literature flourished. A canal was built between the Nile River and the Red Sea. Around 1640 B.C. barbaric invaders, called the *Hyksos*, overran Egypt. The Hyksos fought with horses, horse-drawn chariots, and bronze weapons. These fighting methods were new to the Egyptians, but they soon learned how to use them. About one hundred years later the Egyptians drove out the Hyksos.

"The New Kingdom" lasted from about 1550 B.C. to about 1070 B.C. Egypt enjoyed its last great period of splendor during these years. It was ruled by three dynasties. Tuthmosis III, a member of the 18th dynasty, made Egypt into a powerful empire. Amenophis IV became pharaoh

around 1353 B.C. His queen was the beautiful Nefertiti.

The Egyptians had always believed in many gods. Their pharaohs were thought to be gods, too, and had enormous power. Amenophis IV ordered his subjects to worship only Ra, the sun god. He changed Ra's name to Aten, an ancient name for Ra. He also changed his own name to Akhenaten meaning "Aten is satisfied." Akhenaten's belief in just one god was new and strange, and he upset many Egyptians. They feared he was trying to make himself all-powerful and also blamed him for Egypt's defeats in wars. The people wanted their old gods back, and after Akhenaten's death, the pharaoh Tutankhamen allowed the people to return to their old ways of worship.

▲ **This copy of an Egyptian wall-painting shows a group of Hebrews asking permission to enter Egypt. Jacob, the grandson of Abraham (the first Hebrew according to the Old Testament), led his people to safety in Egypt, when famine struck his own country, Canaan. The Hebrews became the slaves of the Egyptians, until Moses led them back to Canaan.**

| HISTORY OF ANCIENT EGYPT | |
| --- | --- |
| **Prehistory** | Before c. 3000 B.C. |
| **Early Dynastic (Dynasties I-III)** | c. 2920–2575 B.C. |
| **Old Kingdom (Dynasties IV-VIII)** | c. 2575–2134 B.C. |
| **Dynasties IX-XI** | c. 2134–2040 B.C. |
| **Middle Kingdom (Dynasties XII-XIV)** | c. 2040–1640 B.C. |
| **Dynasties XV-XVII** | 1640–1532 B.C. |
| **New Kingdom (Dynasties XVIII-XX)** | 1550–1070 B.C. |
| **Dynasties XXI-XXV** | 1070–712 B.C. |
| **Late Period (Dynasties XXV-XXXI)** | 712–332 B.C. |
| **Greek/Ptolemy Period** | 332–30 B.C. |
| **Roman Period** | 30 B.C.–A.D. 395 |

## GREAT ARCHITECTURAL ACHIEVEMENTS OF THE ANCIENT EGYPTIANS

| Dynasty (B.C.) | Achievement |
| --- | --- |
| **I-III** 2920–2575 | Memphis, the first capital of ancient Egypt, was built. It stood near the site of Cairo, the capital of modern Egypt. The first pyramid, the Step Pyramid, was designed during the reign of Djoser. |
| **IV** 2575–2465 | The three pyramids, including the Great Pyramid, were built at Giza. The Sphinx was built near the second pyramid. It was probably built to protect nearby tombs from evil spirits. |
| **XVIII** 1550–1307 | A splendid temple was built at Deir el-Bahri near Thebes. It honors Hatshepsut, the first great queen known to history. The tomb of Tutankhamen was built near Luxor, one of the first great cities of the ancient world. It was an immense display of jewelry and art. It was not discovered until 1922. |
| **XIX** 1307–1196 | The two great temples of Abu Simbel were built during the reign of the famous ruler, Ramses II. The great temple was carved into the side of a mountain. The splendid temple of Amun-Re was built and improved upon during the 19th dynasty. It honored the main god of ancient Egypt. Beautiful painted columns decorated its great hall. |

Another pharaoh, Ramses II, built the huge temples of Abu Simbel around 1250 B.C.

During the 21st to 31st dynasties, Egypt was overrun by invaders. Libyans and then Assyrians ruled the country. The Persians captured Egypt in 525 B.C. Alexander the Great, a Macedonian, conquered Egypt in 332 B.C. He founded the city of Alexandria, which became one of the greatest cities of the ancient world.

After Alexander's death in 323 B.C., one of his generals, Ptolemy, named himself king of Egypt. Ptolemy's dynasty lasted for almost 300 years and ended with the death of Queen Cleopatra in 30 B.C. In the same year, the Romans captured Egypt and added it to their empire. When the Roman Empire split in two in A.D. 395, the Byzantine, or eastern, part controlled Egypt. Christianity became widespread in Egypt between A.D. 300 and 500 but in the 640s an Arab general, Amr ibn al-As, conquered Egypt, and it eventually became a Muslim country.

▲ **Harvest time. The Egyptians expected to harvest twice a year. The harvested corn was threshed (above), and then the grain was winnowed (right).**

## Egyptian Accomplishments

Most of the people in ancient Egypt lived near the Nile River. Its yearly flooding deposited rich, black soil that was excellent for farming. Egyptian traders traveled by sea and caravan all over the parts of the world known then. The Egyptians developed a system of picture-writing called *hieroglyphics*. They also made writing paper from the *papyrus* reed. Scholars have been able to read hieroglyphics ever since the *Rosetta Stone* was discovered and interpreted in the early 1800s.

The Egyptians believed in a life after death. They placed many objects, such as food, clothing, and doll-like figures of ser-vants, in their tombs. This was to make the afterlife more pleas-ant. They wrapped their dead in layers of cloth and pre-served them as mum-mies, many of which can be seen in muse-ums today. One of the Egyptians' most powerful gods was Osiris, god of the dead. They also wor-shiped many animal gods, including bulls, crocodiles, and cats. The Egyp-tians built mighty temples and stat-ues of stone to honor their god pharaohs. Long after the Egyptian civilization had disappeared, people marveled at their achievements.

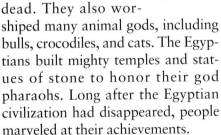

Stomach · Lungs · Intestines · Liver

Many ancient Egyptians were farmers. Originally they owned their own land. As time passed, the farms became the property of nobles and pharaohs. The farmers raised crops of wheat, barley, flax, and grapes on irrigated land. They also raised cattle. Other Egyptians were craftsmen, working with clay, stone, and differ-ent metals to make jars, bowls, jew-elry, and tools. Some wove linen and other materials for clothing. Other Egyptians were soldiers.

Most Egyptians lived in clay huts with flat roofs made from reeds or palm branches. The huts were sparsely furnished with wooden stools and reed mats on the floors. Egyptians ate bread (made from wheat or barley), fish, and vegetables.

▶▶▶▶ **FIND OUT MORE** ◀◀◀◀

Abu Simbel; Ancient Civilizations; Calendar; Cleopatra; Doll; Hieroglyphics; Pyramid; Rosetta Stone; Sphinx

**WHERE TO DISCOVER MORE**

Hart, George. *Ancient Egypt.* New York: Knopf, 1990.
Cohen, Daniel. *Ancient Egypt.* New York: Doubleday, 1989.

## ⚙ EHRLICH, PAUL (1854–1915)

"Physician, heal thyself!" This is what the young German scientist Paul Ehrlich must have thought in 1886. He had been working to find a cure for the disease tuberculosis and had caught it himself. Some cures were found in nature (for instance, quinine was used against malaria), but such medicines were few. Ehrlich was lucky he recovered.

After he was well, Ehrlich tried to find new ways to stain germs (*bacte-ria*) so that they could be seen better through a microscope. He noticed that his dyes often killed the bacteria.

Ehrlich spent years working to find out which dyes killed which bacteria. One dye, *trypan red*, helped fight the bacteria that caused diseases such as sleeping sickness. For this and other work he received a Nobel Prize in 1908. More important, though, was his later discovery of a dye he called *salvarsan*, which killed the bacteria causing syphilis. However, salvarsan is very poisonous except in tiny doses (it contains arsenic) so it is no longer considered safe to use.

Ehrlich had shown that health-restoring drugs could be created by scientists and did not have to come from nature.

▶▶▶▶ **FIND OUT MORE** ◀◀◀◀

Bacteria; Drug

◀ **A group of funeral urns, known as canopic jars, were used to contain the vital organs taken from a body before it was embalmed. The lids show the heads of four minor Egyptian gods called the Sons of Horus, represented as a jackal, a baboon, a hawk, and a man.**

▼ **Paul Ehrlich, German bacteriologist.**

# EINSTEIN, ALBERT
# (1879–1955)

Albert Einstein, one of the most brilliant scientists of all time, was born in Ulm, Germany. As a boy, Einstein was a poor student, but he was destined to change our concept of nature and the universe.

Einstein was a founder of a new branch of physics, called *relativity*. In the 1600s, Sir Isaac Newton set forth what have become known as the "laws of motion." These rules describe how objects move and explain the forces that cause motion. In his "Special Theory of Relativity" article published in 1905, Einstein predicted that objects moving at nearly the speed of light (about 186,000 miles or 300,000 km a second) do not obey Newton's laws. In the years since Einstein announced his ideas, physicists have been able to study the tiny particles (bits) of matter that make up atoms. All these particles move at terrific speeds. Their studies have shown that Einstein's theory is correct.

His theory showed that matter and energy are really two different forms of the same thing. A small piece of matter can be changed into a huge amount of energy. The truth of this bold new idea blazed into reality with the creation and explosion of the first atomic bomb in 1945. Einstein was very sad when he learned that atomic bombs had been dropped on Japan. He was a peaceful man who hated war. Einstein spent the last years of his life urging mankind to use atomic energy for peaceful purposes.

Einstein published his "General Theory of Relativity" article in 1915. This theory tries to explain gravitation. Scientists are still testing the theory. In 1921, Einstein was awarded the Nobel Prize for work done in quantum physics. He left Germany when Adolf Hitler began restricting the activities of Jews in the 1930s.

Einstein became a citizen of the United States. He became director of mathematics at the Institute for Advanced Studies in Princeton, New Jersey, and worked there for the rest of his life. All of his research was aimed at developing a theory that would explain the effects of both electromagnetism and gravitation.

▼ **Albert Einstein, one of the greatest scientific thinkers of all time.**

▶▶▶▶ **FIND OUT MORE** ◀◀◀◀
Atom; Gravity and Gravitation; Light; Newton, Sir Isaac; Nuclear Energy; Physics; Relativity

# EISENHOWER, DWIGHT
# DAVID (1890–1969)

The 34th President of the United States, Dwight Eisenhower, was one of the most popular American leaders of modern times. His nickname was "Ike."

David Dwight Eisenhower was born in Denison, Texas, and grew up in Abilene, Kansas. (He later reversed his names.) Ike got high marks in school. After he graduated from high school, he went to the United States Military Academy at West Point, New York, where he studied to be an army officer. He graduated in 1915, and became a second lieutenant.

Eisenhower served as a member of

General Douglas MacArthur's staff in the Philippines. Eisenhower planned the Louisiana Maneuvers—special training operations held just before the United States entered World War II. He was promoted for his planning abilities. He was a brigadier general in 1941, when the United States entered the war.

The Allied forces had to invade western Europe to win the war, but they knew that the German defenses were very strong. An American general was to lead the invasion. President Franklin Roosevelt and General George Marshall selected Eisenhower for the job. He became commander of all Allied troops in Europe in 1942. Eisenhower was popular with soldiers, and he worked well with military leaders from many countries to plan the invasion. The D-Day invasion (June 6, 1944) was successful. But months of hard fighting followed before Nazi Germany surrendered in May 1945.

Eisenhower was promoted to five-star general in 1944. After the war he served as president of Columbia University from 1948 to 1950. He became commander of the North Atlantic Treaty Organization (NATO) forces in 1950.

Eisenhower's popularity made him a strong candidate to be President of the United States. The Republican Party nominated him in 1952. He won the election and was re-elected in 1956. President Eisenhower worked hard to bring about world peace. He visited Europe, Africa, Asia, and South America. During his presidency, Soviet leader Nikita Khruschev visited the United States. Hawaii and Alaska became states. There was progress on civil rights, and prosperity at home.

Eisenhower was succeeded by John F. Kennedy and retired to his farm near Gettysburg, Pennsylvania.

▶▶▶▶ **FIND OUT MORE** ◀◀◀◀
World War II

# ⚙ ELASTICITY

If you pull a rubber band it stretches. When you let it go, the band immediately springs back to its original size. It does this because it is elastic—it has *elasticity*. A rubber ball is like a rubber band in reverse. If you drop it onto the ground, the part of the ball that hits the ground is squashed flat. Then the ball immediately springs back to its original shape. As this happens, the ball pushes on the ground and it rises into the air—the ball *bounces*.

Elasticity happens because the molecules that make up the elastic material like to remain at a certain distance from each other. If they are pulled apart, as happens when rubber is stretched, the force between the molecules acts to pull them together again. And if the molecules are pushed more tightly together, which happens when rubber is squeezed, the force between the molecules acts to push them apart again.

All solids and liquids have some elasticity, but some have very little. If you drop a wooden ball, it appears not to bounce at all. But although it has little elasticity, it actually does bounce.

If you drop a rubber ball on the floor it bounces—it has elasticity. But many other substances that we don't think of as having elasticity behave in a similar way. If a steel ball is dropped on a concrete floor, it bounces too, although not anything like as high as a rubber ball. As the steel hits the floor the force of the impact squashes it slightly out of shape. Because steel is elastic it quickly regains its original shape and this makes it bounce. But some things are not elastic. If you drop a ball of modeling clay on the floor it does not bounce at all. It simply flattens itself.

▼ Every material has its characteristic "elastic limit." If the strain on the material is too great, the material will remain deformed when the stress has been taken away.

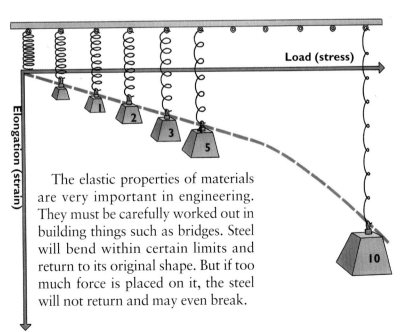

The elastic properties of materials are very important in engineering. They must be carefully worked out in building things such as bridges. Steel will bend within certain limits and return to its original shape. But if too much force is placed on it, the steel will not return and may even break.

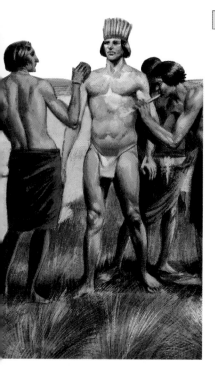

"El Dorado" was actually a man, not the legendary "golden city." According to the legend, once a year the chief of the Chibcha tribe, covered in gold dust, had to dive into the sacred lake Guatavita to appease a god that lived in its depths.

# EL DORADO

When the Spaniards first came to South America, they heard the legend of El Dorado, which means "the gilded man" in Spanish. The legend probably described the Chibcha Native South American tribe of Colombia. It was said that once a year their chief would cover his body with sacred oil and gold dust. Then he would dive into a special lake to wash off the gold. His people would toss gold and emeralds into the lake. The chief became known as El Dorado, and later his village and country acquired the name. Many explorers went to hunt for the fabled golden city, which was sometimes called Monoa. Francisco de Orellana led an expedition in search of El Dorado in 1541. Sir Walter Raleigh set out to look for it in 1595. No one ever found a golden city. Today the name is used to describe any place of legendary riches and wealth.

▶▶▶▶ **FIND OUT MORE** ◀◀◀◀
Conquistador; Exploration;
Raleigh, Sir Walter

# ELEANOR OF AQUITAINE
(about 1122–1204)

Eleanor of Aquitaine was a beautiful French princess who married two kings and was the mother of two more kings. She was born in the province of Aquitaine in southwestern France.

Eleanor was first married at 15 to a prince who, a month later, became King Louis VII of France. They had two daughters. Eleanor and Louis were later divorced. Then, in 1152,

◀ The tomb of Eleanor of Aquitaine, in the abbey church at Frontrevault, in western France. Eleanor's tomb is next to the tomb of Richard I, one of her sons. Her second husband, Henry II, also is buried nearby.

Eleanor married Henry Plantagenet. He became King Henry II of England two years later. Henry and Eleanor had three daughters and five sons.

Eleanor and her sons tried to seize the throne from Henry in 1173. But Henry put down their revolt and forced Eleanor to live in a convent until he released her in 1185. Eleanor made certain that Richard, who was her favorite son, would become the next king. When Henry died in 1189, Richard did become king. He was called Richard the Lion-Hearted because he was a great warrior. During his reign, he went on a crusade to the Holy Land for several years. His mother ruled in his place until he returned. She also kept her son John from seizing the throne during Richard's absence.

Eleanor lived a long life—long enough to see Richard die and John become king. She acted as John's adviser until her death at age 82.

▶▶▶▶ **FIND OUT MORE** ◀◀◀◀
Crusades; English History; Henry, Kings of England; John, King of England; Louis, Kings of France; Richard, Kings of England

# ELECTION

Every year the members of Mrs. Brown's class choose a new president. The president conducts class meetings. This year both John and Anne want to be president. Some class members want Anne for president. Others want John. To decide who will be president, the class holds an election.

In the election, everyone who is a member of the class has one *vote* (can make only one selection for the office of president). Each member writes the name of the person he or she wants to be president on a slip of paper. The slip of paper is called a *ballot*. No one is supposed to see the name someone writes on the ballot, because the vote is secret. Each class member puts a ballot in a special box called the *ballot box*. After everyone has voted, the ballots are counted. Anne has the most votes and becomes class president.

Thousands and thousands of elections are held in the United States each year. Clubs, societies, labor unions, and companies all hold elections. In these elections, voters decide who will be in charge of their organization or company.

Most officials who run the United States are elected. In most cities or towns any citizen living there may vote for the mayor, councilmen, aldermen, or selectmen, and for other officials who will govern the community. Citizens of your state vote for the governor, members of the state legislature, and the other officials who will run the state. A citizen of your state also votes for the President of the United States and for the representatives and senators who will represent your state in the United States Congress.

In order to vote in a city election, a person must live in the city. A person voting in a state election must live in the state. A voter must also be a U.S. citizen who can read and write. The Twenty-sixth Amendment, ratified in 1971, lowered the voting age in all U.S. elections to 18.

Before people can actually vote, they must *register* to vote. They go to a special office for voter registration and prove to the people there that they meet the qualifications. They also tell the people in this office where they live and how long they have lived there. Then the new voter's name is put in a large book called an *election register*. A voter can register as a member of the Democratic or Republican party or as an Independent, or unaffiliated voter (a person who belongs to no political party). A registered member of a party can vote in that party's *primary* election. In a primary election,

members of a political party vote to choose their party's candidates for the general election. Such an election is held before the regular election.

Election Day for the office of President and Vice President of the United States is held on the first Tuesday after the first Monday in November, once every four years. States and communities hold elections once every two years or every year.

When Election Day comes, people go to the polling place in their neighborhoods. The polling place may be a room in a school, a police station, or even in someone's home. The polling place is run by special election officials. The voters give their names, and they are looked up in the election register. The election official then allows the person to vote. In some states, the official gives the voters their ballots, and they take them into the booths. They close the cur-

tain of the booth behind them and vote for whomever they want. When they come out of the booth they put the ballots into a special ballot box. Most states use voting machines with curtains in front of them to make sure people make their choices in secret. The voter pulls a large lever to close the curtain, then presses smaller levers on the machine to select their candidates for each office.

While each person is voting, election officials perform other duties.

In a democracy such as the United States, all citizens who can vote in elections should do so. By voting, they are taking part in the work of government. It is almost as important to vote in elections as it is to obey the laws of the country.

▼ A voter using a voting machine to cast his votes. Normally, voting is done in secret, so no one can see for whom a person votes. But here the curtains have been opened to show the machine.

A ballot printed on one kind of paper listing all candidates in an election was first used in Australia in 1856. Before that, each candidate furnished his own style of ballot. Voters could not keep their choice secret. This uniform ballot is still called the "Australian ballot."

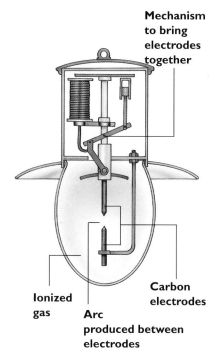

Mechanism to bring electrodes together

Ionized gas

Carbon electrodes

Arc produced between electrodes

▲ The arc lamp, invented by Thomas Wright in 1845, was one of the earliest electric lights. It produces a very bright light when an electric current jumps, or arcs, across the space between two carbon electrodes.

▼ In a toaster, the heater elements are turned on or off by an electric device, which makes, or breaks, an electric circuit. This controls the temperature of the elements.

Heater elements

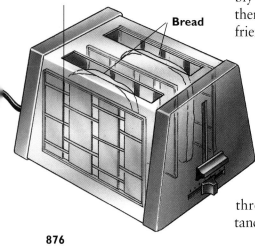

Bread

876

They make sure each voter does not take too much time in the booth. They do not allow people to tell voters how to mark their ballots.

After the polling places close, all the votes are counted in a central place. As various election results are known, they are announced on radio and television, and later in the newspapers. The candidates who have won the most votes are elected.

Elections in other countries differ from those held in the United States. Each government decides what the qualifications are to become a voter. In some countries only one political party is allowed. In others, a dictator rules and decides who shall be members of the government or hold other public offices.

▶▶▶▶ **FIND OUT MORE** ◀◀◀◀
Fascism; Government; Political Party; Socialism; Women's Rights

## ⚙ ELECTRIC APPLIANCE

Look around your home and count the number of appliances that depend upon electricity. Electric appliances provide light, heat, and refrigeration. They do work for us. Power saws, drills, and other electric tools help us do chores quickly and better. Electricity improves our lives in so many ways that it would probably take a whole book just to list them. We enjoy good health, talk to friends around the world, and avoid many kinds of difficult work, all because of machines that run on electricity.

Electric appliances can be divided into two different types that depend on two different characteristics of electricity: 1. Electricity produces heat or both heat and light when it flows through certain wires called resistance wires. 2. Flowing electricity has

a magnetic field around it, which makes electric motors possible.

When electricity flows through resistance wires, heat or both heat and light are produced. *Resistance wires* "resist" or oppose the flow of electricity, and they get hot when electricity passes through them. Some resistance wires resist electricity so strongly that they become white hot. These wires are used for making light bulbs. Appliances that use electricity to make heat or light include toasters, electric stoves, heaters, irons, hot plates, electric frying pans, and light bulbs. The flat wires along the sides of a toaster are resistance wires. You can see them glow red and you can feel their heat when the toaster is operating. Never touch these wires with your fingers or with any piece of metal, such as a knife.

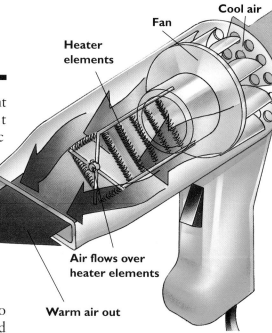

Cool air

Fan

Heater elements

Air flows over heater elements

Warm air out

▲ A hair dryer contains a miniature electric heater which creates warm air. Cool air is sucked in by the fan. It is heated up by the heater elements, and then blown out as warm, dry air.

### Electric Lights

The invention of electric light is one of humanity's greatest achievements. Thomas Alva Edison and Joseph Swan, working separately, succeeded in making the first commercial electric light bulbs in 1879. Swan had worked for over 30 years trying different materials to use as a *filament*. The *filament* is the threadlike wire in an electric bulb. When electric current passes through a filament, so much heat is produced that the filament gets white hot and glows with a brilliant light. Metal filaments will burn in air, so an inert gas (one that does not react easily) must be put into the bulb. Most light bulbs today have tungsten filaments in a bulb containing an inert mixture of argon and nitrogen gases. A tungsten light bulb is a simple device. A glass bulb, a filament, and a screw-in or plug-in base are the main parts.

## Electric Motors

The opposite of resistance wires are *conductive wires*, which *conduct* (carry) electricity very easily and produce very little heat. Conductive wires are essential in all appliances that have electric motors, such as vacuum cleaners, washing machines, air conditioners, fans, sewing machines, mixers, power tools, and many others.

An electric current flows through a coil suspended between the poles of a magnet. The coil produces a magnetic field whose poles move toward the poles of the magnet. The north pole of the coil is attracted toward the magnet's south pole. The south pole of the coil's field similarly moves toward the magnet's north pole. As a result, the coil rotates.

As its poles pass the magnet's poles, the electric current is suddenly reversed and flows in the opposite direction. The commutator causes this to happen. As the current reverses, so does the coil's magnetic field. The south pole becomes the north pole and vice-versa, so the coil is now repelled by the poles of the magnet to which it was previously attracted. In this way, the coil keeps moving. The commutator reverses

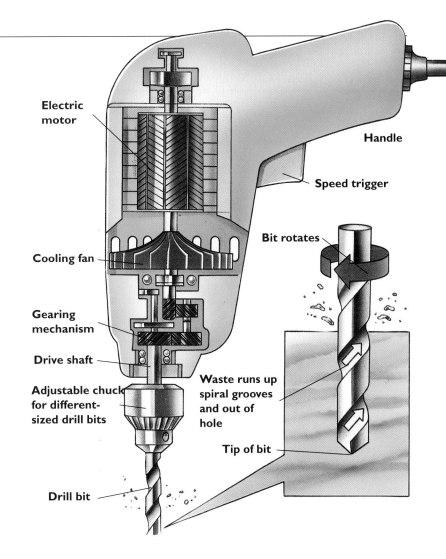

Electric motor

Handle

Speed trigger

Cooling fan

Bit rotates

Gearing mechanism

Drive shaft

Waste runs up spiral grooves and out of hole

Adjustable chuck for different-sized drill bits

Tip of bit

Drill bit

the current flow every half turn.

Electrical appliances are often said to be labor-saving devices. You can see the reason for this if you think about doing the laundry. For thousands of years, this meant hard work. Each piece of laundry had to be washed by hand, rinsed by hand, squeezed, and hung up to dry. The laundry took hours to do. Today, you can place all your laundry into an automatic washer, add detergent, and turn on the switch. In a couple of hours or less, the whole family's laundry can be washed and dried.

Sometimes too many appliances might be attached to one power plug. A lot of current flows along the wire to the power plug, and the wire could get so hot that it could start a fire. This is prevented by one of two special devices, a *fuse* or a *circuit breaker*. A *fuse* is a thin strip of metal

▲ The small electric motor in a drill is extremely powerful, and its turning force is increased as it is slowed down by the gearing mechanism. Many drills have adjustable speeds, either by varying the electric voltage fed to the motor, or by changing the gears.

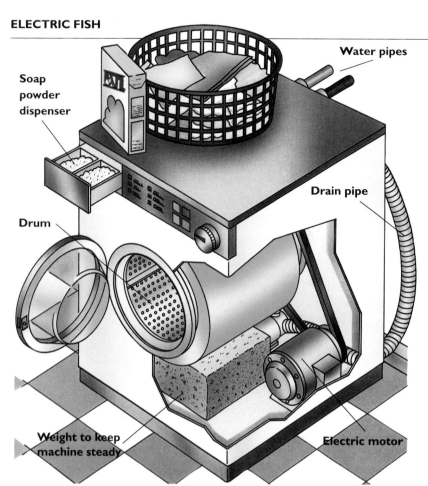

Soap powder dispenser

Water pipes

Drain pipe

Drum

Weight to keep machine steady

Electric motor

▲ An electric motor inside a washing machine turns the drum around to mix the clothes with water and soap. Pipes bring in water, heated to the right temperature by a heating element.

▲ The electric eel uses the electric organs in its tail to stun its prey; it can generate between 500 and 800 volts.

or wire that is placed in the path of the electric current. When the current rises above a certain level, the fuse melts and stops the flow of electricity. Fuses are attached to large individual appliances and to power circuits and outlets. More fuses in the fuse box protect the wiring throughout the house from being overloaded. Without fuses, electrical appliances can cause fires. With fuses, these devices are not dangerous.

A *circuit breaker* is a special kind of switch. When it is "on," current flows through it. But attached to the switch is a device that measures the current. If the current gets too strong, the device throws the switch and stops the current. Houses and buildings constructed today use circuit breakers instead of fuses.

### Appliances in Our World

Many appliances start out as luxuries, but people soon think they are necessities. Refrigerators, for example, were considered a luxury when they first came into use. How well could

you get along without a refrigerator today? Where would you get a cold drink on a hot day? Where would you keep ice cream? If our lights go out in a major storm, we have to scurry around looking for candles and flashlights. Electric lights, along with many other appliances, have become necessary in modern industrial countries. Scientists and engineers work constantly to improve appliances, and to design new ones.

Appliances usually come with a set of instructions. These instructions should always be saved because they tell how the appliance should be operated and cared for. With proper care, most appliances will last for several years.

It may be necessary to repair a plug on an appliance. If you have to do this, always follow the wiring instructions very carefully, as attaching a wire wrongly could make the appliance dangerous.

▶ ▶ ▶ ▶ **FIND OUT MORE** ◀ ◀ ◀ ◀
Electricity; Electric Power;
Electromagnet; Electronics; Fuse;
Magnet; Motor

## ELECTRIC FISH

Did you know some fish can produce electricity? The electric eel of South American rivers is a powerful "living battery." Most of its body is taken up by special muscles that can generate over 500 volts—a lot more than the normal domestic electricity supply. Whenever any muscle is stimulated by its nerves, a small electrical impulse is produced. This would normally cause the muscle to contract, but the nerves and muscles of electric fish are modified so that the muscles concentrate and increase the electrical charges and send them out into the surrounding water. If you touched an electric eel, it could give you a shock strong enough to knock you over. The electric eel uses its high-voltage discharges to kill other fish for food. Smaller discharges of electricity help the fish to navigate in murky water. The electric impulses act as "range finders," or radar, similar to the way bats navigate by sending out high-pitched sounds and listening to the echoes.

Several other kinds of fish generate electricity, although none is as powerful as the electric eel. Many give out shocks to frighten their enemies, and they also use electrical impulses for navigation and communication.

# ELECTRICITY

People have known about the form of energy called electricity for a very long time. The ancient Greeks knew that if they rubbed the material called amber with fur, the amber would attract bits of dust and straw. The Greek word for amber was *elektron*, from which the word "electricity" comes, because the attraction is electrical.

You know that electricity lights your house. It may also heat and cool your house, and refrigerate and cook your food. Electricity carries your friend's voice to you on the telephone, brings your favorite TV show to you, and operates your computer.

Electricity is a form of energy that is stored in *electrons* and *protons*—the tiny particles that go to make up an atom. Electrons and protons each have an equal amount of electric charge, but they are charges of opposite kinds. An electron has a negative charge and a proton has a positive charge. We do not know exactly what an electric charge is, but we know a great deal about what it can do. We know that two negative charges—or two positive charges—repel each other. But opposite charges, a positive and a negative, attract each other.

All matter is made up of atoms, so electricity is present wherever there is matter—in the stars, in the Earth, and in your own body. But in normal atoms there are equal numbers of electrons and protons; the positive and negative charges balance, so we do not notice the presence of the electricity. To make use of its energy we have to create a situation—or make use of a natural one—in which atoms have more electrons than protons or fewer electrons than protons at a particular place and time.

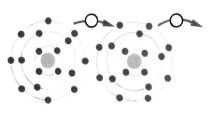

▲ **Electrons orbit round the nucleus of each atom. They carry a tiny negative charge. Electricity flows along a wire when electrons jump from one atom to the next.**

## Two Kinds of Electricity

*Static* electricity and *electric current* are really two forms of the same thing—electric charge. But they are often talked about separately. Static electricity consists of a store of electric charges, either positive or negative, which are not moving.

STATIC ELECTRICITY. Rub a balloon several times against your

**Water is a good conductor of electricity. So is the human body, which is made largely of water.**

## LEARN BY DOING

You can use static electricity to see one of the basic characteristics of electricity. You will need two small balloons tied to bits of string, and a small piece of wool. Rub one of the balloons with the wool. Then hold the ends of both pieces of string in

one hand and let the balloons dangle.
What happens? Now rub the other balloon with wool, and let the balloons dangle again. What happens this time? The balloons push apart because both balloons become negatively charged and similar charges repel each other. What happens if you rub one balloon with wool and the other with nylon? Does this make a difference?

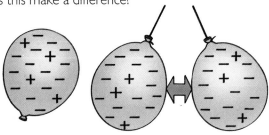

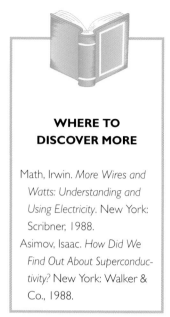

**WHERE TO DISCOVER MORE**

Math, Irwin. *More Wires and Watts: Understanding and Using Electricity*. New York: Scribner, 1988.

Asimov, Isaac. *How Did We Find Out About Superconductivity?* New York: Walker & Co., 1988.

▶ In a circuit, the cell or battery drives the flow of electricity by making the electrons jump from one atom to the next.

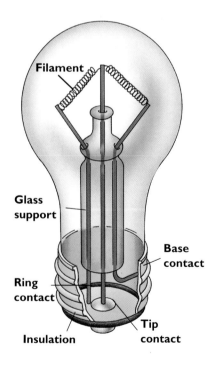

▲ In a light bulb an electric current flows through a thin wire (the filament), which has a high electrical resistance. It gets so hot that it glows white and gives off light.

hair or against a wool sweater. The balloon picks up electrons from your hair. It becomes negatively charged and will stick against a wall, which is unchargeable.

ELECTRIC CURRENT. Electric current can also make objects stick together or give you a shock. But electric current has many valuable uses.

Electric current moves through certain substances called *conductors*. Conductors conduct electricity because they contain free electrons that can move from atom to atom along the substance. Most metals contain many free electrons and make good conductors. Gold and silver are the best conductors. But these are so expensive that normally other metals, usually copper or aluminum, are used instead. Some substances have almost no free electrons. Almost all the electrons are held very tightly in their atoms, and few electrons can move from one atom to another. These substances, such as air, glass, and rubber, are called *insulators* or *nonconductors*. The cords that carry electric current from the wall outlets to the appliances in your home consist of copper (or aluminum) wires to conduct the current and a rubber or plastic coating to protect you from shock. Electric current can be produced by a machine called a *generator*, or by a battery.

### How Electricity Moves

It does not take very long for a light bulb to glow when you turn it on. How fast is electricity? This question has more than one answer. When electricity flows through a wire, the electrons move from atom to atom at a speed of a few feet a second. But the electric signal moves faster— almost at the speed of light, 186,000 miles (300,000 km) a second.

Electric current is related to magnetism. When electrons flow through a wire, a magnetic field develops around the wire. This magnetic effect is useful in making electromagnets, but it is also the basis of the electric motor, which uses the force of two electromagnets to produce work. And when a wire moves in relation to a magnetic field, it causes electrons to flow in the wire. This is how a generator produces electric current.

### Measuring Electricity

Electricity can be measured in many ways. One machine for measuring small electric currents is called a *galvanometer*. The four most common measuring units are *volts*, *amperes*, *ohms*, and *watts*.

VOLTS. *Volts* are units of force. *Voltage* is the force that causes electricity to flow. You can "see" how voltage works if you think of water in a pipe. To make the water move, a pump must work. Take away the pump, and the flow of water stops. It takes work to push electrons through a wire "pipe," too. Take away the battery or other power source, and the electron flow stops. Electrons move through a wire only if there is a difference in voltage, or *potential*, between one end of the wire and the other end. This difference is measured in units called volts. The current that operates appliances in your house is supplied at a potential of 110 volts. (In other parts of the world it may be 240 volts.) A flashlight battery produces $1\frac{1}{2}$ volts. Most automobile batteries produce 12 volts.

AMPERES. It is often useful to measure the "size" of the current, as well as the force that pushes it along. Current is measured in units called *amperes*, or *amps*. A wire will be carrying a 1-amp current if 6,240,000,000,000,000,000 electrons pass any point in the wire in 1 second. In the same piece of wire, doubling the voltage—using a 3-volt battery instead of a $1\frac{1}{2}$-volt battery, for example—doubles the current. Halving the voltage cuts the current in half.

OHMS. Electric appliances often get warm during use, while some (such as electric irons) are designed to produce heat. This happens because electrons crash into atoms of the conductor, which resist the flow of electrons. The better the conductor, the less often collisions happen. But no conductor is perfect. This is called *resistance* and is measured in ohms. Doubling the resistance halves the current, provided the voltage is the same. Several factors affect resistance, including the temperature, thickness, and length of the conductor.

WATTS. Watts measure how much power is generated or used. If you know the voltage and current of an electric circuit, you can find the wattage by multiplying these two figures together. For example, a light bulb of about .909 amps connected to a 110-volt current uses .909 × 110 = 100 watts.

▶▶▶▶ **FIND OUT MORE** ◀◀◀◀

**Basic Principles of Electricity** see Atom; Battery; Electromagnet; Electric Power; Electronics; Energy; Lightning and Thunder; Magnet
**History of Electricity** see Ampère, André; Edison, Thomas Alva; Faraday, Michael; Galvani, Luigi; Watt, James
**Some Uses of Electricity** see Electric Appliance; Motor; Radio; Recording; Television; X ray

▶ Electricity generated at a power station is usually distributed at high voltage and low current. Step-up transformers convert the output of the generators to the high voltage required for distribution. Step-down transformers reduce the voltage to make it suitable for use in factories and homes.

## ⚙ ELECTRIC POWER

Physical strength was the first form of power known to human beings. But human strength alone was not powerful enough to do all the things people wanted to do. So people had to find other forms of power. Over the centuries, people have made use of animals, simple tools, water, wind, and steam to provide power for work. One of the newest and greatest aids has been electricity.

An electric power plant produces electricity from a material, such as coal, oil, gas, or running water. Electric power plants use generators to produce electricity. A *generator* is a device that turns mechanical energy into electrical energy. A generator may supply power to one house, or it may provide electricity for thousands of buildings.

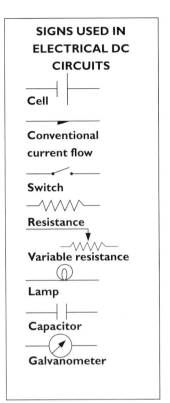

**SIGNS USED IN ELECTRICAL DC CIRCUITS**

Cell

Conventional current flow

Switch

Resistance

Variable resistance

Lamp

Capacitor

Galvanometer

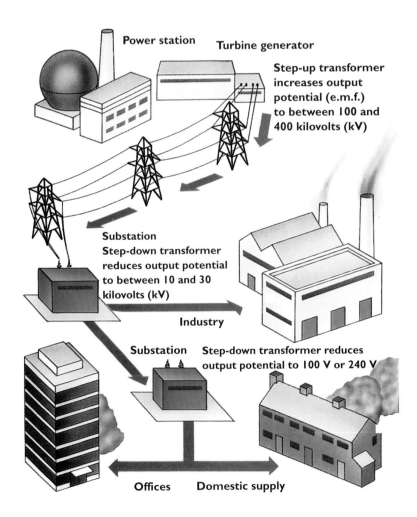

Power station    Turbine generator

**Step-up transformer increases output potential (e.m.f.) to between 100 and 400 kilovolts (kV)**

**Substation Step-down transformer reduces output potential to between 10 and 30 kilovolts (kV)**

Industry

**Substation**    **Step-down transformer reduces output potential to 100 V or 240 V**

Offices    Domestic supply

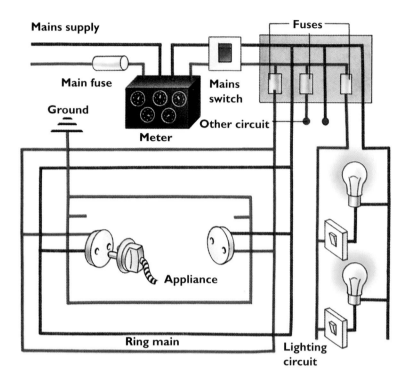

Mains supply

Main fuse

Ground

Meter

Mains switch

Other circuit

Fuses

Appliance

Ring main

Lighting circuit

◄ Electricity supplied to the home is first fed into a meter which records the amount used. The current then flows through a fuse box. If the current is too great for the fuse, the fuse blows and breaks the circuit.

electricity along. Alternating current can be "piped" hundreds of miles at a very high voltage so that little power is lost. Then the voltage is decreased to the lower level at which electric appliances work.

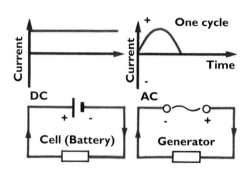

One cycle

Current

Time

Current

DC

AC

Cell (Battery)

Generator

▲ Direct current (DC) flows in one direction only. Alternating current (AC) changes its direction of flow at regularly spaced intervals.

**The United States uses about 700,000 megawatts of electricity each year. (A megawatt is a million watts.) Of this enormous power, about a tenth comes from nuclear power stations, another tenth from hydroelectric stations (waterpower), and the rest comes from burning oil, gas, or coal.**

The first power generators produced *direct current* (DC), a steady flow of electrons in just one direction. Flashlight batteries produce DC. Direct current is used in metal plating, in *electrolysis*—breaking down chemical compounds into elements—and in many processes.

*Alternating current* (AC) flows rapidly back and forth. The current supplied to most houses is called "60-cycle AC," which means that it is alternating current that flows back and forth 60 times a second. The main reason that AC is used so widely is that it is easier to change the *voltage* of AC, using transformers. *Voltage* is the force that pushes

### "Making" Electricity

The simplest kind of generator is a loop of wire that can be turned. The loop is placed between the poles of a magnet. Whenever magnetic lines of force are cut by a wire, electric current is produced in the wire. This is the principle of the electric power generator. A generator with one loop of wire would not produce very much electricity. The generators in a power plant have coils containing thousands of turns of wire in place of a single loop, and magnets of great strength are used to increase the power output.

Several types of energy are used to

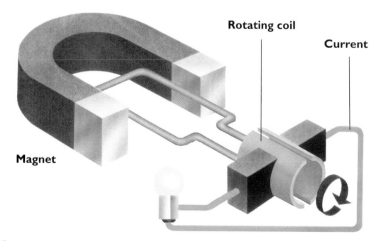

Rotating coil

Current

Magnet

◄ An AC generator. The coil containing loops of wire is rotated between the poles of a magnet. Electric current is generated whenever the wire cuts through the magnetic lines of force.

turn the coils of wire in a generator. Many power plants produce electricity from falling water. Such plants, called *hydroelectric* plants, generate nearly one-fourth of the world's electric power. Heat may be used where there isn't any waterfall. Coal, gas, or oil may be burned to heat water to produce steam to power a turbine, which turns the generator. Nuclear reactors may also be used to produce heat. Nuclear power produces about 16 percent of the world's electricity. However, because of the dangerous materials used in nuclear power plants and the need for high standards of safety, these plants are very expensive to build. They also create hazardous radioactive wastes.

Other devices used to turn small generators include gasoline engines, windmills, and water wheels. Solar furnaces and solar cells use sunlight to make electric power.

Electricity produced in a power plant goes from the generator through a device called a *step-up transformer*. The transformer increases the voltage from about 25,000 volts to as much as 765,000 volts. Then the electricity flows along wires stretched between tall towers. You have probably seen such power lines. At each tower is a sign that says DANGER! HIGH VOLTAGE. Power lines may cross miles of open country to reach a city. At the city, the electricity goes to substations, places where *step-down transformers* lower the voltage to several thousand volts. Other power lines then carry the electricity throughout the city, to buildings, streetlights, and wherever else electric power is needed. Near each power user is another step-down transformer, which lowers the voltage again to between 110 and 240 volts (in the United States).

▶ ▶ ▶ ▶ **FIND OUT MORE** ◀ ◀ ◀ ◀
Battery; Electricity; Energy; Nuclear Energy

# ⚙ ELECTROLYSIS

Do you know how galvanized iron is made? Galvanized iron is covered with a thin coat of another metal, zinc, to protect the iron from corrosion. But how is the zinc fixed onto the iron? One way is by *electrolysis*, the producing of chemical changes by use of an electric current.

Electrolysis depends on the existence of ions. Normally an atom (or molecule) has no overall electrical charge, but if for some reason it has lost an electron it will have a positive electrical charge. Likewise, if it has an extra electron it will be negatively charged. These charged particles are called *ions*.

To galvanize iron we need to make a solution of a zinc-containing substance. Into it we put a piece of iron and a piece of zinc, and we wire these into an electric circuit. When we switch on the current, positively charged zinc ions travel through the solution to coat the iron. This process is called *electroplating*.

There are many other uses of electrolysis, but all depend on this same principle. One important use is to separate metals from the ores in which they have been found.

▶ ▶ ▶ ▶ **FIND OUT MORE** ◀ ◀ ◀ ◀
Atom; Electricity

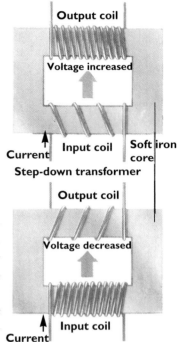

**Step-up transformer**

**Output coil**

**Voltage increased**

**Input coil** — **Current** — **Soft iron core**

**Step-down transformer**

**Output coil**

**Voltage decreased**

**Input coil** — **Current**

▲ In a transformer, a current flows through the input coil and induces a current with a different voltage in the output coil. In the step-up transformer, there are more turns of the output coil than of the input coil, so the voltage is increased. The process is reversed in the step-down transformer so the voltage is decreased.

---

## LEARN BY DOING

Attach wires to the ends of two pencils, which are sharpened at both ends. The pencils are the electrodes. Connect the other ends of the wires to a 6 or 9 volt battery. Place the pencils (with a card support) in a jar of water with a little salt added. The process of electrolysis will break up the water ($H_2O$) into its two components of hydrogen gas and oxygen, which will collect as bubbles around each pencil tip.

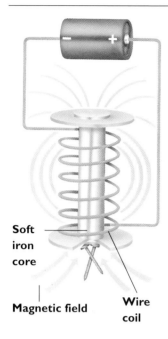

**Soft iron core**

**Magnetic field**

**Wire coil**

▲ An electromagnet is a kind of magnet worked by electricity. Its magnetism can be switched on and off. It contains a coil of wire wound around an iron bar. When an electric current flows through the coil, the bar becomes magnetic.

# ELECTRON

SEE ATOM

# ELECTROMAGNET

An *electromagnet* is a device that uses electricity to produce magnetism. Scrapyards have very powerful electromagnets to pick up loads of scrap metal. Electric motors contain electromagnets too, and so do loudspeakers in radio and television sets and earphones in cassette players.

When an electric current flows through a wire, the wire becomes magnetic. The magnetic field is stronger if the wire is in a coil. It is stronger still if an iron bar is placed in the center of the coil. You can make a simple electromagnet by winding some insulated electrical wire around a large screw or nail. Connect the ends of the wire to a battery and the screw or nail becomes magnetic. Disconnect the wire and the magnetism disappears.

In an electric motor, such as the motor in an electric drill, two electromagnets produce strong magnetic fields that turn the shaft of the motor. In a loudspeaker, an electric signal causes an electromagnet to vibrate and produce sound.

▶▶▶▶ **FIND OUT MORE** ◀◀◀◀
Electricity; Magnet

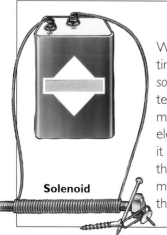

**Solenoid**

### LEARN BY DOING

Wind a length of plastic-insulated wire many times around a nail to make what is called a *solenoid*. Connect the ends of the wire to the terminals of a battery. Try picking up small metal objects with this electromagnet. As the electricity flows through the tight coils of wire, it creates magnetic forces from one end of the coil to the other. The nail is turned into a magnet because the magnetic force causes all the magnetic particles in the nail to line up.

# ELECTRONIC MUSIC

If you have ever gone to a concert, you know that every musician must play his or her instrument at exactly the right moment. You also know that a trumpet always sounds like a trumpet, and not like a violin. A snare drum does not sound like a piccolo. In an orchestra, a number of instruments, each making a distinctive sound, are grouped together. The instruments make their sounds by vibrating the air in various ways: for example, the bowing of a violin's strings causes them to vibrate and produce sound.

The electronic instrument called the *synthesizer* differs in two ways from more familiar instruments. First, the synthesizer can imitate the sound of any other musical instrument—a guitar, a harmonica, a clarinet, a bell, or an organ. The synthesizer can also make a variety of sounds that no other musical instrument has ever made, such as scratching, whirring, and ticking sounds.

Second, a synthesizer can be connected to a computer. This means that the musician can play an instrument long before a concert, because the computer can play the instrument again, at the right time.

The musician can sit in the audience and listen to the concert. He or she can even be hundreds of miles away, eating dinner or taking a nap. But the synthesizer is quite a difficult instrument to master. Ideally, it should be played, like any other instrument, by someone who knows music and has the skill to play the instrument properly.

Composers sometimes write music only for synthesizers. To do this, they first decide what kinds of sounds they want in their music. Then they figure out how to make the synthesizer play the sounds in the desired loudness, pitch, and tone. Composers also write music to be played by synthesizers and other musical instruments.

Many familiar instruments have been built with electronic parts. You can hear how different the electronic keyboards of a rock band sound from the older pipe organ used in churches. Electronics has created many such new sounds from old instruments. Some composers, such as John Cage, combine these new sounds with taped sounds. Electronic music is a modern form of musical expression.

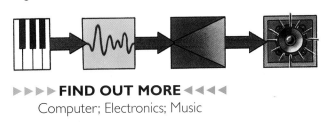

▶ ▶ ▶ ▶ **FIND OUT MORE** ◀ ◀ ◀ ◀
Computer; Electronics; Music

## ⚙ ELECTRONICS

Cassette players, pocket calculators, digital watches, portable radios, video recorders, television sets, home computers, telephones—all these marvels are powered by electronics. The workings of many familiar machines, such as automatic washing machines and cameras, are controlled by electronics. Without electronics, space travel would be impossible, and we would not have flown to the moon nor obtained superb pictures of distant planets. Air travel would be much less safe without radar, another electronic invention, to guide aircraft. Electronics affect our lives in many ways.

Machines such as calculators and television sets are not the only machines that are powered by electricity. Electric heaters, stoves, drills, cleaners, and lights all use electricity. However, these are *electric* appliances, not *electronic* machines. Electric appliances use electricity mainly to produce movement, heat, or light; they convert electrical energy into another form of energy. Electronic machines use electricity to create electric signals and then handle these signals in various ways. The signals can produce sound in a radio, cassette player, or telephone, a picture in a television set, or figures in the display of a digital watch, for example. In a computer, the electric signals are code signals that can represent letters, numbers, and even pictures.

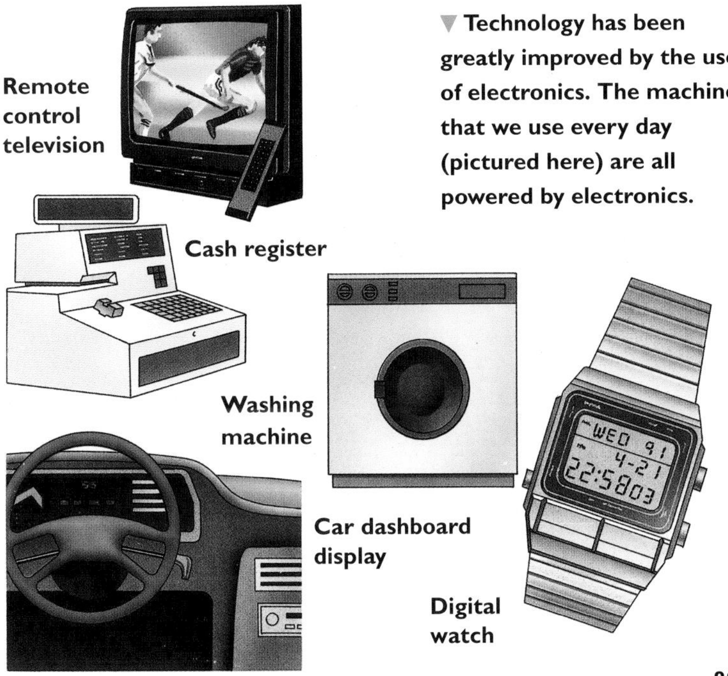

Remote control television

Cash register

Washing machine

Car dashboard display

Digital watch

▲ Electronic music sounds are created on tape using electronics and computers. The sound from the keyboard is changed into an electronic signal. This signal is passed through an amplifier and made louder, and is then played through loudspeakers. This is the sound we hear.

▼ Technology has been greatly improved by the use of electronics. The machines that we use every day (pictured here) are all powered by electronics.

▼ Inside a television is a form of cathode-ray tube. It changes the vision signal into an image on the screen. The signal controls the strength of an electron beam as it scans the fluorescent screen, line by line.

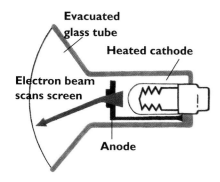

Evacuated glass tube

Heated cathode

Electron beam scans screen

Anode

The number of microscopic transistors that can be put on a tiny chip has increased rapidly year by year. It is now possible to put more than a million of them on a single chip. Each of these million parts does the job that a large glass tube did only a few years ago.

These machines are called electronic because the electric signals consist of *electrons*. *Electrons* are tiny particles of electricity that move along a wire when an electric current flows through the wire. As the signals pass, the current varies so that the number of electrons in the signals changes all the time. In television, for example, a signal with lots of electrons may give a bright part of the picture and a signal with fewer electrons may give a dark part.

## How Electronic Machines Work

The first step taken by any electronic machine is to produce the electric signals that make it carry out a certain task. Let's first look at machines that produce sound or pictures. A microphone, like that in a telephone mouthpiece, converts the sound of a voice or music into electric signals called *audio signals*. A television camera changes the light and color in a scene into electric *video signals*. A microphone contains a device like an electromagnet that vibrates as sound waves strike it and changes the vibrations into audio signals. A television camera contains a light-sensitive

radio's or television's antenna. Alternatively, these signals may come along a cable. In cassette or disc players or video recorders, audio or video signals come from the parts of the machine that play the discs or tapes, such as the pickup in a disc player or the tape head in a video recorder.

The next step is to turn these signals back into sound and pictures. However, the signals have first to be treated in various ways. They must be *amplified*, or made more powerful, and they may need to be improved in quality. The signals go to electronic components like transistors that carry out these actions.

Audio signals then go to a loudspeaker or earphone that turns them into sound. These contain electromagnets that vibrate as signals pass through them, and produce sound waves. In a television set, the video signals go to a cathode ray tube in which the electrons in a signal strike a screen and cause it to light up and show a picture.

Electronic machines such as computers and calculators work in a different way. Operating the keys, and feeding programs and data into a computer from a tape or disk, causes electric code signals to be produced. The signals can be stored in electronic components inside, and other components then handle the code signals to make calculations or do other tasks. Because the signals travel quickly, these tasks are done very rapidly. The signals finally go to units like a display screen, or printer, which decode them to produce letters and numbers, for example. A digital watch is similar, except that the electronic components inside automatically create code signals all the time to change the display every second, minute, hour, and day.

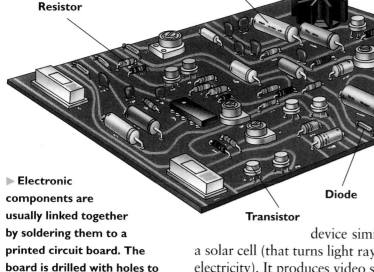

Resistor

Capacitor

Silicon chip

Diode

Transistor

▶ Electronic components are usually linked together by soldering them to a printed circuit board. The board is drilled with holes to take the wire leads of the components, which are joined by a pattern of metal tracks printed on the board.

device similar to a solar cell (that turns light rays into electricity). It produces video signals as light rays strike it.

A radio or television set creates audio or video signals as radio waves from the transmitter strike the

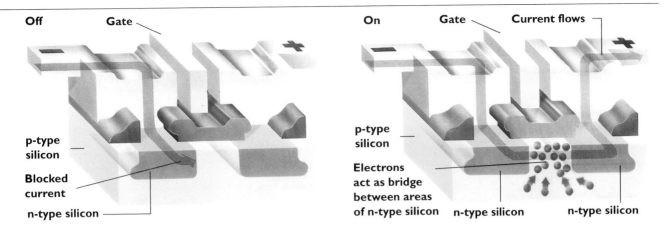

**Off**   **Gate**

p-type
silicon

**Blocked
current**

n-type silicon

**On**   **Gate**   **Current flows**

p-type
silicon

**Electrons
act as bridge
between areas
of n-type silicon**   **n-type silicon**   **n-type silicon**

## Analog and Digital

There are two basic kinds of electronic machines—*analog* and *digital*. Computers and calculators are digital, as are watches. Most machines that produce sound and pictures are analog. However, sound and pictures are becoming digital because digital electronics give very high quality of reproduction.

The difference between analog and digital is in the kind of electric signals that are used. Analog signals are copies of things; an analog audio signal is an electrical copy of the original sound wave, for example. As the original sound gets louder or softer, the electric signal copying it continually gets stronger or weaker in the same way.

A digital signal consists of code signals that represent numbers. In digital sound and pictures, each number is a measure of the strength of the original—for example, the loudness of a sound—at a particular instant. The measurements are made thousands of times a second, so the numbers represent the original very accurately. Digital machines are generally better than analog systems because it is much easier to record or transmit a series of code numbers accurately than it is to record or transmit a changing analog signal.

**Chip in its package**

**Pins**

## Electronic Components

The earliest electronic components were vacuum tubes. The most important of them were invented in the early 1900s. The simplest is the *diode*, which can be used to change alternating current electricity (AC) to direct current (DC). The diode has two electrodes, a *filament* or *cathode* that gives off electrons, and a *cold plate* or *anode* that attracts and collects electrons.

The *X-ray tube* is a kind of diode. When the current to the anode is very strong, electrons are drawn to the anode with great force. When they hit it, they stop suddenly, and X rays are given off.

The *cathode ray tube*, or CRT, produces the pictures in a television set or visual display. It is also used to provide the pictures taken through an electron microscope, and to give a visible pattern of a sound or an electric signal on an oscilloscope.

The anodes inside a cathode ray tube attract electrons, which are then fired, by means of an electron gun arrangement of filament and anodes, along the tube at very high speeds. When the electrons crash into a screen coated with fluorescent material, each collision produces a tiny flash of light. By aiming the stream of electrons at the right part of the screen, the collisions are made to form a picture.

The components used in modern

▲ Silicon chips can control the flow of current by acting like switches, or transistors. When the switch is "off" (left), the current is blocked. When the switch is "on" (right), the current flows.

◄ The heart of a microprocessor is a silicon chip integrated circuit, mounted on a base with two rows of pins or terminals. A microprocessor is the control center and electronic calculator of a computer.

▼ Electronic circuits are built with such tiny components that they have to be greatly magnified when being designed, so that the parts can be accurately placed.

The most common element in the universe is hydrogen. Scientists think that 90 percent of all matter is hydrogen. The commonest element in the Earth's crust is oxygen. It makes up about half of the crust by weight. The rarest element on Earth is astatine. There is only about one-hundredth of an ounce (0.30 gram) of it in all the Earth's crust. The heaviest element is osmium. A cubic foot of osmium weighs 1,410 pounds (a cubic cm weighs 22.6 grams). No weight lifter could raise a cubic foot of the metal.

▶ Ancient scientists thought that there were only four elements: earth, water, fire and air. These, in turn, gave rise to the properties of dry, wet, hot, and cold.

◀ An early list of elements made by John Dalton (1766–1844). He discovered that each element had its own kind of atoms. Elements cannot be broken down into simpler substances, but in certain nuclear reactions one element can be changed into another.

electronic equipment, such as transistors and microchips, are made of materials called *semiconductors*. Unlike conductors, which allow electrons to move freely through them, semiconductors can control the movement of the electrons in an electric current to produce signals.

In a *transistor*, for example, a current arrives at one end and travels through a sandwich of different layers of semiconductors. A controlling signal goes to the central layer, and the electrons in the signal change the conductivity of this layer. In this way, the current is made to vary in step with the control signal as it passes through the transistor, so that the transistor either switches the current rapidly on and off or amplifies the control signal.

The *microchips* in computers and other electronic machines contain thousands of tiny components, such as transistors, linked together. Electric codes flash among them, enabling the microchips to perform complex operations at high speed. For example, an electronic English/French dictionary the size of a pocket calculator can give you the French translation of an English word literally at the touch of a button.

▶▶▶▶ **FIND OUT MORE** ◀◀◀◀
Atom; Computer; Electricity; Magnet; Lasers and Masers; Radio; Recording; Semiconductor; Television; Transistor; Video; X Ray

Earth

Cold · Wet

Air · Water

Dry · Hot

Fire

## ⚙ ELEMENT

What are things made of? This is a question that has puzzled people for thousands of years. Today we know that a few substances, called *elements*, make up all others.

### First Ideas

Thales, a scientist of ancient Greece, was the first person to state an idea about the source of elements. He said that everything is made of water. He had seen water as ice, steam, fog, rain, and dew. If water could take all these forms, might it not take the form of any material? Thales thought it could, so he said that water is the element of which everything is made.

But other Greeks disagreed. One said that air is the only element; another said fire; and still another, earth. Democritus said that everything is made up of extremely small, hard particles called *atoms*. One of the greatest of Greek scientist-philosophers, Aristotle, named four elements—water, air, fire, and earth. For about the next 2,000 years, people believed that all things were made up of these four "elements."

### The Road to Chemical Changes

During the Middle Ages, alchemists in Europe and Asia spent much effort trying to change "base" (cheap) metals, such as lead, into precious gold. This was impossible, but they learned that certain substances could be changed into more than one material. Other substances, such as gold, silver, lead, copper, tin, antimony, mercury, carbon, and sulfur, could not be divided or broken down. This understanding gave a good definition of what an *element* is: "a substance that cannot be broken down into simpler substances."

Air, for example, is not an element

because it is made up of several substances. Oxygen is one of them. It is mixed in the air with another gas, nitrogen, and other gases. Often an element is found *combined* (joined) with another in what is known as a *compound*. Water, for instance, is a compound; it consists of oxygen (an element) combined with hydrogen (another element). Water itself is not an element.

## Dalton's Theory

In 1804, an English schoolmaster, John Dalton, revived Democritus's idea that all substances are made up of tiny particles called atoms. Dalton

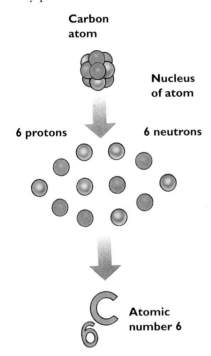

**Carbon atom**

**Nucleus of atom**

**6 protons**          **6 neutrons**

**Atomic number 6**

said that all the atoms of any chemical element are exactly alike, having the same weight, size, and form, and that the atoms of one element are different from those of all other elements. This idea gives us another definition of an element: "a substance made up entirely of atoms of the same kind."

## Atomic Numbers

Scientists worked out a new idea of an atom soon after the beginning of

the 1900s. Each atom has a central part called a *nucleus*. Very small particles called *electrons* orbit around the nucleus. Inside the nucleus itself are two kinds of particles, *neutrons* and *protons*. The hydrogen atom, which is the lightest of all atoms, has one proton. Each succeeding heavier atom has one more proton than the atom before it. The number of protons in the nucleus of an atom is called the *atomic number* of that element. Every atom has the same number of protons and electrons, so the atomic number also tells the number of electrons.

Scientists found that the idea of atomic numbers gave a more exact definition of an element: "a substance made up of atoms all having the same atomic number."

## Atomic Weight

Chemists have learned that electrons have almost no weight at all. The

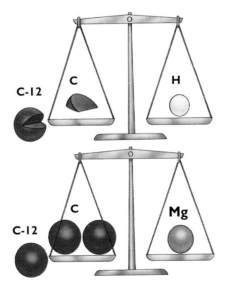

C-12    C          H

C-12    C          Mg

◄ **Dalton's model of the atom. John Dalton is best known for his atomic theory to explain the structure of matter. This theory became one of the foundations of modern chemistry.**

◄ **Every element has its own atomic number. The atomic number is the same as the number of protons. The nucleus of a carbon atom has six protons and six neutrons, and so has an atomic number of six. It also has six electrons spinning around the nucleus.**

◄ **Atomic weight is a ratio of the average mass of the atoms of an element. Carbon which has an atomic weight of 12, has been used as the reference point since 1961. Hydrogen (H) is one-twelfth the weight of a carbon-12 atom and so its atomic weight is one. Magnesium (Mg) is the weight of two carbon atoms, so its atomic weight is 24.**

### LEARN BY DOING

Some substances are easier to break down into elements than others. Ask an adult to help you burn a marshmallow. You cannot see the oxygen and hydrogen that are driven off in the smoke of the fire. But the black material that is left is carbon. The heat has caused a chemical change.

▲ **Dmitri Mendeleyev (1834–1907), the Russian chemist who devised the periodic table of elements.**

weight of an atom is concentrated in its nucleus. Protons all weigh the same, as do neutrons. And a neutron weighs as much as a proton. A proton (or neutron) weighs more than 1,800 times as much as an electron.

The weight of an atom (in *atomic mass unit*) can be found by adding the number of protons and neutrons in its nucleus. An atom of hydrogen has one proton and no neutrons in its nucleus, so the atom's *atomic weight* is 1. The nucleus of a carbon atom contains six protons and six neutrons. Its atomic weight is 12. A uranium atom has 92 protons and 146 neutrons. What is its atomic weight?

Not all atoms of an element are

the same. Atoms with the same atomic number but different weights are called *isotopes*. Nearly all the elements have been found to have more than one isotope.

**The Periodic Table**

In 1869, a Russian chemist, named Dmitri Mendeleyev, arranged all the elements that were then known into a table according to their increasing atomic weights.

If you look up the properties of all the elements, you will find that the elements in each vertical row of the table below have similar chemical properties. In the horizontal rows, the properties of the elements repeat themselves in each row. On the left of each row is a light metal, then follow heavier metals, then nonmetals, and finally one or two gases. This repetition caused Mendeleyev to say that the properties of the elements repeat in definite periods as their atomic weights increase. In the modern *periodic table*, elements are listed in order of increasing atomic numbers.

TRANSURANIUM ELEMENTS. Some elements are extremely rare in

## PERIODIC TABLE

▶ **The periodic table contains all the known elements in order of increasing atomic number. Elements of atoms with similar structures have similar properties and so are positioned close to each other. Elements can be divided into metals and non-metals.**

| | |
|---|---|
| **I** | Atomic number |
| **Hydrogen** | Name of element |
| **H** | Chemical symbol |

Across →

▲ **The size of the atoms increases across the table. Elements change from metals to non-metals.**

Down ↓

▶ **The size of the atoms increases down the table. All elements in a group have the same number of electrons.**

| 1 Hydrogen H | | | | | | | | |
|---|---|---|---|---|---|---|---|---|
| **1** | **2** | | | | | | | |
| 3 Lithium Li | 4 Beryllium Be | | | | | | | |
| 11 Sodium Na | 12 Magnesium Mg | | | | | | | |
| 19 Potassium K | 20 Calcium Ca | 21 Scandium Sc | 22 Titanium Ti | 23 Vanadium V | 24 Chromium Cr | 25 Manganese Mn | 26 Iron Fe | 27 Cobalt Co |
| 37 Rubidium Rb | 38 Strontium Sr | 39 Yttrium Y | 40 Zirconium Zr | 41 Niobium Nb | 42 Molybdenum Mo | 43 Technetium Tc | 44 Ruthenium Ru | 45 Rhodium Rh |
| 55 Caesium Cs | 56 Barium Ba | 57–71 Lanthanide series | 72 Hafnium Hf | 73 Tantalum Ta | 74 Tungsten W | 75 Rhenium Re | 76 Osmium Os | 77 Iridium Ir |
| 87 Francium Fr | 88 Radium Ra | 89–103 Actinide series | 104 Element 104 | 105 Element 105 | 106 Element 106 | 107 Element 107 | 108 Element 108 | 109 Element 109 |

| 57 Lanthanum La | 58 Cerium Ce | 59 Praseodymium Pr | 60 Neodymium Nd | 61 Prometheum Pm | 62 Samarium Sm | 63 Europium Eu | 64 Gadolinium Gd | 65 Terbium Tb |
|---|---|---|---|---|---|---|---|---|
| 89 Actinium Ac | 90 Thorium Th | 91 Protactinium Pa | 92 Uranium U | 93 Neptunium Np | 94 Plutonium Pu | 95 Americium Am | 96 Curium Cm | 97 Berkelium Bk |

nature but can be made in the laboratory. Chemists made the first synthetic element, *neptunium*, in 1940. This was done by bombarding uranium with neutrons. Neptunium has an atomic number of 93, one more proton than uranium. Scientist claim to have made thirteen more synthetic elements since 1940. Because all are heavier than uranium, the new elements are called *transuranium* elements. *Trans* is Latin for "beyond" or "heavier than" so transuranium means heavier than uranium. Only small quantities of transuranium atoms have been made. More unknown elements await discovery.

CHEMICAL SYMBOLS. The known elements range from atomic number 1 to atomic number 103. There are 92 different, named elements that occur in nature: 79 of which occur as solids, 11 as gases, and 2 as liquids. The other elements are made in particle accelerators, or "atom-smashers."

Chemists use special abbreviations, or *symbols*,

to name the elements. For instance, instead of writing out "hydrogen," the chemist writes H. The symbol for an element may be the first letter of its name, as N for nitrogen and S for sulfur. But the names of many elements begin with the same letter (11 elements begin with the letter C). So the symbols for most elements are made up of the first letter and one more, as Ca for calcium. The symbols for some elements are abbreviations of their Latin names, for example, Fe for *ferrum*, the Latin word for iron. Symbols used to describe a combination of elements are called a *formula*.

▶▶▶▶ **FIND OUT MORE** ◀◀◀◀
Atom; Chemistry; Particle Accelerator; Radioactivity

### WHERE TO DISCOVER MORE

Bronowski, Jacob. *Biography of an Atom*. New York: Harper & Row, 1965.
Cobb, Vicki. *Chemically Active!: Experiments You Can Do at Home*. Philadelphia, Pennsylvania: J B Lippincott Co., 1985.

There is a tradition that the person who discovers an element has the right to suggest a name. New elements are named for famous scientists.

▼ The metal elements are divided into three groups: alkali metals, transitional metals, and the inner transition series. Elements higher than element 92, uranium, are called transuranium elements and are all highly unstable and radioactive.

| | | | 8 |
|---|---|---|---|
| | | | 2<br>Helium<br>He |

| 3 | 4 | 5 | 6 | 7 | |
|---|---|---|---|---|---|
| 5<br>Boron<br>B | 6<br>Carbon<br>C | 7<br>Nitrogen<br>N | 8<br>Oxygen<br>O | 9<br>Fluorine<br>F | 10<br>Neon<br>Ne |
| 13<br>Aluminium<br>Al | 14<br>Silicon<br>Si | 15<br>Phosphorus<br>P | 16<br>Sulphur<br>S | 17<br>Chlorine<br>Cl | 18<br>Argon<br>Ar |

| 28<br>Nickel<br>Ni | 29<br>Copper<br>Cu | 30<br>Zinc<br>Zn | 31<br>Gallium<br>Ga | 32<br>Germanium<br>Ge | 33<br>Arsenic<br>As | 34<br>Selenium<br>Se | 35<br>Bromine<br>Br | 36<br>Krypton<br>Kr |
|---|---|---|---|---|---|---|---|---|
| 46<br>Palladium<br>Pd | 47<br>Silver<br>Ag | 48<br>Cadmium<br>Cd | 49<br>Indium<br>In | 50<br>Tin<br>Sn | 51<br>Antimony<br>Sb | 52<br>Tellurium<br>Te | 53<br>Iodine<br>I | 54<br>Xenon<br>Xe |
| 78<br>Platinum<br>Pt | 79<br>Gold<br>Au | 80<br>Mercury<br>Hg | 81<br>Thallium<br>Tl | 82<br>Lead<br>Pb | 83<br>Bismuth<br>Bi | 84<br>Polonium<br>Po | 85<br>Astatine<br>At | 86<br>Radon<br>Rn |

| 66<br>Dysprosium<br>Dy | 67<br>Holmium<br>Ho | 68<br>Erbium<br>Er | 69<br>Thulium<br>Tm | 70<br>Ytterbium<br>Yb | 71<br>Lutetium<br>Lu |
|---|---|---|---|---|---|
| 98<br>Californium<br>Cf | 99<br>Einsteinium<br>Es | 100<br>Fermium<br>Fm | 101<br>Mendelev-<br>ium<br>Md | 102<br>Nobelium<br>No | 103<br>Lawrencium<br>Lr |

☐ Alkali metals          ☐ Inner transition series

☐ Transition metals      ☐ Non-metals

▼ The African elephant is the largest animal on land. It has larger ears and tusks than the Indian, or Asian, elephant. It also has a different shaped back.

## ELEPHANT

The elephant is the largest living land mammal. Ancestors of modern elephants lived on all continents except Australia. The *woolly mammoth* was a long-haired animal about 10 feet (3 m) tall with long, curved tusks. The ancestors of Native Americans probably knew the *mastodon*. It was about the same size as the woolly mammoth but had straight tusks and less hair. Today, however, only two species of elephants exist: the *Asian* or *Indian* and the larger *African*. (See table, page 893.)

It might be awkward for you to have a nose that touched the ground. But the elephant finds its trunk, or *proboscis*, a very handy tool. Nostrils at the end of the trunk are used in breathing. Below the nostrils in the open end of the tubelike trunk is at least one tiny fingerlike piece jutting up. The elephant uses the "finger" to pick up small objects. An elephant picks up the masses of plant food it eats in its hollow trunk and then curves the trunk into its mouth, dropping the food down its throat. It drinks water the same way. Poking out from most elephants' mouths

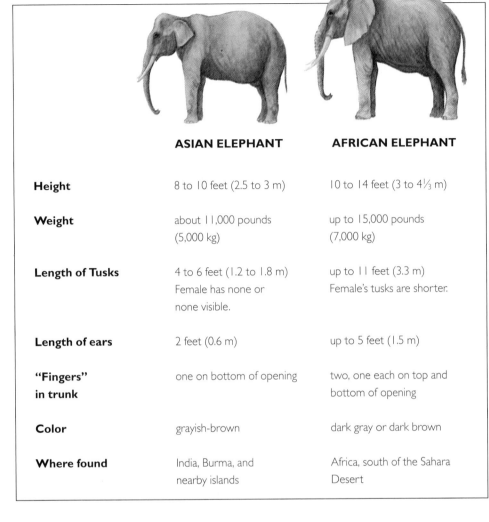

| | ASIAN ELEPHANT | AFRICAN ELEPHANT |
|---|---|---|
| **Height** | 8 to 10 feet (2.5 to 3 m) | 10 to 14 feet (3 to 4⅓ m) |
| **Weight** | about 11,000 pounds (5,000 kg) | up to 15,000 pounds (7,000 kg) |
| **Length of Tusks** | 4 to 6 feet (1.2 to 1.8 m) Female has none or none visible. | up to 11 feet (3.3 m) Female's tusks are shorter. |
| **Length of ears** | 2 feet (0.6 m) | up to 5 feet (1.5 m) |
| **"Fingers" in trunk** | one on bottom of opening | two, one each on top and bottom of opening |
| **Color** | grayish-brown | dark gray or dark brown |
| **Where found** | India, Burma, and nearby islands | Africa, south of the Sahara Desert |

> The elephant lives longer than any other land mammal, excluding humans. A few specimens have lived to be 70 years old, and there are stories of longer-lived elephants.

under the trunk are two long tusks. They are enlarged teeth. The tusks are used for defense and, like teeth, they may wear down or be broken off. An elephant's call is a trumpeting sound that echoes through the forest or across the grasslands.

An elephant's massive body is supported by four legs shaped like thick tree trunks. Usually five hooflike toenails grow on each foot, although the toes don't show. An elephant's knees are in the middle of the legs like a person's (the knees of most mammals are tucked into the top of the legs where they join the body). But full-grown elephants are so heavy they often prefer not to go to the effort of bending their knees to lie down on the ground and so they sleep standing up.

Elephants live in groups, called *herds*. Within the herd, they appear to have rules and customs that gov-

ern each member, from the old female leader, called the *matriarch*, to the youngest baby or *calf*. They defend a wounded member of the herd. A calf drinks its mother's milk for almost a year and stays close to her for five years. Elephants reach adolescence at age 14, like human beings, and live to be 65 to 70 years old.

▼ The elephant herd has a female (the *matriarch*) in charge. She is the oldest female. All adult females live with their offspring; young adult males form bachelor herds. Older males roam on their own and meet the females only at mating time.

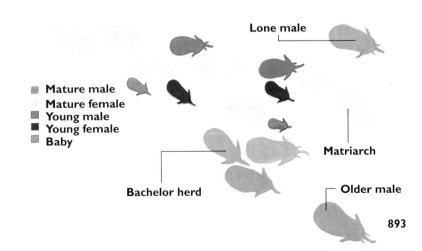

Lone male

- ■ Mature male
- Mature female
- ■ Young male
- ■ Young female
- ■ Baby

Matriarch

Bachelor herd

Older male

## BREEDING CYCLES

When elephant numbers are low and conditions are good, females usually give birth to a calf every three or four years. If conditions deteriorate, or if the numbers rise and the elephants become crowded, the gap between calves becomes longer. This helps to stabilize the population. Most female elephants are able to breed by 10 to 15 years of age. They have most of their calves between the ages of 25 and 45. Few female elephants over the age of 50 are able to breed. The pregnancy of an elephant lasts 18 to 22 months—the longest of any mammal. The baby elephants are called calves. They are very hairy when they are born and can walk when they are only one hour old. The calves stand no taller than a big dog. They will be fully grown after 20 years.

**Water is very important to elephants. They are very good swimmers and spend much of their time in water. Because elephants do not have any sweat glands in their skin, water provides a way for them to cool off.**

Female elephants are called *cows*; male elephants are called *bulls*. Sometimes a male elephant will decide to live away from the rest of the herd. These bulls are often aggressive males that have been driven off by the rest of the herd. Some male African elephants can weigh as much as eight family cars and need over 440 pounds (200 kg) of food a day.

Elephants do not live in one place. They usually roam about in their herds looking for food and water. In the wild, elephants have no natural enemies. But people kill elephants for their ivory tusks. As a result, the numbers of elephants in the wild has been greatly reduced. It is hoped that now that ivory hunting has been banned, the numbers of elephants will begin to increase again. Elephants are protected by organizations such as the World Wildlife Fund.

Elephants have been used by people for many centuries. Elephants once carried warriors into battles. Even today in Asia, elephants are ridden on important occasions. Passengers sit inside an ornamented box called a *howdah* on the elephant's back. Elephants have been used in Asian forests to move heavy logs of teak wood. Elephants are sometimes still seen in zoos and circuses, although African elephants have rarely been tamed by humans.

▶▶▶▶ **FIND OUT MORE** ◀◀◀◀
Circus; Hannibal; Mammal; Mammals of the Past

▼ **Elephants greet other elephants within their herd, by shaking trunks. An elephant's trunk is a combined nose and upper lip. It is used to breathe, smell, feed and drink, and even to make noises.**

# ELEVATORS AND ESCALATORS

Tall buildings, or skyscrapers, stretch upward in every large city. In New York City, giant buildings of 100 stories or more look down on buildings only 50 stories high. But look at a picture of New York City in 1850. The buildings were small. Most buildings had only two to four floors. The biggest buildings were only a little higher. Tall buildings were constructed only rarely before the invention of the elevator in the 1850s.

Elisha Graves Otis first showed his elevator at the 1854 New York World's Fair. He designed this elevator for freight. It hung from strong ropes. The ropes ran up to a large drum powered by a steam engine. The drum turned one way to lower the elevator. It turned the other way to pull the elevator up. Otis also invented a safety device to stop the elevator from falling to the ground if the lift rope broke.

Factories and warehouses soon began installing freight elevators. And in 1857, Otis put his first passenger elevator in a New York City building. It was an immediate success. People no longer had to walk up many steps. Taller buildings soon began to be built and improved elevators appeared. The hydraulic elevator was first used in 1871. The elevator car sat on top of a long metal plunger. The plunger went into a cylinder at the bottom. When water was forced into the cylinder, the plunger moved up. When water was released, the plunger moved down. Hydraulic elevators moved more smoothly than the earlier steam-engine elevators. Another type of hydraulic elevator went into the tallest buildings. The elevator car hung from ropes or cables. The cables went through pulleys to a short hydraulic plunger. As the plunger moved in or out, the cables pulled the car up or down.

▶ Elisha Otis demonstrated the first elevator to have an automatic safety device, in 1854. If the hoisting ropes broke, the elevator would not fall.

Modern elevators powered by electric motors began replacing other elevators in the 1890s. Electric elevators hung from long steel cables. Powerful motors pulled the cables swiftly up or down. An elevator operator rode in the car. He controlled the car by a switch that ran the electric motors at the top of the elevator shaft. Automatic elevators have mostly replaced elevators with

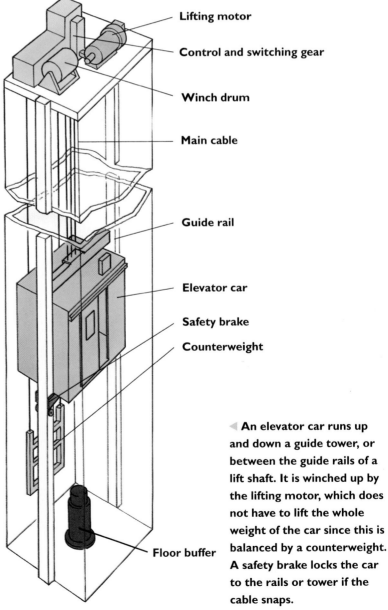

- Lifting motor
- Control and switching gear
- Winch drum
- Main cable
- Guide rail
- Elevator car
- Safety brake
- Counterweight
- Floor buffer

◀ An elevator car runs up and down a guide tower, or between the guide rails of a lift shaft. It is winched up by the lifting motor, which does not have to lift the whole weight of the car since this is balanced by a counterweight. A safety brake locks the car to the rails or tower if the cable snaps.

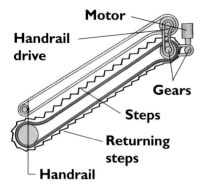

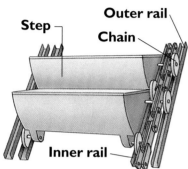

◄ The machinery inside an escalator drives a continuous loop of steps. The same principle is used for travelators or moving walkways. Escalators can move as fast as 13 feet (4 m) a second.

operators. In an automatic elevator, passengers push a button for the floor number they want. The button is an electric switch that stops the elevator at the right floor. The newest automatic elevator systems have computers to control elevator operation.

Escalators are moving stairs used in stores, railroad and airline terminals, and other places where there is a lot of pedestrian traffic. One of the first escalators was installed at the Paris Exposition of 1900. Escalator steps connect to a chain or belt. The chain travels endlessly around electric-powered gears, or drive shafts. Steps flatten out at the top and bottom of the escalator to line up with a solid platform. Steps on an "up" escalator then curve around and go down. At the bottom, they curve back up.

Escalators move about 90 feet (27 m) per minute. This is much slower than elevators. Different types of elevators move at different speeds. Some move at 100 feet (30 m) per minute, but others can travel at speeds up to 1,700 feet (518 m) per minute. For going up or down only a few floors, escalators are often easier.

## QUIZ ANSWERS

### Desert quiz, page 775
1. No. Desert just means dry, not necessarily hot or sandy.
2. The second-largest desert in the world is the Sahara in North Africa. It is about 3,500,000 square miles (9,065,000 sq. km).
3. The Painted Desert is called "painted" because millions of years of erosion has made the rocks and exposed sandstone in this region turn many different shades of red, yellow, pink, and purple. It is located in northern Arizona.
4. Yes. An oasis is a region within a hot desert that is green, wet, and fertile. Its pool is fed by an underground stream. A mirage, on the other hand, is not real: it is an optical illusion caused by waves of heat in the air, which may look like a pool of water.
5. The camel stores fat and moisture in its hump (or humps—the Arabian camel has one hump, the Bactrian camel has two). This stored fuel helps it survive in arid desert climates.

### Dinosaur quiz, page 791
1. Different dinosaurs ate different things. Some were carnivores (meat-eaters) and some were herbivores (plant-eaters).
2. The sharp teeth of the meat-eating *Tyrannosaurus rex* were 6 inches (15 cm) long.
3. Both the *Stegosaurus* and the *Triceratops* were cloaked in spiny armor. Their bony outer shells helped regulate their temperature and protected them from enemies.
4. Most scientists would say that the dinosaurs were extinct by about 65 million years ago.

### Driving quiz, page 825
1. A car with an automatic transmission changes gears for the driver, unless the driver wants to go in reverse or have some extra power going up hills. A car with a manual transmission means that the gears have to be changed manually (by hand)— or actually by the combination of a hand on the gear stick and left foot on the clutch. Automatic cars are easier in some ways, but manuals offer the driver more control. All race cars as well as most heavy transportation vehicles (tractors, trucks, etc.) have manual transmissions for this reason.
2. In Great Britain the steering wheel is on the right side and people drive on the left side of the road. This is the exact reverse of the way we drive in the United States, but the same way cars and roads are designed in Australia and Japan.
3. The two pedals on the floor of a car with an automatic transmission are the accelerator and the brake. The third pedal, seen only in a manual car, is the clutch.
4. The legal age to drive in most states is 16. The exceptions to this are Hawaii, Louisiana, Montana, and New Mexico (15), Idaho (16½), New Jersey (17), and Colorado and Vermont (18). In many of these states you can only get a license at 16 if you have completed a driver's education course. Otherwise you need to be 18, in most cases. In some states you can get your license as young as 14—or even 13 in Montana—as long as you have your parents' consent.
5. Warning signs are diamond-shaped.

### Earth quiz, page 843
1. Roughly 29 percent of the Earth's surface is covered by land.
2. The biosphere is the region of the Earth and its atmosphere— from the bottom of the oceans to the outermost part of the atmosphere—that is the home of all life on the planet.
3. There are three Earth layers: the crust, the mantle, and the core.
4. The Earth is made up of oxygen, magnesium, potassium, sodium, calcium, iron, aluminum, and silicon. Elements in the Earth's atmosphere include hydrogen, nitrogen, and carbon dioxide.
5. It takes the Earth one day to make a full rotation on its axis. It takes the Earth a year to orbit (make a full turn around) the sun.